Ukrainian pocket dictionary

English-Ukrainian & Ukrainian-English

John Shapiro

Ukrainian pocket dictionary
by John Shapiro

First edition: March 2017

ENGLISH-UKRAINIAN

A

abacus • *n* рахівниця *(f)*, абак *(m)*

abandon • *v* покидáти, покúнути

abandoned • *adj* покúнутий *(m)*

abandonment • *n* відмóва *(f)*, абандóн *(m)*, абандон *(m)*, залишення *(n)*

abattoir • *n* бóйня *(f)*

abbess • *n* абатúса *(f)*

abbot • *n* абáт *(m)*

abbreviate • *v* скорóчувати, скороти́ти

abbreviation • *n* абревіатýра *(f)*

abdomen • *n* живіт *(m)*

abiogenesis • *n* абіогенез *(m)* /(abiogenez)/

abjuration • *n* зрéчення *(n)*, аб'юрáція *(f)*

abolish • *v* касувáти /(kasuváty)/, скасувати /(akasuváty)/

abolitionist • *n* аболіціоніст *(m)*

aboriginal • *adj* аборигенський /(aboryhéns'kyj)/, тубільний /(tubíl'nyj)/, автохтонний /(avtoxtónnyj)/, туземський /(tuzéms'kyj)/

aborigine • *n* аборигéн *(m)*

above • *prep* над /(nad)/

abridge • *v* скорóчувати, скороти́ти

abrogate • *v* касувáти /(kasuváty)/, скасувати /(skasuváty)/

abrupt • *adj* раптóвий *(m)*

absent • *adj* відсýтній

absinthe • *n* абсент *(m)*

absolute • *adj* необмежений /(neobmézhenyj)/, абсолютний /(absoljútnyj)/, цілковитий

absorb • *v* поглинáти, погли́нути

abstractionism • *n* абстракціонізм *(m)*

acacia • *n* акáція *(f)*

academical • *adj* академíчний *(m)*

accelerate • *v* прискóрювати, приско́рити, прискóрюватися

acceleration • *n* прискóрення *(n)*, прискóрення *(n)*

accent • *n* нáголос *(m)*

accept • *v* приймáти, прийня́ти

accession • *n* вступ *(m)*, приéднання *(n)*

accident • *n* ви́падок *(m)*, авáрія *(f)*, катастрóфа *(f)*

accolade • *n* аколáда *(f)*

accordion • *n* акордеóн *(m)*, гармóнія *(f)*

account • *n* рахýнок *(m)*

accountant • *n* бухгáлтер *(m)*, бухгáл-терка *(f)*, рахівни́к *(m)*, рахівни́ця *(f)*

accurate • *adj* точний /(tóčnyj)/, доклáдний /(dokládnyj)/

accusative • *n* знахíдний відмíнок *(m)*, знахíдний *(m)*

accuse • *v* звинувачувати /(zvynuváčuvaty)/, звинуватити /(zvynuvátyty)/

acetone • *n* ацетóн *(m)*

ache • *v* болíти, хворíти, захворíти • *n* біль *(m)*

achieve • *v* досягáти /(dosjaháty)/, досягти /(dosjahtý)/

acid • *n* кислотá *(f)*

acidity • *n* кислотність *(f)*

aconite • *n* борець /(borets')/

acorn • *n* жолудь *(m)* /(žólud□)/

acquaint • *v* знайóмити, познайóмити

acrobatic • *adj* акробатíчний *(m)*

acrobatics • *n* акробатика *(f)*

acromegaly • *n* акромегáлія *(f)*

act • *v* діяти, чинити, грати, поводи́тись • *n* акт *(m)*, вчинок *(m)*, дія *(f)*

actinium • *n* актиній *(m)*

actinometer • *n* актинометр *(m)*

activist • *n* активíст *(m)*, активíстка *(f)*

actor • *n* актóр *(m)*, актрúса *(f)*

actress • *n* актрúса *(f)*

acupuncture • *n* акупунктýра *(f)*

add • *v* додавáти, додáти

adder • *n* змія *(f)*, гадю́ка *(f)*

additional • *adj* додаткóвий *(m)*

address • *n* адреса *(f)*

adduce • *v* представляти /(predstavljáti)/, наводити /(navodíti)/

adjectival • *adj* прикметник *(m)*

adjective • *n* прикметник *(m)*

admiration • *n* захóплення *(n)*

admire • *v* захоплюватися /(zahoplyuvatysja)/

adolescent • *n* підлíток *(m)*

adrenaline • *n* адреналíн *(m)*

adult • *n* дорóслий *(m)* • *adj* дорóслий

adultery • *n* перелю́бство *(n)*, адюльтéр *(m)*

advantage • *n* кóристь *(f)*, ви́года *(f)*, перевáга *(f)*

advantageous • *adj* вигідний, сприятливий

adventurism • *n* авантюрíзм *(m)*

adverb • *n* прислíвник *(m)*

advertisement • *n* реклáма *(f)*, оголо-

́шення (n), анонс (m), заява (f)

advice • n рада (f), порада (f)

advise • v радити, порадити

aerial • n антена (f)

aerolite • n аероліт (m) /(aerolít)/

aeroscopy • n аероскопія

afflict • v дошкуляти, причиняти

afford • v дозволяти собі

again • adv знову, знов, ще раз

against • prep проти

agave • n агава (f)

age • n вік (m), епоха (f), ера (f), час (m)

aggression • n агресія (f)

aggressive • adj агресивний

aggressor • n агресор (m)

agouti • n агуті

agree • v погоджуватися, погодитися, згоджуватися, згодитися

agriculture • n сільське господарство (n), землеробство (n), агрикультура (f)

aha • interj агá

air • n повітря (n)

air-to-air • adj повітря-повітря

air-to-surface • adj повітря-земля

aircraft • n літак (m)

airline • n авіакомпанія (f), авіалінії

airliner • n пасажирський літак (m), авіалайнер (m)

airmail • n повітряна пошта (f), авіапошта (f)

airplane • n літак (m), аероплан (m)

airport • n аеропорт (m), литовище (n)

akin • adj споріднений, подібний

alarm • n тривога (f) /(tryvóha)/

albumen • n білок (m)

alcohol • n алкоголь (m), спирт (m)

alcoholism • n алкоголізм (m), алкого́льне отру́єння (n)

aldehyde • n альдегід (m)

ale • n ель (m)

alga • n во́дорость (f)

algebra • n а́лгебра (f)

algorithm • n алгоритм (m)

alienation • n відчуження, відчужування, віддалення, збайдужування, відчуженість, божевілля, збайдужіння, психоз

alive • adj живий

allergy • n алергія (f)

alley • n провулок (m), алея (f)

alliance • n союз (m) /(sojúz)/

alligator • n алігатор (m)

allotropic • adj алотропічний /(alotropíčnyj)/

allow • v дозволяти, дозволити

allure • n шарм (m), привабливість (f)

almost • adv майже, сливе

aloe • n алое (n)

alone • adv один, сам

aloofness • n відчуженість, нетовариськість, замкнутість

aloud • adv вголос

alpha • n альфа (f)

alphabet • n абетка (f), алфавіт (m), азбука (f), альфабет (m)

already • adv уже, вже, раніше

also • adv так само, теж, також

altar • n вівтар (m)

alter • v змінювати, змінити

altruist • n альтруїст (m) /(al□trujíst)/, альтруїстка (f) /(al□trujístka)/

always • adv завжди, завше

amanita • n мухомор (m) /(muxomór)/

ambassador • n посол (m)

amber • n бурштин (m), янтар (m)

ambergris • n амбра (f) /(ámbra)/

ambitious • adj амбіційний /(ambitsíjnyj)/

ambulance • n швидка допомога (f)

americium • n америцій (m)

among • prep серед, між

ampere-hour • n ампер-година (f)

amphibian • n земноводне (n), амфі́бія (n)

amylase • n амілаза

anachronism • n анахронізм (m) /(anaxronízm)/

anaconda • n анаконда (f) /(anakónda)/

anagram • n анаграма (f)

analgesic • n анальгетик (m)

anarchy • n анархія (f)

ancestor • n предок (m)

anchor • n якір (m)

ancient • adj стародавній

and • conj і, й /(j)/, та, й, а

anemia • n недокрів'я, малокрів'я

angel • n ангел (m), янгол (m)

anger • n гнів, злість (f)

angle • n кут (m), вугол (m)

anglicism • n англіцизм (m)

angry • adj сердитий, злий

animal • n тварина (f), звір (m)

anime • n аніме (n)

animosity • n ворожість (f)

ankle • n кісточка (f), щиколотка (f)

annex • v анексувати, приєднувати, приєднати

annexation • n анексія (f), приєднання (n), аншлюс (m)

annihilate • v знищувати, знищити

anniversary • n річниця (f), ювілей (m)

announce • *v* оголо́шувати, оголоси́-ти, заявля́ти, заяви́ти, повідомля́ти, повідо́мити

annul • *v* касувати /(*kasuváty*)/, скасувати /(*skasuváty*)/

anode • *n* ано́д (*m*)

answer • *n* ві́дповідь (*f*) • *v* відповіда́ти, відповісти́

ant • *n* мура́шка (*f*), мура́ха (*f*)

anteater • *n* мурахої́д (*m*)

antepenultimate • *adj* передпередоста́нній

anthem • *n* гімн (*m*)

anther • *n* пиляк (*m*)

anthill • *n* мура́шник (*m*)

anthrax • *n* сибірка (*f*)

anthropology • *n* антропологія

anthropomorphism • *n* антропоморфі́зм (*m*)

antibiotic • *n* антибіо́тик (*m*)

antichrist • *n* антихрист (*m*)

antidepressant • *n* антидепреса́нт (*m*)

antimony • *n* сурма́ (*f*)

antitank • *adj* протита́нковий (*m*)

antler • *n* ріг (*m*)

anus • *n* а́нус (*m*), відхі́дник (*m*), за́дній прохі́д (*m*)

anvil • *n* кова́дло (*f*)

anxiety • *n* занепоко́єння (*n*), триво́га (*f*), неспокі́й (*m*)

anything • *pron* що-не́будь, ніщо́

aorist • *n* аорист (*m*)

aorta • *n* ао́рта (*f*)

apartment • *n* кварти́ра (*f*), апартаме́нт (*m*)

apatite • *n* апатит

ape • *v* мавпувати • *n* ма́впа (*f*)

aphid • *n* тля (*f*) /(*tlja*)/, попелиця (*f*) /(*popelýcja*)/

aphorism • *n* афоризм (*m*)

apiary • *n* пасіка (*f*)

apologize • *v* вибача́тися, ви́бачитися, перепро́шувати, перепроси́ти

apology • *n* ви́бачення (*n*)

apostrophe • *n* апостроф (*m*) /(*apostrof*)/

apothegm • *n* апофтегма

apparent • *adj* очеви́дний, я́вний

appear • *v* з'явля́тися, з'яви́тися

appetite • *n* апети́т (*m*)

apple • *n* я́блуко (*n*)

approximately • *adv* прибли́зно, ма́йже

apricot • *n* абрикос (*m*) /(*abrykós*)/

apron • *n* фа́ртух (*m*)

aptitude • *n* схильність (*f*), здібність (*f*)

aquarium • *n* аква́ріум (*m*)

aquatic • *adj* во́дний

araba • *n* арба́ (*f*)

archbishop • *n* архієпи́скоп (*m*)

archer • *n* лу́чник (*m*)

archipelago • *n* архіпела́г (*m*)

architect • *n* архіте́ктор (*m*)

architectural • *adj* архітекту́рний

architecture • *n* архіте́ктура (*f*)

argent • *n* срі́бло (*n*)

arginine • *n* аргінін

argon • *n* арго́н (*m*)

arise • *v* встава́ти

ark • *n* ковче́г (*m*)

arm • *n* рука́ (*f*), збро́я (*f*)

armchair • *n* крі́сло (*n*), фоте́ль (*m*)

armful • *n* обере́мок (*m*)

armistice • *n* припине́ння вогню́ (*n*), переми́р'я (*n*)

armpit • *n* па́хва (*f*), паха́ (*f*)

army • *n* а́рмія (*f*), ві́йсько (*n*)

arnica • *n* арніка (*f*) /(*arnika*)/

arrest • *v* арешто́вувати, заарешто́вувати, арештува́ти, заарештува́ти • *n* аре́шт (*m*)

arrival • *n* прибуття́ (*n*), приї́зд (*m*), прихі́д (*m*), прилі́т (*m*)

arrive • *v* дохо́дити, дійти́, доїжджа́ти, дої́хати, прихо́дити, прийти́, приїжджа́ти, приї́здити, приї́хати

arrow • *n* стріла́ (*f*), стрі́лка (*f*)

arsenic • *n* миш'я́к (*m*)

art • *n* мисте́цтво (*n*)

arthropod • *n* членистоно́ге (*n*)

artichoke • *n* артишо́к (*m*)

article • *n* стаття́ (*f*)

artillery • *n* артилерія (*f*)

artist • *n* худо́жник (*m*), арти́ст (*m*)

as • *adv* як, так, насті́льки • *conj* як, коли, як ті́льки, поки, у той час як, оскі́льки • *prep* як, у ро́лі

ascetically • *adv* аскетично

asceticism • *n* аскетизм (*m*) /(*asketýzm*)/

asexuality • *n* асексуальність /(*aseksual'níst*)/

ash • *n* по́піл (*m*), зола́ (*f*)

ashtray • *n* попільни́чка (*f*)

ask • *v* пита́ти, запита́ти, проси́ти, попроси́ти

asparagus • *n* спа́ржа (*f*)

aspic • *n* холодець (*m*) /(*xolodéc*□)/

ass • *n* сра́ка (*f*), ду́па (*f*), жо́па (*f*), за́дниця (*f*)

asshole • *n* засра́нець (*m*), муда́к (*m*), гад (*m*), козе́л (*m*), підора́с (*m*), гівнюк (*m*), сволота́ (*f*), хуйло́ (*n*)

assist • *v* допомага́ти, допомогти́, сприя́ти, посприя́ти

assistance • *n* допомо́га (f)

assure • *v* запевня́ти, запе́внити

astatine • *n* аста́т (m)

asterisk • *n* зі́рочка (f)

asteroid • *n* астеро́їд (m)

asthma • *n* а́стма (f)

astronaut • *n* космона́вт (m), астрона́вт (m)

astronomy • *n* Астроно́мія

asylum • *n* приту́лок (m)

at • *prep* у, в, при, бі́ля

atelier • *n* ательє́ (n)

atheism • *n* атеїзм

atmosphere • *n* атмосфе́ра (f)

atoll • *n* атол (m)

atom • *n* а́том (m), неді́лка

attack • *v* напада́ти, напа́сти, атакува́ти • *n* на́пад (m), ата́ка (f)

attempt • *v* про́бувати, намага́тися • *n* спро́ба (f)

attention • *n* ува́га (f)

attitude • *n* ста́влення (n)

attraction • *n* по́тяг (m)

attribute • *n* атрибу́т (m)

auction • *n* аукціо́н (m)

aunt • *n* ті́тка (f), тьо́тя (f)

author • *n* а́втор (m)

authority • *n* вла́да (f)

autobiographical • *adj* автобіографі́чний

autobiography • *n* автобіогра́фія (f) /(avtobiográfija)/

automobile • *n* автомобі́ль (m), маши́на (f) /(mašýna)/, автомаши́на (f) /(avtomašýna)/, авто́ (n) /(avtó)/

autopilot • *n* автопіло́т (m)

autotomy • *n* автотомія (f) /(avtotomíja)/

autumn • *n* о́сінь (f) • *adj* осі́нній

available • *adj* досту́пний (m)

avoid • *v* уника́ти, уни́кнути, ухиля́тися, ухили́тися

await • *v* чека́ти, жда́ти, очі́кувати

awake • *v* просипа́тися

away • *adv* геть, пріч

awl • *n* ши́ло (n)

awning • *n* наві́с (m), козиро́к

awry • *adv* хибно /(khýbno)/

aye-aye • *n* ай-ай (m) /(aj-áj)/

B

baby • *n* дити́на (f), ля́лька (f), немовля́ (n)

baccarat • *n* баккара /(bakkara)/

bachelor • *n* холостя́к (m), парубо́к (m)

bacillus • *n* баци́ла (f)

back • *n* спи́на (f) • *adv* наза́д

backgammon • *n* нарди /(nárdy)/

backpack • *n* рюкза́к (m), ра́нець (m)

bacon • *n* беко́н (m)

bactericide • *n* бактерицид (m)

bad • *adj* пога́ний, ке́пський, злий

badger • *n* борсу́к (m)

badminton • *n* бадмінто́н (m)

bag • *n* су́мка (f), мішо́к (m), то́рба (f)

bagpipes • *n* волинка

bake • *v* пекти́, випіка́ти

baker • *n* пе́кар (m), пе́карка (f)

bakery • *n* пека́рня (f)

baklava • *n* пахлава́ (f), баклава́ (f)

balalaika • *n* балала́йка (f)

balance • *n* рівнова́га (f)

balcony • *n* балко́н (m)

bald • *adj* лисий

bale • *n* тюк (m)

ball • *n* ку́ля (f), м'яч (m), ядро́ (n), яйце́ (n), яє́чко (m)

ballerina • *n* балери́на (f)

ballet • *n* бале́т (m)

balloon • *n* бало́н (m) /(balón)/

baluster • *n* баля́сина (f)

balustrade • *n* балюстра́да (f)

ban • *v* забороня́ти, заборони́ти

banana • *n* банан (m) /(banán)/

bandit • *n* банди́т (m), розбі́йник (m)

banish • *v* виганя́ти, виго́нити, ви́гнати, висила́ти, ви́слати

banjo • *n* ба́нджо (n)

bank • *n* банк (m), бе́ріг (m), бе́рег (m)

banner • *n* пра́пор (m), стяг (m), флаг (m), знамено

banquet • *n* банке́т, пир (m)

baptism • *n* хреще́ння (n)

bar • *n* бар (m), пивна́ (f), каба́к (m), кна́йпа (f), пивни́ця (f)

barbarian • *n* ва́рвар (m), ва́рварка (f) • *adj* варварський

barbarism • *n* варваризм (m)

barbell • *n* штанга (f) /(štánha)/

barbershop • *n* перука́рня (f)

barefoot • *adv* босоніж

barge • *n* ба́ржа (*f*)

barium • *n* ба́рій (*m*)

bark • *v* бреха́ти, га́вкати • *n* кора́ (*f*)

barley • *n* ячмі́нь (*m*)

barrack • *n* каза́рма (*f*), бара́к (*m*)

barrage • *n* гре́бля (*m*)

barrel • *n* бо́чка (*f*)

basalt • *n* база́льт (*m*)

baseball • *n* бейсбо́л (*m*)

basically • *adv* в основному /(*v osnovnómu*)/

basin • *n* таз (*m*) /(*taz*)/, басейн (*m*) /(*baséjn*)/

basket • *n* ко́шик (*m*)

basketball • *n* баскетбо́л (*m*), кошикі́вка (*f*), баскетбо́льний м'яч (*m*), м'яч до кошикі́вки (*m*)

bass • *n* окунь (*m*) /(*ókun*☐)/

bassoon • *n* фаго́т (*m*)

bast • *n* лико (*n*) /(*lýko*)/, луб (*m*) /(*lub*)/, мачула (*f*) /(*mačúla*)/

bat • *n* кажа́н (*m*), летю́ча ми́ша (*f*)

bath • *n* ва́нна (*f*), лазни́чка (*f*), купа́льня (*f*), ва́нна кімна́та (*f*), ку́пиль (*f*), купа́ння (*n*), ла́зня (*f*)

bathe • *v* купати /(*kupátysja*)/ • *n* купання (*n*) /(*kupánnja*)/

bathhouse • *n* ла́зня (*f*), ба́ня (*f*)

bathroom • *n* ва́нна кімна́та (*f*), ва́нна (*f*)

bathtub • *n* ва́нна (*f*)

bathyscaphe • *n* батискаф (*m*)

batik • *n* батик

battery • *n* батаре́йка (*f*), батаре́я (*f*), акумуля́тор (*m*), батарея (*f*)

battle • *n* би́тва (*f*), бій (*m*)

baud • *n* бод (*m*) /(*bod*)/

bay • *n* зали́в (*m*), бу́хта (*f*)

bayonet • *n* багне́т (*m*)

bazaar • *n* ри́нок (*m*), база́р (*m*)

be • *v* бу́ти

beach • *v* посади́ти на мілину́, направля́ти на бе́рег, битягати на бе́рег • *n* пляж (*m*), пля́жа (*f*), бе́рег (*m*), надмо́р'я (*n*), узмо́р'я (*n*), обмі́лина (*f*), мілина́ (*f*)

beak • *n* дзьоб (*m*)

beam • *n* балка (*f*) /(*bálka*)/, промінь (*m*) /(*prómin*☐)/

bean • *n* біб (*m*), квасо́ля (*f*), фасо́ля (*f*)

bear • *n* ведмі́дь (*m*) • *v* носи́ти, нести́

beard • *n* борода́ (*f*)

bearing • *n* підши́пник (*m*)

beast • *n* звір (*m*)

beat • *v* би́ти, поби́ти, вдаря́ти, уда-
ря́ти, вда́рити, уда́рити

beautiful • *adj* вродли́вий, краси́вий, га́рний

beauty • *n* краса́ (*f*), вро́да (*f*), красу́ня (*f*)

beaver • *n* бобе́р (*m*)

because • *conj* бо, тому́, тому́ що, та́к як, оскі́льки, а́дже, внаслі́док, унаслі́док

become • *v* става́ти, ста́ти

bed • *n* лі́жко (*f*), лі́жко (*n*), по́стіль (*f*)

bedbug • *n* постільний клоп (*m*), клоп (*m*)

bedouin • *n* бедуї́н (*m*)

bedroom • *n* спа́льня (*f*)

bee • *n* бджола (*f*) /(*bdžolá*)/

beech • *n* бук (*m*)

beef • *n* яловичина (*f*)

beefsteak • *n* біфште́кс (*m*)

beehive • *n* ву́лик (*m*)

beekeeping • *n* бджільни́цтво (*n*)

beer • *n* пи́во (*n*)

beet • *n* буря́к (*m*)

beetle • *n* жук (*m*)

beetroot • *n* буря́к (*m*)

begin • *v* почина́ти, поча́ти, почина́тися, поча́тися

beginning • *n* поча́ток (*m*)

begonia • *n* бегонія

behave • *v* поводитися /(*povódytysja*)/

behaviorism • *n* біхевіоризм (*m*) /(*bixeviorýzm*)/

behind • *prep* за, поза

being • *n* істо́та (*f*), тварь (*f*), твари́на (*f*), ство́ріння (*n*), існува́ння (*n*), буття́ (*n*)

bel • *n* бел (*m*)

belch • *v* рига́ти

belief • *n* ві́ра (*f*)

believe • *v* ві́рити

believer • *n* ві́руючий (*m*), ві́руюча (*f*)

bell • *n* дзвін (*m*), дзво́ник (*m*)

belle • *n* красу́ня (*f*)

belles-lettres • *n* худо́жня літерату́ра (*f*), белетри́стика (*f*)

belly • *n* живі́т (*m*), бру́хо (*n*)

below • *prep* під, нижче, південні́ше

belt • *n* по́яс (*m*), ремі́нь (*m*)

bench • *n* ла́вка (*f*), ла́вочка (*f*)

bend • *v* згина́ти, гну́ти

beneath • *prep* під

beneficial • *adj* корисний, вигідний, благотворний

benzene • *n* бензол (*m*)

berkelium • *n* берке́лій (*m*)

berry • *n* я́года (*f*)

beryl • *n* берил *(m)* /(beril)/
beryllium • *n* берилій *(m)*
betray • *v* зраджувати, зрадити
better • *adj* ліпше /(lípše)/
between • *prep* між
beverage • *n* напій *(m)*, напиток *(m)*
bewitch • *v* зачаровувати, зачарувати
bicameral • *adj* двопалатний
bicycle • *n* велосипед *(m)*
bid • *v* наказувати, наказати
bigamy • *n* бігамія *(f)*
bikini • *n* бікіні *(n)*
bilberry • *n* чорниця *(f)* /(čornýcja)/
bile • *n* жовч *(f)* /(žovč)/
bill • *n* дзьоб *(m)*, рахунок *(m)*
billiards • *n* більярд *(m)*
bingo • *n* бінго *(n)* /(bíngo)/
binnacle • *n* нактоуз *(m)*
binoculars • *n* бінокль *(m)*
biochemistry • *n* біологічна хімія *(f)*, біохімія *(f)*
biography • *n* біографія *(f)*
biology • *n* біологія *(f)*
birch • *n* береза *(f)*
bird • *n* птах *(m)*, птиця *(f)*
birdie • *n* пташка *(f)* /(ptáška)/
birth • *n* пологи, народження *(n)*
birthday • *n* день народження *(m)*
birthmark • *n* родимка *(f)*
bisexuality • *n* бісексуальність *(f)*
bishop • *n* єпископ *(m)*, слон *(m)*, офіцер *(m)*
bismuth • *n* вісмут *(m)*
bison • *n* зубр *(m)*, бізон *(m)*, американський бізон *(m)*, американський зубр *(m)*
bistro • *n* бістро
bitch • *n* сука *(f)*, стерва *(f)*
bite • *v* кусати, укусити
bitter • *adj* гіркий
bittern • *n* бугай
bittersweet • *n* Паслін солодко-гіркий
black • *n* чорний *(m)*, мурин *(m)*, муринка *(f)*, негр *(m)*, негритянка *(f)* • *adj* чорний
blackberry • *n* ожина *(f)*
blackbird • *n* чорний дрізд *(m)*
blackboard • *n* дошка *(f)*
blacklist • *n* чорний список *(m)*
blackmail • *n* шантаж *(m)*, вимагання *(n)*
blacksmith • *n* коваль *(m)*
bladder • *n* міхур *(m)* /(mixúr)/
blanket • *n* ковдра *(f)*, покривало *(n)*
blasphemy • *n* богохульство *(n)*, блюзнірство *(n)*

blazer • *n* блейзер *(m)* /(bléjzer)/
bleak • *n* верховодка *(f)*
blind • *adj* сліпий
blini • *n* млинці /(mlyncí)/
bliss • *n* блаженство *(n)* /(blažénstvo)/
blockade • *n* блокада *(f)*
blockbuster • *n* блокбастер *(m)* /(blokbáster)/
blood • *n* кров *(f)*
bloodshed • *n* кровопролиття *(n)*
bloodthirsty • *adj* кровожерливий
bloom • *v* цвісти
blow • *v* дути, віяти
blue • *n* синій /(sýnij)/, блакитний /(blakýtnyj)/ • *adj* синій /(sýnij)/, блакитний /(blakýtnyj)/
blues • *n* блюз *(m)*
blunderbuss • *n* мушкетон
blunt • *adj* тупий /(tupýj)/
boa • *n* удав *(m)*
boar • *n* кабан *(m)*
boat • *n* човен *(m)*, лодь *(f)*
body • *n* тіло *(n)*
bodyguard • *n* тілоохоронець
bog • *n* болото *(n)*
boil • *v* варити
bolt • *n* болт *(m)*
bomb • *n* бомба *(f)*
bombard • *v* бомбардувати
bombardment • *n* бомбардування *(n)*, бомбування *(n)*
bone • *n* кістка *(f)* /(kístka)/
bonfire • *n* багаття *(n)*, вогнище *(n)*
boob • *n* цицька *(f)*
booger • *n* коза
book • *n* книжка *(f)*, книга *(f)*
bookcase • *n* книжкова шафа *(f)*
bookshop • *n* книгарня *(f)*
boot • *n* чобіт *(m)*, черевик *(m)*
border • *n* кордон *(m)*, границя *(f)*
boron • *n* бор
borrow • *v* позичати, позичити
borscht • *n* борщ *(m)*
botanize • *v* ботанізіровать
botany • *n* ботаніка *(f)*
botfly • *n* овід *(m)* /(óvid)/
bottle • *n* пляшка *(f)*
bottom • *n* дно *(n)*
botulism • *n* ботулізм *(m)*
bougainvillea • *n* бугенвілія *(f)*
bough • *n* сук *(m)*, гілка *(f)*
boundary • *n* кордон *(m)*, межа *(f)*
bouquet • *n* букет *(m)*
bow • *n* лук *(m)*, смичок *(m)*
bowl • *n* чаша *(f)*, миска *(f)*
bowstring • *n* тятива *(f)*

box • *n* коробка (*f*), ящик (*m*), скриня (*f*)

boxing • *n* бокс (*m*)

boy • *n* козачок (*m*), хлопець (*m*), хлопчик (*m*)

boyar • *n* боярин (*m*), буй (*m*)

boycott • *n* бойкот (*m*) /(bojkót)/

boyfriend • *n* коханий (*m*), парубок (*m*), хлопець (*m*), друг (*m*), приятель (*m*)

bra • *n* бюстгальтер (*m*), ліфчик (*m*)

bracelet • *n* браслет (*m*)

brain • *n* мозок (*m*)

brake • *v* гальмувати, загальмувати • *n* гальмо (*n*)

brambling • *n* в'юрок (*m*) /(v⎤jurók)/

branch • *n* вітка (*f*), галузь (*f*), галузка (*f*), гілка (*f*), гілочка (*f*), філія (*f*)

brandy • *n* бренді (*n*), коньяк (*m*)

brass • *n* латунь (*f*)

brave • *adj* хоробрий, відважний

bravery • *n* хоробрість (*f*), сміливість (*f*), відвага (*f*)

bread • *n* хліб (*m*) /(xlib)/, хліб (*m*)

breakfast • *n* сніданок (*m*)

breakwater • *n* хвилеріз (*m*) /(xvyleríz)/

breast • *n* грудь (*f*), груди

breathe • *v* дихати

breeze • *n* бриз (*m*), вітерець (*m*)

breviary • *n* требник (*m*) /(trébnik)/

brewer • *n* пивовар (*m*), пивоварка (*f*)

brewery • *n* броварня (*f*)

bribe • *n* хабар (*m*), підкуп (*m*)

brick • *n* цегла (*f*)

bride • *n* наречена (*f*), молода (*f*)

bridegroom • *n* жених (*m*)

bridge • *n* міст (*m*), перенісся (*n*), брідж (*m*)

bridle • *n* вуздечка (*f*)

brie • *n* брі (*m*)

briefcase • *n* портфель (*m*)

bright • *adj* яскравий, світлий

bring • *v* приносити, принести, приводити, привести, привозити, привезти

bromine • *n* бром (*m*)

brooch • *n* брошка (*f*)

broom • *n* мітла (*f*), віник (*m*)

brothel • *n* бордель (*m*), будинок розпусти (*m*), публічний будинок (*m*), дім розпусти (*m*)

brother • *n* брат (*m*)

brother-in-law • *n* дівер (*m*), шурин (*m*)

brown • *n* коричневий • *adj* коричневий, карий, каштановий, бурий

bruise • *n* синяк (*m*)

brush • *n* щітка (*f*)

bubble • *n* пузир (*m*), міхур (*m*)

bucket • *n* відро (*n*)

buckwheat • *n* гречка (*f*)

buffalo • *n* буйвол (*m*), бізон (*m*)

bug • *n* клоп (*m*)

build • *v* будувати, збудувати

building • *n* будівництво (*n*), будинок (*m*), споруда (*f*), дім (*m*)

bulb • *n* цибулина (*f*)

bull • *n* бик (*m*), бугай (*m*)

bulldozer • *n* бульдозер (*m*)

bullet • *n* куля (*f*)

bullock • *n* віл (*m*) /(vil)/

bulwark • *n* хвилеріз (*m*)

bumblebee • *n* джміль (*m*)

bun • *n* булочка (*f*)

bunker • *n* бункер (*m*)

bunting • *n* вівсянка (*f*) /(vivsjánka)/

buoy • *n* буй (*m*)

burden • *n* тягар (*m*)

bureaucracy • *n* бюрократія (*f*)

burgundy • *adj* вишневий /(vyšnévyj)/, бордовий /(bordóvyj)/

burn • *v* горіти, згоріти, палити, спалити

burp • *v* ригати • *n* відрижка (*f*)

burrow • *n* нора (*f*) /(norá)/

bus • *n* автобус (*m*)

bush • *n* кущ (*m*)

business • *n* підприємство (*n*), бізнес (*m*)

businessman • *n* бізнесмен (*m*), підприємець (*m*)

busy • *adj* зайнятий

but • *conj* крім, але /(alé)/, а /(a)/, алé

butt • *n* сідниця (*f*), зад (*m*), попа (*f*), дупа (*f*), жопа (*f*)

butter • *n* масло (*n*)

butterfly • *n* метелик (*m*)

buttermilk • *n* маслянка (*f*)

buttock • *n* сідниця (*f*), сидня (*f*)

button • *n* ґудзик (*m*), кнопка (*f*)

buy • *v* купувати, купити

buzzard • *n* канюк (*m*) /(kanjúk)/

byte • *n* байт (*m*)

C

cabaret • *n* кабаре (*n*)

cabbage • *n* капуста (*f*) /(*kapústa*)/

cabinet • *n* кабінет (*n*)

cable • *n* кабель (*m*)

cacao • *n* какао

cadmium • *n* кадмій (*m*)

cafeteria • *n* їдальня (*f*)

caffeine • *n* кофеїн (*m*)

cage • *n* клітка (*f*)

cake • *n* торт (*m*), тістечко (*n*), кекс (*m*), пирожне (*n*)

calcium • *n* кальцій (*m*)

calculator • *n* калькулятор (*m*)

calendar • *n* календар (*m*)

calendric • *adj* календарний

calf • *n* теля (*n*)

californium • *n* каліфорній (*m*)

caliph • *n* халіф (*m*)

caliphate • *n* халіфат (*m*)

call • *v* клікати, покликати, звати, позвати, дзвонити, подзвонити • *n* відвідування (*n*), візит (*m*), візита (*f*)

calmness • *n* спокій (*m*) /(*spokíj*)/

calumny • *n* наклеп (*m*)

calyx • *n* чашечка

camel • *n* верблюд (*m*)

camera • *n* фотоапарат (*m*), камера (*f*), відеокамера (*f*)

camp • *n* табір (*m*)

campaign • *n* кампанія (*f*)

campus • *n* кампус (*m*)

can • *v* могти, змогти, вміти, уміти, зуміти

canal • *n* канал (*m*)

cancer • *n* рак (*m*)

candle • *n* свічка (*f*)

candy • *n* цукерка (*f*)

cannabis • *n* конопля (*f*)

cannon • *n* гармата (*f*)

canteen • *n* їдальня (*f*)

canyon • *n* каньйон (*m*)

caoutchouc • *n* каучук (*m*)

capacious • *adj* просторий /(*prostóryj*)/, місткий /(*mistkýj*)/

cape • *n* мис (*m*)

capercaillie • *n* глухар

capital • *n* капітал (*m*), багатство (*n*)

capitalism • *n* капіталізм (*m*)

capsicum • *n* стручковий перець (*m*)

captive • *n* полонений (*m*), бранець (*m*)

car • *n* автомобіль (*m*), машина (*f*), автомашина (*f*), авто (*n*), вагон (*m*)

caramel • *n* карамель (*m*)

caraway • *n* кмин (*m*)

carbon • *n* вуглець

carburetor • *n* карбюратор (*m*)

card • *n* карта (*f*), картка (*f*)

cardamom • *n* кардамон (*m*)

cardboard • *n* картон (*m*)

carefully • *adv* обережно

cargo • *n* вантаж (*m*)

caricature • *n* карикатура (*f*), шарж (*m*)

carnival • *n* карнавал (*m*)

carp • *n* короп (*m*)

carpenter • *n* тесля (*m*), столяр (*m*)

carpet • *n* килим (*m*), диван (*m*)

carriage • *n* вагон (*m*)

carrier • *n* носій (*m*)

carrot • *n* морква (*f*)

carry • *v* носити, поносити, нести, понести, возити, повозити, везти, повезти

cartilage • *n* хрящ (*m*)

case • *n* скриня (*f*)

cash • *n* готівка (*f*), гроші

casino • *n* казино (*n*)

cassock • *n* ряса (*f*)

cast • *n* гіпс (*m*)

castle • *n* замок (*m*)

cat • *n* кіт (*m*), кішка (*f*)

cataclysm • *n* катаклізм (*m*)

catalyst • *n* каталізатор (*m*)

catch • *v* ловити, піймати

caterpillar • *n* гусениця (*f*)

catfish • *n* сом (*m*)

cathedral • *n* собор (*m*)

cathode • *n* катод (*m*)

catnip • *n* котовник

cattle • *n* бидло (*n*), скотина (*f*), бугай (*m*), бик (*m*), корова (*f*), худоба

cauliflower • *n* кучерява капуста (*f*), цвітна капуста (*f*)

cave • *n* печера (*f*)

caviar • *n* кав'яр (*m*), чорний кав'яр (*f*)

ceiling • *n* стеля (*f*)

celeriac • *n* селера (*f*), селера пахуча (*f*)

celery • *n* селера (*f*), салера (*f*)

celesta • *n* ☐☐☐☐☐

cell • *n* камера (*f*), клітина (*f*)

cellar • *n* льох (*m*), підвал (*m*), погріб (*m*)

cello • *n* віолончель

censor • *v* цензурувати

cent • *n* цент (*m*)

centaur • *n* кентавр (*m*)

centenary • *adj* столітній /(*stolítnij*)/

center • *n* центр (*m*), середина (*f*)

centipede • *n* сороконіжка (*f*)

centrifuge • *n* центрифуга (*f*)

/(centryfúha)/

century • n століття (n)

ceramic • n кераміка (f) /(keramika)/

cerebral • adj мозковий

ceremony • n церемонія (f)

cerium • n церій (m)

chaff • n полова (f), січка (f)

chain • n ланцюг (m) /(lancjúh)/, ланцюжок (m) /(lancjužók)/

chair • n стілець (m), крісло (n)

chalcedony • n халцедон /(halcedon)/

chalk • n крейда, крейда (f)

chameleon • n хамелеон (m)

chamois • n серна (f), сарна (f)

champagne • n шампанське (n)

chance • n шанс (m), можливість (f)

chancellor • n канцлер (m)

change • v змінюватися, змінитися, переодягатися, переодягнутися, пересідати, пересісти

channel • n пролив (m), протока (f), канал (m)

chanterelle • n лисичка (f)

chaos • n хаос (m)

chapel • n каплиця (f)

chapter • n глава (f), розділ (m)

charlatan • n дурисвіт (m), пройдисвіт (m)

chase • v ганяти, поганяти, гнати, погнати

chassis • n шасі (n)

chastity • n цнотливість (f), непорочність (f), невинність (f)

chat • v балакати • n розмова (f), бесіда (f), чат (m)

chauffeur • n шофер (m), водій (m)

check • n рахунок (m)

checkmate • n мат (m) • interj мат (m), шах і мат

cheek • n щока (f)

cheers • interj будьмо

cheese • n сир (m)

cheetah • n гепард (m)

chemistry • n хімія (f)

cheque • n чек (m) /(ček)/

cherry • n черешня (f), вишня (f)

chess • n шахи

chest • n груди

chestnut • n каштан (m)

chew • v жувати

chickadee • n синиця (f)

chicken • n курча, курка

chiefly • adv в основному, головним чином, особливо, в першу чергу

child • n дитина (f), дитя (n)

childbirth • n роди

childhood • n дитинство (n)

chilly • adj прохолодний

chimney • n димова труба (f), димохід (m)

chimpanzee • n шимпанзе (f)

chin • n підборіддя (n), борода (f)

chisel • n долото (n), зубило (n), стамеска (f)

chivalry • n лицарство (n)

chlorine • n хлор (m) /(xlor)/

chloroform • n хлороформ (m) /(xlorofórm)/

chocolate • n шоколад (m)

choir • n хор (m)

choose • v вибирати, вибрати

chromium • n хром (m)

chrysanthemum • n хризантема (f) /(xryzantéma)/

church • n церква (f)

ciao • interj чао /(čáo)/

cigarette • n сигарета (f), цигарка (f), папірос (m), папіроса (f)

cinema • n кінотеатр (m) /(kinoteátr)/, кіно (n)

circle • n круг (m), окружність (f), коло (n)

circumcision • n обрізання (n)

circus • n цирк (m)

cirque • n цирк (m)

citizen • n громадянин (m), громадянка (f)

citizenship • n громадянство (n)

city • n місто (n)

civilization • n цивілізація (f)

clabber • n кисляк (m) /(kyslják)/

clairvoyance • n ясновидіння (n) /(jasnovýdinnja)/

clarinet • n кларнет (m)

clarity • n ясність (f) /(jásnist□)/

class • n клас (m)

classification • n класифікація (f) /(klasyfikácija)/

classroom • n клас (m), класна кімната (f)

claw • n кіготь (m), клішня (f)

clean • v чистити, почистити • adj чистий

cleanliness • n чистота (f), чистість (f)

clergy • n духовенство (n)

clever • adj розумний

cliff • n скеля (f), кліф (m)

climate • n клімат (m)

climatology • n кліматологія (f)

climb • v лазити, полазити, лізти, полізти

clinic • n клініка (f)

clitoral • *adj* кліторний
clitoris • *n* клітор (*m*) /(*klítor*)/
clock • *n* годинник (*m*)
cloister • *n* клуатр (*f*)
close • *v* зачиняти, зачинити, закривати, закрити • *adj* близький, ближній
closed • *adj* зачинений (*m*), закритий (*m*), замкнений (*m*)
closely • *adv* тісно /(*tísno*)/, близько /(*blýz□ko*)/
closet • *n* шафа (*f*)
clothes • *n* одяг (*m*), одежа (*f*)
clothing • *n* одяг (*m*), одежа (*f*)
cloud • *n* хмара (*f*) /(*xmára*)/
cloudy • *adj* хмарний, облачний
clover • *n* конюшина (*f*)
clown • *n* клоун (*m*)
club • *n* клуб (*m*)
coal • *n* вугілля (*n*), кам'яне вугілля (*n*)
coast • *n* побережжя
coat • *n* пальто (*n*), піджак
cobalt • *n* кобальт (*m*)
cobra • *n* кобра (*f*)
cock-a-doodle-doo • *interj* кукуріку /(*kukuriku*)/
cockade • *n* кокарда (*f*) /(*kokárda*)/
cockchafer • *n* хрущ (*m*) /(*xrušč*)/, травневий жук (*m*) /(*travnévyj žuk*)/, травневий хрущ (*m*) /(*travnévyj xrušč*)/
cockle • *n* серцевидка (*f*) /(*sercevýdka*)/
cockroach • *n* тарган (*m*)
coconut • *n* кокос (*m*), кокосовий горіх (*m*)
cocoon • *n* кокон (*m*)
cod • *n* тріска (*f*)
code • *n* код (*m*)
coercion • *n* примус (*m*) /(*prýmus*)/
coffee • *n* кава (*f*)
coffin • *n* труна (*f*) /(*truná*)/, гроб (*m*) /(*hrob*)/
cognac • *n* коньяк (*m*)
coin • *n* монета (*f*)
cola • *n* кола (*f*)
colander • *n* друшляк (*m*)
cold • *n* простуда (*f*), застуда (*f*) • *adj* холодний
collaborator • *n* колабораціоніст (*m*), колабораціоністка (*f*)
collar • *n* комір (*m*), комірець (*m*)
colleague • *n* колега (*f*), співробітник (*m*), співробітниця (*f*)
collect • *v* збирати, зібрати
collectivization • *n* колективізація (*f*)
collocation • *n* словосполучення (*n*) /(*slovospolúčennja*)/

cologne • *n* одеколон (*m*)
colonization • *n* колонізація (*f*)
colony • *n* колонія (*f*)
color • *n* колір (*m*), фарба (*f*)
colostrum • *n* молозиво (*n*)
colt • *n* лоша (*n*) /(*lošá*)/
columbine • *n* водозбір /(*vodosbir*)/
coma • *n* кома (*f*)
come • *v* приходити, прийти, приїжджати, приїхати
comedy • *n* комедія (*f*)
comestible • *adj* їстівний
comet • *n* комета (*f*)
comical • *adj* смішний (*m*)
comma • *n* перетинка (*f*), кома (*f*)
command • *n* наказ (*m*), команда (*f*)
commandment • *n* заповідь (*f*)
commemorative • *n* мемориал, меморіал /(*Memoryal, memorial*)/
commence • *v* починати, почати, починатися, початися
commerce • *n* торгівля (*f*), комерція (*f*)
committee • *n* комітет (*m*) /(*komitét*)/
communism • *n* комунізм (*m*)
company • *n* товариство (*n*), діло (*n*), компанія (*f*), фірма (*f*), підприємство (*n*), сотня (*f*), ланка (*f*)
compare • *v* порівнювати, порівняти
comparison • *n* порівняння (*n*), ступені порівняння
compass • *n* компас (*m*), бусоля (*f*)
compatriot • *n* співвітчизник (*m*), співвітчизниця (*f*)
complete • *adj* повний
compliment • *n* комплімент, похвала, люб'язність
component • *n* компонент (*m*)
composer • *n* композитор (*m*)
compromise • *n* компроміс (*m*) /(*kompromís*)/
compulsory • *adj* обов'язковий (*m*)
computer • *n* комп'ютер (*m*)
comrade • *n* товариш (*m*)
conception • *n* зачаття (*n*)
concert • *n* концерт (*m*)
concrete • *n* бетон (*m*)
concubine • *n* наложниця (*f*)
condiment • *n* приправа (*f*)
condition • *n* умова (*f*), стан (*m*)
condom • *n* презерватив (*m*)
condor • *n* кондор (*m*)
cone • *n* шишка (*f*)
confederation • *n* конфедерація (*f*)
confessional • *n* сповідальня (*f*)
conflagration • *n* пожежа (*f*), згарище (*n*)

conflict • *n* конфлíкт *(m)*

congratulate • *v* поздоровля́ти, поздоро́вити

congratulations • *interj* вітати

conjunction • *n* сполу́чник *(m)*

connect • *v* з'є́днувати, під'є́днувати

conquer • *v* підко́рювати, перемага́ти

conscience • *n* со́вість *(f)* /(sóvist')/, сумлíння *(n)* /(sumlínnja)/

consonant • *n* приголо́сний *(m)*, шелестíвка *(f)*, приголо́сна *(f)*

constellation • *n* сузір'я *(n)*

construct • *v* буду́вати /(budaváty)/, збуду́вати /(zbudaváty)/, конструюва́ти /(konstrujuváty)/, зконструю́вати /(zkonstrujuváty)/

consulate • *n* ко́нсульство *(n)*

consumer • *n* спожива́ч *(m)* /(spožyváč)/

consumptive • *adj* виснажливий *(m)*, руйнівний *(m)*, сухотний *(m)*

contagion • *n* інфе́кція *(f)*

container • *n* контейнер *(m)* /(kontéjner)/

contemporary • *n* суча́сник *(m)*, суча́сниця *(f)*

continent • *n* контине́нт *(m)*, матери́к *(m)*

continue • *v* продовжувати /(prodóvžuvaty)/, продовжити /(prodóvžyty)/

contract • *n* контра́кт *(m)*, до́говір *(m)*

contradict • *v* суперечити, заперечувати

contradictory • *adj* суперечли́вий

controversial • *adj* спíрний

contumely • *n* обра́за *(f)*

convenient • *adj* зру́чний

convention • *n* конвенція *(f)* /(konvéncija)/

conversation • *n* розмо́ва *(f)*, бесíда *(f)*

converse • *v* розмовля́ти, розмо́вити

convoy • *n* конво́й *(m)*

cook • *v* готува́ти, кухова́рити, вари́ти • *n* куха́р *(m)*, куха́рка *(f)*

cool • *adj* прохоло́дний

cooling • *n* охолодження *(n)* /(oxolódžennja)/

copper • *n* мідь *(f)*

copra • *n* копра *(f)*

cordial • *n* сироп *(m)* /(syróp)/

corkscrew • *n* штопор *(n)* /(shtopor)/

cormorant • *n* баклан *(m)*

corolla • *n* віно́чок *(m)*

corporation • *n* корпорація *(f)*

corpse • *n* труп *(m)*, мертве́ць *(m)*, мрець *(m)*

correct • *v* виправля́ти • *adj* пра́вильний

corridor • *n* коридор *(m)* /(korydór)/

corruption • *n* кору́пція *(f)*

corvette • *n* корвет *(m)*

cosmic • *adj* космічний /(kosmíčnyj)/

cosmos • *n* ко́смос *(m)*, всесвіт *(m)*

cost • *v* ко́штувати

cotton • *n* баво́вник *(m)* /(bavóvnyk)/, бавовна *(f)* /(bavóvna)/ • *adj* баво́вняний, бавовня́ний

cough • *v* ка́шляти • *n* ка́шель *(m)*

count • *v* рахува́ти, лічи́ти

counterespionage • *n* контррозвідка *(f)*

country • *n* краї́на *(f)*, земля́ *(f)*, держа́ва *(f)*, село́ *(n)*, провíнція *(f)*

courage • *n* смíливість *(f)*, хоро́брість *(f)*, му́жність *(f)*, відва́га *(f)*

court • *n* двір *(m)*, суд, суд *(m)*

courteous • *adj* вві́чливий /(vvíčlyvyj)/

cousin • *n* двою́рідний брат *(m)*, брат у пе́рших *(m)*, двою́рідна сестра́ *(f)*, кузе́н *(m)*, кузи́на *(f)*

cover • *v* покрива́ти, покри́ти, прикрива́ти, прикри́ти, укрива́ти, вкрива́ти, укри́ти, вкри́ти • *n* кри́шка *(f)*

cow • *n* коро́ва *(f)*

coward • *n* боягу́з *(m)*, боягу́зка *(f)*

cowbell • *n* тронка *(f)* /(tronka)/

cowboy • *n* ковбо́й *(m)*

crab • *n* краб *(m)*

cradle • *n* колíска *(f)*, лю́ля *(f)*, лю́лька *(f)*

crag • *n* скéля *(f)*

cranberry • *n* журавлина *(f)* /(žuravlýna)/

crane • *n* жураве́ль *(m)*, кран *(m)*, двигу́н *(m)*

crash • *n* ава́рія *(f)*, катастро́фа *(f)*

crawl • *v* по́взати, повзти́

crayfish • *n* рак *(m)*

cream • *n* смета́на *(f)*, вершки́, крем *(m)*, мазь *(f)*, масть *(f)*, масти́ло *(n)*, пома́да *(f)* • *adj* сметанко́вий *(m)*, сметанко́вого кольо́ру, кремо́вий *(m)*, кремо́вого кольо́ру

crease • *v* м'яти /(mjáty)/

creative • *adj* тво́рчий

creature • *n* істо́та *(f)*, тварь *(f)*, твари́на *(f)*, створíння *(n)*

crematorium • *n* кремато́рій *(m)*

cricket • *n* цвірку́н *(m)*

crime • *n* зло́чин *(m)*

criminal • *n* злочи́нець *(m)*, злочи́нниця *(f)*

crisis • *n* кри́за *(f)*

criticism • *n* критика */(krytyka)/*

crocodile • *n* крокоди́л *(m)*

cross • *n* хрест *(m)*, хрест *(m)* */(xrest)/*, розп'яття *(f)* */(rozp'játtja)/*, хресне зна-мення *(n)*

crossbow • *n* арбале́т *(m)*

crossing • *n* перехрестя *(n)*, пере-тин *(m)*, перехрещення *(n)*, схреще-ння *(n)*, роздоріжжя *(n)*, перехре-щування *(n)*, переї́зд, перехід *(m)* */(perekhid)/*, переправа *(f)* */(perepráva)/*, хрест *(m)* */(khrest)/*, перехрещення *(n)* */(perekhreshennia)/*

crossroads • *n* перехре́сток *(m)*, пере-хре́стя *(n)*

crow • *n* воро́на *(f)*, ґава, ґа́ва *(f)*

crowd • *n* натовп *(m)* */(nátovp)/*, купа *(f)* */(kúpa)/*

crown • *n* коро́на *(f)*, тім'я *(n)*, ма́ківка *(f)*

cruel • *adj* жорстокий */(žorstókyj)/*

crumb • *n* кри́хта *(f)*

crustacean • *n* ракоподібні

cry • *v* пла́кати

cube • *n* куб *(m)*

cubism • *n* кубізм *(m)* */(kubízm)/*

cuckoo • *n* зозу́ля *(f)*

cucumber • *n* огіро́к

cuff • *n* манже́та *(f)*, обшла́ґ *(m)*

culinary • *adj* куха́рський *(m)* */(kúcharśkyj)/*, куховарський *(m)* */(kuchovárśkyj)/*

cult • *n* культ *(m)*, се́кта *(f)*

culture • *n* культу́ра *(f)*

cunt • *n* пизда́ *(f)*, пі́ська *(f)*

cup • *n* ча́шка *(f)*

cupboard • *n* буфет *(m)* */(bufét)/*, сер-вант *(m)* */(servánt)/*, шафа *(f)* */(šáfa)/*

curiosity • *n* цікавість *(f)* */(cikávist☐)/*, рі́дкість *(f)* */(rídkist☐)/*, дивина *(f)* */(dyvýna)/*

curious • *adj* ціка́вий *(m)*, допи́тливий *(m)*

curium • *n* кюрій *(m)*

currant • *n* смородина *(f)* */(smorodyna)/*, сморо́дина *(f)* */(smoródyna)/*

curtain • *n* завіса *(f)*, занаві́ска *(f)*, кур-ти́на *(f)*, портьє́ра *(f)*

cushion • *n* подушка *(f)* */(podúška)/*, бу-фер *(m)* */(búfer)/*, борт *(m)* */(bort)/*

custom • *n* звича́й *(m)*, обичай *(m)*

cut • *v* рі́зати, руба́ти

cuttlefish • *n* карака́тиця *(f)*

cyborg • *n* кі́борг *(m)*

cynicism • *n* цинізм *(m)* */(cynízm)/*

D

dacha • *n* дача *(f)* */(dáča)/*

dachshund • *n* такса *(f)* */(táksa)/*

dactylic • *adj* дактилі́чний

dad • *n* та́то *(m)*, та́тусь *(m)*, па́па *(m)*

daddy • *n* та́то *(m)*, та́тусь *(m)*

dagger • *n* кинджа́л *(m)*

daikon • *n* дайкон *(m)* */(dajkon)/*, япон-ська редька *(f)* */(japóns☐ka réd☐ka)/*, ки-тайська редька *(f)* */(kitájs☐ka réd☐ka)/*

dale • *n* долина *(f)* */(dolýna)/*

dam • *n* гребля *(f)*, да́мба *(f)*

dance • *v* танцюва́ти • *n* та́нець *(m)*, та́нок *(m)*

dancer • *n* танцюри́ст *(m)*, танцюри́с-тка *(f)*

dandelion • *n* кульба́ба *(f)*

dandruff • *n* лупа́ *(f)*

danger • *n* небезпе́ка *(f)*, загро́за *(f)*

dangerous • *adj* небезпе́чний

dark • *adj* те́мний

darkness • *n* темрява *(f)*, тьма *(f)*, мо-рок *(m)*, темнота *(f)*

data • *n* да́ні

database • *n* ба́за да́них *(f)*

date • *n* фі́нік *(m)*, да́та *(f)*

daughter • *n* дочка́ *(f)*

daughter-in-law • *n* неві́стка *(f)*

dawn • *n* зоря́ *(f)*, світа́нок *(m)*

day • *n* день *(m)*, до́ба *(f)*, день

deacon • *n* дия́кон *(m)*

dead • *adj* ме́ртвий

deaf • *adj* глухи́й

dear • *adj* дороги́й

death • *n* смерть *(f)*

debt • *n* борг *(m)*, зобов'яза́ння

decade • *n* десятилі́ття *(n)*, десятиріч-чя *(n)*

decadence • *n* декада́нс *(m)*

deceive • *v* обма́нювати, обману́ти

deception • *n* обма́н *(m)*

decide • *v* вирі́шувати, ви́рішити

deep • *adj* глибокий */(hlybókyj)/*

deer • *n* оле́нь *(m)*

defamatory • *adj* наклепницький, який гань́бить

defeat • *n* поразка *(f)*

defeatism • *n* дефетизм *(m)* /*(defetýzm)*/

defend • *v* обороняти, оборонити, захищати, захистити

defender • *n* захисник *(m)*, захисниця *(f)*

defense • *n* оборона *(f)*, захист *(m)*

defenseless • *adj* беззахисний

definition • *n* означення *(n)*, визначення *(n)*, дефініція *(f)*

degree • *n* градус *(m)* /*(gradus)*/

deism • *n* деїзм *(m)*

deity • *n* божественність *(f)* /*(božéstvennist⁻)*/

deliberate • *adj* навмисний /*(navmýsnyj)*/, умисний /*(umýsnyj)*/

deliberately • *adv* навмисно, свідомо, нароком, умисно, зумисно, нарошне, знарошне, нарочито, знарошна, назнарошне, назнарошки, поволі, повільно, звагом, проквольисто, несквапно, неквапливо, виважено

delicious • *adj* смачний

delirium • *n* бред *(m)*

delivery • *n* роди /*(ródy)*/

demagogue • *n* демагог /*(demahoh)*/

democracy • *n* демократія *(f)*

demon • *n* біс *(m)* /*(bis)*/, демон *(m)* /*(démon)*/, чорт *(m)* /*(čort)*/

demonstrator • *n* демонстрант *(m)*, демонстрантка *(m)*, маніфестант *(m)*, маніфестантка *(f)*

denial • *n* заперечення *(n)*, відмова *(f)*

denominator • *n* знаменник *(m)*

dentist • *n* зубний лікар *(m)*, дантист *(m)*

depart • *v* відправлятися, відправитися

departure • *n* відправлення *(n)*, виїзд *(m)*, від'їзд *(m)*, виліт *(m)* /*(výlit)*/, відхилення *(n)*, смерть *(f)*, відхід *(m)*, упокоєння *(n)*, упокій *(m)*

deport • *v* висилати, вислати

deportation • *n* депортація *(f)*, висилка *(f)*

depression • *n* депресія *(f)* /*(deprésija)*/

depth • *n* глибина *(f)*

dervish • *n* дервіш *(m)*

descend • *v* спускатися, спуститися

descendant • *n* нащадок *(m)*

describe • *v* описувати /*(opýsuvaty)*/, описати /*(opysáty)*/

description • *n* опис *(m)*

desert • *n* пустеля *(f)*, пустиня *(f)*

desertion • *n* дезертирство, залишення, занедбаність

designer • *n* дизайнер *(m)*

desire • *v* бажати • *n* бажання *(n)*

despise • *v* зневажати /*(znevažáty)*/

despotism • *n* деспотизм *(m)* /*(despotýzm)*/

dessert • *n* десерт *(m)* /*(desért)*/

destiny • *n* доля *(f)*, льос *(m)*

detachment • *n* відділення /*(viddilenia)*/, відокремлення /*(vidokremlenia)*/, відірваність /*(veedeervahnist')*/, відчуження /*(vidchuzhenia)*/, роз'єднання /*(rozyednania)*/, відчуженість /*(vidchuzhenist')*/, безстрасність /*(bezstrasneest')*/, безсторонність /*(bezstoroneest')*/, загін /*(zaheen)*/

detail • *n* деталь *(f)* /*(detál')*/, наряд /*(narjád)*/

develop • *v* розвиватися, розвинутися

device • *n* пристрій *(m)*

devil • *n* чорт *(m)*, біс *(m)*, диявол *(m)*

dew • *n* роса *(f)*

diabetes • *n* діабет *(m)* /*(diabét)*/

diagnostic • *adj* діагностичний

dialect • *n* діалект *(m)*, наріччя *(n)*, говір *(m)*

dialogue • *n* діалог *(m)*, розмова *(f)*, бесіда *(f)*

diametrically • *adv* діаметрально /*(diametrál'no)*/

diamond • *n* алмаз *(m)*, діамант *(m)*

diary • *n* щоденник *(m)*

dick • *n* хуй *(m)*, пісюн *(m)*

dictator • *n* диктатор *(m)* /*(dyktátor)*/

dictatorship • *n* диктатура *(f)* /*(dyktatúra)*/

dictionary • *n* словник *(m)*

die • *v* умирати, умерти, померти • *n* кістка *(f)*

diet • *n* дієта *(f)*, їжа *(f)*

difference • *n* різниця *(f)*

different • *adj* інший, відмінний, різний

difficult • *adj* важкий, трудний

dig • *v* копати, рити

digest • *v* перетравлювати /*(peretrávljuvaty)*/, травити /*(travýty)*/

digestion • *n* травлення *(n)* /*(trávlennja)*/

digitization • *n* оцифровування *(n)*

dignified • *adj* гідний

dignity • *n* достоїнство *(n)*, гідність *(f)*

dildo • *n* фалоімітатор *(m)* /*(faloimitátor)*/

dilemma • *n* дилема *(f)* /*(dyléma)*/

dilettantism • *n* дилетантизм *(m)*

dill • *n* кріп *(m)*, окрі́п *(m)*

dine • *v* вечеряти /*(večérjaty)*/, повечеряти /*(povečérjaty)*/

dinner • *n* вече́ря *(f)*, обі́д *(m)*

dinosaur • *n* диноза́вр *(m)*

diocese • *n* єпархія *(f)* /*(jepárxija)*/, діоцез *(m)* /*(diocéz)*/, діє́цезія *(f)* /*(dijecézija)*/

diploma • *n* диплом /*(dyplóm)*/

direction • *n* напря́мок *(m)*, на́прям *(m)*

director • *n* директор *(m)* /*(dyréktor)*/, режисер *(m)* /*(režysér)*/

dirt • *n* бруд *(m)*

dirty • *adj* бру́дний

disappear • *v* зникати /*(znikáty)*/

disaster • *n* катастро́фа *(f)*, ли́хо *(n)*, неща́стя *(n)*, го́ре *(n)*, біда́ *(f)*

discount • *n* зни́жка *(f)*

discovery • *n* відкриття *(n)* /*(vidkrýttja)*/

discrimination • *n* дискримінація *(f)* /*(dyskryminácija)*/

discuss • *v* дискутувати /*(dyskutuváty)*/, обгово́рювати, обговори́ти

discussion • *n* розмова /*(rozmóva)*/, дискусія /*(dyskúsija)*/

disease • *n* хворо́ба *(f)*

disgrace • *n* ганьба́ *(f)*

disgust • *n* відраза *(f)* /*(vidráza)*/

dish • *n* тарі́лка *(f)*, ми́ска *(f)*

dishwasher • *n* посудоми́йна маши́на *(f)*

disk • *n* диск *(m)*, пласти́нка *(f)*

disobedient • *adj* непокі́рний, неслухня́ний

dispel • *v* розві́ювати /*(rozvíjuvaty)*/, розсі́ювати /*(rozsíjuvaty)*/

display • *v* пока́зувати, показа́ти

disservice • *n* ведме́жа по́слуга *(f)*

dissident • *n* дисиде́нт *(m)*, дисиде́нтка *(f)*

distance • *n* відда́лення *(n)*, ві́дстань *(f)*, ві́ддаль *(f)*, дистанція *(f)*

distant • *adj* дале́кий

distress • *n* го́ре *(n)*, лихо *(n)*, стражда́ння *(n)*, небезпека *(f)*, загроза *(f)*

ditch • *n* рів *(f)* /*(riv)*/, канава *(f)* /*(kanáva)*/

diurnal • *adj* денний, добовий, щоденний

dive • *v* ниря́ти

diver • *n* гагара *(f)*

divide • *v* ділити

divinity • *n* божественність *(f)* /*(božéstvennist)*/

do • *v* роби́ти, зроби́ти

dobra • *n* добра /*(dobra)*/

doctor • *n* лі́кар *(m)*, до́ктор *(m)*, до́ктор

document • *n* докуме́нт *(m)*

documentary • *n* документа́льний фільм *(m)* • *adj* документа́льний

documentation • *n* документа́ція *(f)*

dodecahedron • *n* додекаедр *(m)* /*(dodekáedr)*/

dog • *n* собака *(f)* /*(sobáka)*/, пес *(m)* /*(pes)*/, пес *(m)*, собáка *(f)*, собака

doge • *n* дож *(m)* /*(dož)*/

dogmatism • *n* догматизм *(m)*

doll • *n* ля́лька *(f)*

dollar • *n* до́лар *(m)*

dolphin • *n* дельфі́н *(m)*

dominoes • *n* доміно *(n)* /*(dominó)*/

donkey • *n* осе́л *(m)*, віслюк *(m)*, іша́к *(m)*

door • *n* две́рі

dormouse • *n* соня *(f)* /*(sonja)*/

dose • *n* доза *(f)* /*(dóza)*/

dot • *n* крапка *(f)* /*(krápka)*/, точка *(f)* /*(tóčka)*/, дот *(m)* /*(dot)*/

doubt • *v* сумніва́тися • *n* су́мнів *(m)*

dough • *n* тісто *(n)*

doughnut • *n* по́нчик *(m)*, пампу́шка *(f)*

dove • *n* голуб *(m)* /*(hólub)*/

down • *adv* вниз, дони́зу, внизу́

downpour • *n* злива *(f)* /*(zlýva)*/

doze • *v* дріма́ти

dozen • *n* дю́жина *(f)*

drachma • *n* драхма *(f)* /*(dráxma)*/

dragon • *n* змій *(m)*, змі́їха *(f)*, драко́н *(m)*

dragonfly • *n* стрекоза́ *(f)*, ва́жка *(f)*, ба́бка *(f)*

drain • *v* спуска́ти, спусти́ти, висушувати, висна́жувати

draughts • *n* ша́шки

draw • *v* рисува́ти, нарисува́ти, малюва́ти, намалюва́ти

drawing • *n* рисунок *(m)* /*(rysúnok)*/, малюнок *(m)* /*(maljúnok)*/

dream • *n* сон *(m)*, сновиді́ння *(n)*, мрі́я *(f)*

dress • *v* одяга́ти, одяга́тися • *n* пла́ття *(n)*, су́кня *(f)*, оде́жа *(f)*, о́дяг *(m)*

drink • *v* пи́ти, ви́пити

drinkable • *adj* питни́й

drinker • *n* п'яни́ця *(f)*

drive • *v* гна́ти, ганя́ти

driver • *n* во́дій *(m)*, шофе́р *(m)*

dromedary • *n* дромадéр *(m)*

drone • *n* трýтень *(m)*, безпілóтник *(m)*

drop • *n* крáпля *(f)*

drought • *n* зáсуха *(f)*

drum • *n* барабáн *(m)* /(barabán)/

drunk • *adj* п'я́ний

dry • *adj* сухий /(suxýj)/

dryer • *n* сушарка *(f)* /(sušárka)/

duchess • *n* герцогиня *(f)* /(hercohýnja)/, княгиня *(f)* /(knjahýnja)/

duchy • *n* герцогство *(n)* /(hércohstvo)/, князівство *(n)* /(knjázivstvo)/

duck • *v* поринáти, занýрювати, заглúблювати, ухиля́ти • *n* кáчка *(f)*, парусúна *(f)*, грýбе полотнó *(n)*

duel • *n* дуель *(f)* /(duél□)/, поєдинок *(m)* /(pojedýnok)/

duke • *n* гéрцог *(m)*, князь *(m)*

dulcimer • *n* цимбали /(cimbali)/

dull • *adj* тупúй

duma • *n* дýма *(f)*

dumbbell • *n* гантель *(f)*

dumpling • *n* пельмéнь *(m)*, клéцька *(f)*, галýшка *(f)*

dune • *n* дюна *(f)*, бархáн *(m)*

dung • *n* гній *(m)*, кал *(m)*, екскремéнти

durian • *n* дуріан *(m)*

during • *prep* прóтягом, під чáс

dust • *n* пил *(m)*

dustpan • *n* совóк *(m)*

duty • *n* борг *(m)*, обов'язок *(m)* /(obov'jázok)/

dwarf • *n* кáрлик *(m)*, гном *(m)*

dwell • *v* мéшкати, жúти, проживáти

dwelling • *n* житло *(n)* /(žytló)/, помешкання *(n)* /(poméškannja)/

dynamite • *n* динамíт *(m)*

dyslexia • *n* дислексія /(dysleksija)/

dysprosium • *n* диспрóзій *(m)*

E

eagle • *n* орéл *(m)*

ear • *n* вýхо *(n)*, кóлос *(m)*

eardrum • *n* барабáнна перетинка *(f)* /(barabánna peretýnka)/

early • *adj* рáнній, завчáсний • *adv* рáно, завчáсно

earring • *n* сергá *(f)*, серéжка *(f)*

earth • *n* земля́ *(f)*

earthquake • *n* землетрýс *(m)*

easement • *n* сервітут

easily • *adv* легко /(léhko)/

east • *n* схід *(m)*

easterly • *n* схíдний вíтер *(m)* • *adj* схíдний *(m)*

eastern • *adj* схíдний /(sxídnyj)/

eastward • *adv* на схід

easy • *adj* легкúй

eat • *v* íсти

echo • *n* лунá *(f)*, вíдгук *(m)*, відгómін *(m)*

ecology • *n* екологія *(f)* /(ekolóhija)/

economics • *n* еконóміка *(f)*

economy • *n* еконóміка *(f)*, господáрство *(n)*

ecosystem • *n* екосистема *(f)* /(ekosystéma)/

edible • *adj* їстівнúй

education • *n* освíта *(f)*

eel • *n* вугóр *(m)*

egg • *n* яйцé *(n)*, яйцеклíтина *(f)*

eggplant • *n* баклажан *(m)* /(baklažán)/

egoism • *n* егоїзм *(m)* /(ehojízm)/

eider • *n* гага *(f)* /(háha)/

eight • *n* вісíмка *(f)*

eighteenth • *adj* вісімнáдцятий *(m)*

eighth • *adj* восьмий *(m)* /(vós'myj)/

einsteinium • *n* ейнштейнíй *(m)* /(ejnštéjnij)/

eisteddfod • *n* айстедфед

ejaculation • *n* сíм'явиверження /(sim"javiveržennja)/, еякуляція /(ejakuljacija)/

elastic • *adj* еластичний /(elastychny)/

elbow • *n* лíкоть *(m)*

elder • *adj* старший /(stáršyj)/ • *n* бузина *(f)*, бузинá *(f)*

elderberry • *n* бузинá *(f)*

election • *n* вибор

electricity • *n* елéктрика *(f)*

electrification • *n* електрифікáція *(f)* /(elektryfikácija)/

electromagnetism • *n* електромагнетúзм *(m)*

electron • *n* електрон *(m)* /(elektrón)/

electronics • *n* елéктрóніка *(f)*

elephant • *n* слон *(m)*, слонúха *(f)*

eleventh • *adj* одинáдцятий *(m)*

elision • *n* елíзія *(f)* /(elízija)/

ellipse • *n* елíпс

em • *n* ем /(em)/

embassy • *n* посóльство *(n)*

embrasure • *n* амбразура *(f)*

emerald • *n* смара́гд *(m)*, смара́гдовий • *adj* смара́гдовий

emir • *n* емі́р *(m)*

emotion • *n* емо́ція *(f)*, почуття́ *(n)*

empire • *n* імпе́рія *(f)*

empiricism • *n* емпіризм *(m)*

empty • *adj* поро́жній, пусти́й

emu • *n* ему *(m)* /(ému)/

enamel • *n* ема́ль *(f)* /(emál')/

encounter • *n* зустрі́ч *(f)* /(zústrič)/

encyclopedia • *n* енциклопе́дія *(f)*

end • *v* закі́нчувати, закі́нчити, кінча́ти, скі́нчити • *n* кіне́ць *(m)*, край *(m)*

endogamy • *n* ендогамія /(endogamija)/

enemy • *n* во́рог *(m)*, проти́вник *(m)*, супроти́вник *(m)*, не́друг *(m)*

energy • *n* ене́ргія *(f)*

engine • *n* двигу́н *(m)*, мото́р *(m)*

engineer • *n* інжене́р *(m)*, машині́ст *(m)*

enrage • *v* скажені́ти /(skaženity)/, розлютовувати /(rozljutovuvati)/

enslave • *v* понево́лювати

enter • *v* входи́ти, уходи́ти, ввійти́, увійти́

enteritis • *n* ентерит *(m)*

enterprise • *n* підприє́мство *(n)*

enthrall • *v* зачаро́вувати, понево́лювати, підко́рювати

enthusiasm • *n* ентузіазм *(m)*, запал *(m)*

enthusiast • *n* ентузіаст *(m)*, ентузіа́стка *(f)*

entire • *adj* ці́лий, весь, по́вний

entomology • *n* ентомологія *(f)* /(entomolóhija)/

entrails • *n* внутрощі /(vnútrošči)/

entrance • *n* вхід *(m)* /(vxid)/, в'їзд *(m)* /(v"jizd)/

entrepreneur • *n* підприє́мець *(m)*, підприє́мниця *(f)*

entresol • *n* антресоль *(f)*

entropy • *n* ентропія *(f)* /(entropíja)/

envelope • *n* конверт *(m)* /(konvért)/

episode • *n* епізо́д *(m)*

epithelium • *n* епіте́лій *(n)* /(epitelij)/

epopee • *n* епопея

equation • *n* рівня́ння *(n)*

equator • *n* екватор *(m)*

equilibrium • *n* рівнова́га *(f)* /(rivnováha)/

erase • *v* стира́ти, сте́рти

eraser • *n* гу́мка *(f)*, гу́мка *(f)*

erbium • *n* е́рбій *(m)*

erection • *n* ере́кція *(f)* /(erékcija)/

ermine • *n* горностай *(m)* /(hornostáj)/

erotic • *adj* еротичний

err • *v* помиля́тися, помили́тися

erudition • *n* ерудиція /(erudýcija)/, багаж, знань, розумовий

escalator • *n* ескала́тор *(m)*

essence • *n* су́тність *(f)*, суть *(f)*

establishment • *n* істеблішмент *(m)*

estrangement • *n* розрив, розлучення, відчуження, віддалення, відчуженість

eternity • *n* вічність *(f)* /(víčnist□)/

ether • *n* ете́р *(m)*, діетилете́р *(m)*, не́бо *(n)*

ethics • *n* е́тика *(f)*

ethnocentrism • *n* етноцентризм *(m)* /(etnocentrýzm)/

etymology • *n* етимоло́гія *(f)*

eukaryote • *n* імперія Ядерні *(f)* /(impérija Jaderni)/

eulogy • *n* надгробна промова *(f)*, панегірик *(m)*, вихваляння *(n)*

euphemism • *n* евфемізм *(m)*

euphuism • *n* евфуїзм *(m)*

europium • *n* євро́пій *(m)*

euthanasia • *n* евтаназія *(f)* /(evtanázija)/

evening • *n* ве́чір *(m)*

event • *n* поді́я *(f)*

everybody • *pron* усі́, всі, ко́жний

everyone • *pron* усі́, всі, ко́жний

everything • *pron* усе /(usé)/, все /(vse)/

everywhere • *adv* усюди /(usjúdy)/, повсюди /(povsjúdy)/

evil • *n* зло *(n)*, лихо *(n)* /(lýxo)/ • *adj* злий

evolution • *n* еволю́ція *(f)*

ewe • *n* вівця́ *(f)*

ewer • *n* глек *(m)*, глечик *(m)*, дзбан *(m)*

exact • *adj* точний /(tóčnyj)/, докла́дний /(dokládnyj)/

exactly • *adv* точно

examination • *n* екза́мен *(m)*, і́спит *(m)*

example • *n* при́клад *(m)*

excavator • *n* екскава́тор *(m)*

excellent • *adj* відмінний /(vidmínnyj)/, чудовий /(čudóvyj)/

except • *prep* крім /(krim)/, за винятком /(za výnjatkom)/

exceptional • *adj* винятковий *(m)*, винятковий *(m)*, відмінний *(m)*

exclamation • *n* вигук *(m)* /(výhuk)/

excrement • *n* ви́порожнення *(n)*, екскре́менти, кал *(m)*, фека́лії

excursion • *n* екскурсія *(f)* /(ekskúrsija)/

executioner • *n* кат *(m)* /(kat)/

exercise • *n* вправа *(f)* /(vpráva)/

exhibitionism • *n* ексгібіціонізм *(m)* /(eks-hibicionízm)/
exile • *v* висилáти, вúслати
exist • *v* існувати /(isnuváty)/
existence • *n* існувáння *(n)*, буття́ *(n)*
existentialism • *n* екзистенціалізм *(m)*
exit • *n* вúхід *(m)*, вúїзд *(m)*
expensive • *adj* дорогúй
experience • *n* дóсвід
explain • *v* поясни́ти
express • *v* виражáти, вúразити
expression • *n* вислів *(m)*, вираз *(m)*
expressionism • *n* експресіонізм *(m)*
exterminate • *v* винищувати /(vyný̌sčuvaty)/, виводити /(vyvódyty)/

extreme • *adj* крáйній /(krájnij)/, далекий /(dalékyj)/, надмірний /(nadmírnyj)/, екстремáльний /(ekstremál'nyj)/
extremism • *n* екстремізм *(m)* /(ekstremízm)/
eye • *n* óко *(n)*, вý̆шко *(n)*
eyeball • *n* óчне я́блуко *(n)*
eyebrow • *n* брóва *(f)*
eyelash • *n* вія *(f)*
eyelid • *n* повіка *(f)*, віко *(n)*
eyesight • *n* зір *(m)*
eyewitness • *n* очевидець

F

fable • *n* бáйка *(f)*, кáзка *(f)*
face • *n* обли́ччя *(n)*, лицé *(n)*, вúраз обли́ччя *(m)*
fact • *n* факт *(m)*
factory • *n* фáбрика *(f)*, завóд *(m)*
faculty • *n* професура *(f)* /(profesúra)/, професорсько-викладáцький склад *(m)* /(profésors'ko-vykladác'kyj sklad)/, факультет *(m)* /(fakul'tét)/, відділ *(m)* /(viddíl)/, дар *(m)* /(dar)/, здібність *(f)* /(zdíbnist')/
fag • *n* підорáс *(m)*, пі́дор *(m)*, пéдик *(m)*, пéдік *(m)*, гóмік *(m)*
faience • *n* фаянс *(m)*
faith • *n* вíра *(f)*
faithful • *adj* вірний /(vírnyj)/, віддáний /(víddanyj)/, віруючий /(vírujučyj)/
falcon • *n* сóкіл *(m)*
fall • *v* пáдати, упáсти
fame • *n* слáва *(f)* /(sláva)/, відомість *(f)* /(vidómist□)/
familial • *adj* родинний, сімейний
familiar • *adj* знайóмий, відóмий
family • *n* сім'я́ *(f)*, родúна *(f)*
famine • *n* гóлод *(m)*, голодомóр *(m)*
fan • *n* вентилятор *(m)*
fancy • *v* уявляти /(ujavljáty)/, уяви́ти /(ujavýty)/, хотіти /(xotíty)/, бажати /(bažáty)/
far • *adj* далéкий • *adv* далéко
farad • *n* фарáд *(m)*
farm • *n* фéрма *(f)*
farmer • *n* фермер *(m)* /(férmer)/, селянин *(m)* /(seljányn)/, землероб *(m)* /(zemleró́b)/
fart • *v* пердíти
fascinate • *v* захóплювати, зачарóву-

вати, чарувáти /(čaruváty)/
fascism • *n* фашизм *(m)* /(fašý̆zm)/, нацизм *(m)* /(nacý̆zm)/
fascist • *n* фаши́ст *(m)*, фаши́стка *(f)* • *adj* фаши́стський
fashion • *n* мóда *(f)*
fast • *adj* швидки́й • *adv* швúдко • *interj* Припини́ти вогóнь *(m)*
fat • *n* жир *(m)* • *adj* тóвстий, жи́рний, дебéлий
fate • *n* дóля *(f)*, льос *(m)*
father • *n* бáтько *(m)*, отéць *(m)*, тáто *(m)*
father-in-law • *n* свéкор *(m)*, тесть *(m)*
fatherland • *n* батьківщина *(f)* /(bát□kivščýna)/
fawn • *n* оленятко *(n)* /(olenjátko)/
fax • *n* факс *(m)*
fear • *n* страх *(m)*
feather • *n* перó
feces • *n* фекáлії, вúпорожнення *(n)*, екскремéнти, кал *(m)*
federation • *n* федерáція *(f)*
feed • *v* годувáти, харчувáти, корми́ти
feel • *v* відчувáти, відчýти, почувáти, чýти, почýти
feeling • *n* почуття́ *(n)*
fellatio • *n* фелляція *(f)*, мінет
female • *n* жі́нка *(f)*, сами́ця *(f)*, сáмка *(f)*
feminine • *n* жінóчий рід *(m)* • *adj* жінóчий
feminism • *n* фемінізм *(m)* /(feminízm)/
fence • *n* паркан *(m)* /(parkán)/, огорóжа *(f)* /(ohoróža)/, тин *(m)* /(tyn)/
fermium • *n* фéрмій *(m)*

fern • *n* папороть *(f)* /*(paporot)*/
ferret • *n* тхір *(m)*
ferry • *n* поро́м *(m)*
fertilize • *v* удобрювати, живити, за-
плі́днювати, запліднити
fertilizer • *n* добриво *(n)*, мінеральне
добриво *(n)*, міндобриво *(n)*
fever • *n* жар *(m)*, температу́ра *(f)*, ли-
хома́нка *(f)*
fiasco • *n* фиаско *(m)* /*(fyasko)*/
field • *n* по́ле *(n)*
fifteenth • *adj* п'ятна́дцятий *(m)*
fifth • *adj* п'я́тий *(m)*
fiftieth • *adj* п'ятидеся́тий
fight • *v* би́тися, боро́тися • *n* бі́йка *(f)*,
бій *(m)*, сути́чка *(f)*, би́тва *(f)*, боротьба́
(f)
file • *n* річ /*(rič)*/, напилок *(m)*
/*(napýlok)*/, пилка *(f)* /*(pýlka)*/
film • *n* плі́вка *(f)*, кіноплі́вка *(f)*
filth • *n* бруд *(m)*
finally • *adv* зре́штою
finch • *n* зя́блик *(m)* /*(zjáblyk)*/
find • *v* знахо́дити, знайти́
fine • *n* штраф *(m)* /*(štraf)*/, пеня *(f)*
/*(penjá)*/
finger • *n* па́лець *(m)*
fingernail • *n* ні́готь *(m)*
finish • *v* закі́нчувати, закі́нчити, кін-
ча́ти, скі́нчити
fir • *n* яли́ця *(f)*, яли́на *(f)*, пі́хта *(f)*
fire • *n* вого́нь *(m)*, поже́жа *(f)*, піч *(f)*
firefly • *n* світля́к *(m)* /*(svitlják)*/
firewood • *n* дро́ва
first • *n* пе́рший • *adj* пе́рший
fish • *n* ри́ба *(f)*
fisherman • *n* риба́лка *(m)*, риба́к *(m)*
fishing • *n* риба́лка *(f)*
fishy • *n* рибка *(f)* /*(rýbka)*/
fist • *n* кула́к *(m)*
fitness •   *n*   придатність   *(f)*
/*(prydátnist□)*/
flag • *v* прикраша́ти пра́пором, си-
гналізува́ти пра́пором, сигналізува́-
ти пра́пором, повиснути, пони́кнути,
сла́бшати, зме́ншувати, зме́ншувати-
ся, мости́ти, брукува́ти, вистила́ти,
прокла́дати • *n* пра́пор *(m)*, стяг *(m)*,
знамено *(n)*, флаг *(m)*, фля́га *(f)*, фля́га
(f), хоругва́ *(f)*, хоругва́ *(f)*, іри́с *(m)*, пі-
́вники, коси́ця *(f)*, плита́ *(f)*, плитня́к
(m), тротуа́р *(m)*
flagellum • *n* джгу́тик *(m)*
flail • *n* ціп *(m)* /*(cip)*/
flame • *n* по́лум'я *(n)*
flamethrower • *n* вогнеме́т *(m)*

flamingo • *n* флама́нго *(m)*
flashlight • *n* лі́хтарик *(m)*, лі́хтар *(m)*
flat • *adj* пло́ский, рі́вний, поло́гий
flea • *n* блоха́ *(f)*
fleece • *n* руно́ *(n)*, шерсть *(f)*, во́вна *(f)*
fleeting • *adj* швидкоплинний
flight • *n* полі́т *(m)*, рейс *(m)*
flip-flop • *n* в'єтна́мки
flock • *n* стая *(f)* /*(stája)*/, зграя *(f)*
/*(zhrája)*/
floe • *n* крижина *(f)* /*(kryžýna)*/
flood • *n* пові́нь, пото́п *(m)*
floor • *n* підло́га *(f)*
floriculture • *n* квітникарство, квіткар-
ство
flounder • *n* камбала *(f)* /*(kámbala)*/
flour • *n* бо́рошно *(n)*, мука́ *(f)*
flow • *v* текти́
flower • *n* кві́тка *(f)*, цвіт *(m)*
flu • *n* грип *(m)*
fluorine • *n* фтор *(m)*
flute • *n* фле́йта *(f)*
fly • *n* муха *(f)*, му́ха *(f)*, блешня́ *(f)*
flyer • *n* листі́вка *(f)* /*(lystívka)*/
foal • *n* лоша́ *(n)*, жеребе́ць *(m)*
foam • *n* пі́на *(f)*
fog • *n* тума́н *(m)*, імла́ *(f)*
folklore • *n* фольклор
fondue • *n* фондю́ /*(fondyu)*/
font • *n* шрифт *(m)* /*(šryft)*/
fontanelle • *n* джере́льце *(n)*, тім'ячко
(n)
food • *n* ї́жа *(f)*, харчува́ння *(n)*
fool • *n* ду́рень *(m)*
foolish • *adj* дурни́й
foot • *n* нога́ *(f)*, ступня́ *(f)*, фут *(f)*
football • *n* футбо́л *(m)*, со́кер *(m)*, ко-
́паний м'яч *(m)*
footwear • *n* взуття́ *(n)*
for • *prep* для
forbid • *v* заборони́ти, заборони́ти
force • *v* зму́сити /*(zmúsyty)*/, мусити
/*(músyty)*/ • *n* міць *(f)* /Mić/, загін *(m)*
/*(zahín)*/
ford • *n* брід *(m)* /*(brid)*/
forebrain • *n* передній мозок
forecast • *n* прогно́з *(m)*, передба́чен-
ня *(n)*
forefinger • *n* вказі́вний па́лець *(m)*
forehead • *n* лоб *(m)*, чоло́ *(n)*
foreign • *adj* іноземний
foreigner • *n* інозе́мець *(m)*, інозе́мка
(f)
foresight • *n* передба́чення *(n)*
forest • *n* ліс *(m)*
forethought • *n* продума́ність *(f)*, обду-

маність (f), передбачливість (f)

forethoughtful • *adj* передбачливий, завбачливий

forever • *adv* назавжди /(*nazávždy, nazavždý*)/, навік /(*navík*)/, вічно /(*vícno*)/

forget • *v* забувати, забути

forget-me-not • *n* незабудка (f) /(*nezabúdka*)/

forgive • *v* прощати, простити, пробачати, пробачити

fork • *n* виделка (f), вилка (f)

formidable • *adj* грізний /(*hríznyj*)/

fort • *n* форт (*m*)

fortieth • *adj* сороковий

fortress • *n* фортеця (f)

fountain • *n* фонтан (*m*), водограй (*m*), джерело (*n*) /(*džereló*)/

fourteenth • *adj* чотирнадцятий (*m*)

fourth • *adj* четвертий (*m*)

fox • *n* лис (*m*), лисиця (f)

fracture • *v* ламати /(*lamáty*)/, зламати /(*zlamáty*)/, ламатися /(*lamátysja*)/, зламатися /(*zlamátysja*)/

fragrance • *n* аромат (*m*)

francium • *n* францій (*m*)

freak • *n* дивак

freckle • *n* веснянка (f)

free • *adj* вільний

freedom • *n* свобода (f), вільність (f)

freeway • *n* автострада (f) /(*avtostráda*)/

freeze • *v* заморожувати, заморожу-

ватися

frequent • *adj* частий /(*částyj*)/

fresh • *adj* свіжий

friend • *n* друг (*m*), приятель (*m*), подруга (f), приятелька (f)

friendly • *adj* дружній

friendship • *n* дружба (f)

frog • *n* жаба (f)

from • *prep* від /(*vid*)/, з /(*z*)/

frost • *n* іній (*m*) /(*ínij*)/, мороз (*m*) /(*moróz*)/

frozen • *adj* заморожений /(*zamoróženyj*)/, морожений /(*moróženyj*)/

fruit • *n* плід (*m*), фрукт (*m*)

fry • *v* жарити, смажити

fuck • *v* їбати, їбатися

fuel • *n* паливо (*n*) /(*pályvo*)/

fulcrum • *n* точка опори (f)

full • *adj* повний, ситий

fun • *n* потіха (f) /(*potíxa*)/, забава (f) /(*zabáva*)/, розвага (f) /(*rozváha*)/

function • *n* функція

funeral • *n* похорони, погреб (*m*)

fungus • *n* гриб (*m*), грибок

funnel • *n* воронка (f)

fur • *n* хутро (*n*), хутро (*n*)

furniture • *n* меблі

furrow • *n* борозна (f)

future • *n* майбутнє (*n*) • *adj* майбутній

G

gadolinium • *n* гадоліній (*m*)

galaxy • *n* галактика (f)

gall • *n* гал (*m*) /(*hal*)/

galleon • *n* галіон (*m*)

gallery • *n* галерея (f)

gallicism • *n* галліцизм (*m*)

gallium • *n* галій (*m*)

gallows • *n* шибениця (f)

galosh • *n* калоша (f)

game • *n* гра (f), ігра (f)

gander • *n* гусак (*m*) /(*husák*)/

gang • *n* банда (f)

gangrene • *n* гангрена (f)

garage • *n* гараж (*m*)

garbage • *n* сміття (*n*)

garden • *n* сад (*m*), город (*m*)

garlic • *n* часник (*m*)

gas • *n* газ (*m*)

gasoline • *n* бензин (*m*)

gastritis • *n* гастрит (*m*)

gate • *n* ворота, брама (f)

gather • *v* збирати, зібрати

gaucho • *n* гаучо (*m*)

gauze • *n* марля (f) /(*márlja*)/

gay • *n* гей (*m*), гей (*m*), гомосексуаліст (*m*)

gecko • *n* гекон (*m*)

geisha • *n* гейша (f)

gem • *n* дорогоцінний камінь (*m*) /(*dorohocínnyj kámin'*)/, самоцвіт (*m*) /(*samocvít*)/

gender • *n* рід (*m*), стать (f)

generation • *n* покоління (*n*)

generosity • *n* щедрість (f) /(*ščédrist□*)/

genitive • *n* родовий відмінок (*m*), родовий (*m*)

genocide • *n* геноцид (*m*) /(*henocýd*)/

gentleman • *n* пан (*m*) /(*pan*)/

geography • *n* географія (f)

geology • *n* геологія (f)

geometry • *n* геоме́трія (*f*)

geophysics • *n* геофізика (*f*)

germ • *n* заро́док (*m*), ембріо́н (*m*), мі-кро́б (*m*), зáв'язь (*f*)

germanium • *n* герма́ній (*m*)

get • *v* діставáти, діста́ти, отри́мувати, оде́ржувати

geyser • *n* гейзер (*m*) /(héjzer)/

gherkin • *n* корнішо́н (*m*) /(kornišón)/

ghetto • *n* ге́тто (*n*)

ghost • *n* приви́д (*m*), примáра (*f*), мáра (*f*), фантóм (*m*), мáрево (*n*)

gift • *n* подарýнок (*m*), дар (*m*), талáнт (*m*)

gill • *n* зя́бра /(zjábra)/, жáбри /(žábry)/

gin • *n* джин (*m*) /(džyn)/

giraffe • *n* жирáфа (*f*), жирáф (*m*)

girl • *n* ді́вчина (*f*)

girlfriend • *n* кохáна (*f*), ді́вчина (*f*), подрýга (*f*), прия́телька (*f*)

give • *v* давáти, дáти, дарувáти, подарувáти

glacier • *n* льодови́к (*m*)

glade • *n* поля́на (*f*) /(poljána)/

gland • *n* залоза (*f*) /(záloza)/

glanders • *n* сап (*m*)

glans • *n* голі́вка статевого члена (*f*) /(holivka statevogo člena)/

glass • *n* скло (*n*), шкло (*n*), скля́нка (*f*)

glitter • *v* блищати /(blyščáty)/, ся́я-ти /(sjájaty)/ • *n* блиск (*m*), сяйво (*n*) /(sjájvo)/

globe • *n* гло́бус (*m*)

gloomy • *adj* похмурий (*m*), сумний (*m*)

glory • *n* слáва (*f*) /(sláva)/, велич (*f*) /(velýč)/, честь (*f*) /(čest□)/, слáва (*f*)

glove • *n* рукави́ця (*f*), перчáтка (*f*)

gluck • *v* бýлькати /(búl′katy)/

glue • *n* клей (*m*) /(klej)/

gnaw • *v* гризти /(hrýzty)/

gneiss • *n* гнейс (*m*)

go • *v* ходити /(xodýty)/, іти /(itý)/, йти /(jty)/, піти /(pitý)/, їздити /(jízdyty)/, їхати /(jíxaty)/

goal • *n* ворота /(voróta)/, гол (*m*) /(hol)/

goalkeeper • *n* воротар (*m*) /(vorotár)/, голкіпер (*m*) /(holkíper)/

goat • *n* козá (*f*), козéл (*m*), цап (*m*)

god • *n* бог (*m*)

goddess • *n* богиня (*f*) /(bohýnja)/

godless • *adj* безбо́жний /(bezbóžnyj)/

gold • *n* зо́лото (*n*)

golden • *adj* золотий /(zolotýj)/

goldfinch • *n* щиглик (*m*) /(ščýhlyk)/, щиго́ль (*m*)

goldfish • *n* золота рибка (*f*) /(zolotá rýbka)/

golf • *n* гольф (*m*)

gondola • *n* гондола (*f*)

gonorrhea • *n* гонорéя (*f*)

good • *adj* до́брий, хоро́ший, гáрний, добрий, хороший • *n* добрó (*n*)

goodbye • *interj* до побáчення

goose • *n* гýска (*f*), гусáк (*m*)

gooseberry • *n* агрус

gopher • *n* ховрáх (*m*), ховрашóк (*m*)

gorilla • *n* горила (*f*) /(horýla)/

gory • *adj* кривавий /(kryvávyj)/

goshawk • *n* я́струб вели́кий (*m*), те-терев'я́тник (*m*)

gospel • *n* єванге́ліє (*n*)

gouache • *n* гýáш (*f*)

goulash • *n* гуля́ш (*m*) /(huljáš)/

government • *n* ýряд (*m*)

governmental • *adj* урядовий /(ur′adóvyj)/

grain • *n* зерно (*n*) /(zernó)/, збíжжя (*n*) /(zbížžja)/, жито (*n*) /(žýto)/

gram • *n* грам (*m*) /(hram)/

grammar • *n* грамáтика (*f*)

gramophone • *n* грамофóн (*m*), пате-фóн (*m*), програвáч (*m*)

granary • *n* шпіхлíр (*m*) /(špixlír)/

granddaughter • *n* внýчка (*f*), онýчка (*f*)

grandfather • *n* дід (*m*), дідýсь (*m*)

grandmother • *n* бабýся (*f*), бáба (*f*)

grandson • *n* онýк (*m*), внук (*m*)

granny • *n* бабуся (*f*), бабуня (*f*)

grape • *n* виногрáд (*m*)

grapeshot • *n* картéч (*f*)

grappa • *n* граппа

grass • *n* травá (*f*)

grasshopper • *n* кóник (*m*)

grateful • *adj* вдячний /(vdjáčnyj)/

grater • *n* тéрка (*f*)

grave • *n* могила (*f*)

gravy • *n* підли́вка (*f*), сóус (*m*)

gray • *adj* сíрий

graze • *v* пасти /(pastý)/

grease • *n* масло (*n*) /(máslo)/, сало (*n*) /(sálo)/, мастило (*n*) /(mastýlo)/, мазило (*n*) /(mazýlo)/, мазь (*f*) /(maz□)/

great • *adj* вели́кий, прекрáсний, чу-дóвий, чудéсний

grebe • *n* пірникоза (*f*)

green • *n* зелéний (*m*) • *adj* зелéний (*m*)

greenhouse • *n* тепли́ця (*f*), оранже-рéя (*f*)

grenade • *n* гранáта (*f*)

griffin • *n* гриф (*m*)

grind • *v* молоти, товкти, шліфувати

gringo • *n* грінго *(f)*, грінго *(f)*

grosz • *n* грош *(m)* */(hroš)/*

ground • *n* земля *(f)* */(zemljá)/*

group • *n* гру́па *(f)*

grove • *n* гай *(m)*, лісо́к *(m)*

grow • *v* рости́, ви́рости

gruel • *n* ка́ша *(f)*

guard • *n* охоро́нець *(m)*, захисни́к *(m)*, ва́рта *(f)*, охоро́на *(f)*, гва́рдія *(f)*

guardian • *n* охоро́нець *(m)*

guava • *n* гуая́ва *(f)*, гуа́ва *(f)*

guerrilla • *n* партиза́н *(m)*, партиза́нка *(f)*

guess • *v* вга́дувати, вгада́ти

guest • *n* гість *(m)*

guffaw • *v* реготати */(rehotáty)/*, іржа́ти */(iržáty)/* • *n* регіт *(m)* */(réhit)/*

guide • *v* проводи́ти, вести́, бу́ти провідник

guilt • *n* вина́ *(f)*

guitar • *n* гіта́ра *(f)*

gulf • *n* зато́ка *(f)*, зали́в *(m)*

gull • *n* чайка *(f)* */(čájka)/*, мартин *(m)* */(mártyn)/*

gum • *n* десна́ *(f)*, ясна́ *(f)*

gun • *n* пістоле́т *(m)*

gunpowder • *n* по́рох *(m)*

gymnastics • *n* гімнастика *(f)* */(himnástyka)/*

gynecology • *n* гінекологія *(f)* */(hinekolóhija)/*

gypsy • *n* циган *(m)* */(cyhán)/*, циганка *(f)* */(cyhánka)/*

gyrfalcon • *n* кре́чет *(m)*

gyrus • *n* зви́вина *(f)*

H

habit • *n* зви́чка *(f)*, ря́са *(f)*

habitation • *n* ме́шкання *(n)*, прожива́ння *(n)*, поме́шкання *(n)*

hacker • *n* хакер *(m)* */(xáker)/*

hafnium • *n* га́фній *(m)*

hail • *n* град *(m)*

hair • *n* волосся *(n)* */(volóssja)/*, волос *(m)* */(vólos)/*, волоси */(vólosy)/*, волосина *(f)* */(volosýna)/*

hairdresser • *n* перука́р *(m)*, перука́рка *(f)*

hairless • *adj* безволо́сий *(m)*

hairy • *adj* волоса́тий *(m)*

hajj • *n* хадж *(m)*

half • *n* полови́на *(f)*

halibut • *n* палтус *(m)*

hallelujah • *interj* алілу́я, алилу́я

ham • *n* о́корок *(m)*, ши́нка *(f)*

hamburger • *n* га́мбургер *(m)*

hammer • *n* мо́лот *(m)*, молото́к *(m)*

hammock • *n* гамак *(m)* */(hamák)/*, підвісне ліжко */(pidvísne ližko)/*

hamster • *n* хом'як *(m)*

hand • *n* рука *(f)* */(ruká)/*, стрілка *(f)* */(strílka)/*

handball • *n* гандбол *(m)* */(handból)/*

handbook • *n* довідник *(m)* */(dovidnýk)/*

handcuffs • *n* нару́чники

handful • *n* жме́ня *(f)*

handicraft • *n* ремесло *(n)* */(remesló)/*

handkerchief • *n* носова́ ху́стка *(f)*, ху́стка *(f)*, ху́сточка *(f)*

handsaw • *n* ножівка *(f)* */(nožívka)/*

hang • *v* висіти */(visíty)/*, вішати, пові́сити

hangover • *n* похмі́лля *(n)*

happen • *v* статися */(státysja)/*

happiness • *n* ща́стя *(n)*

happy • *adj* щасли́вий

hard • *adj* тве́рдий

hardly • *adv* ле́две */(lédve)/*

hare • *n* за́єць *(m)*

harm • *n* шкода *(f)* */(škóda)/*

harmful • *adj* шкідли́вий */(škidlývyj)/*, небезпе́чний

harness • *v* запрягати, приборкувати • *n* у́пряж *(f)*, збру́я *(f)*

harp • *n* а́рфа *(f)*

harpoon • *n* гарпун *(m)* */(harpún)/*

harpsichord • *n* клавесин *(m)* */(klavesýn)/*

harpsichordist • *n* клавесиніст *(m)*, клавесиністка *(f)*

harrier • *n* лунь *(m)*

harrow • *n* борона́ *(f)*

harvestman • *n* коса́рик *(m)* */(kosáryk)/*

hashish • *n* гашиш *(m)* */(hašiš)/*

hat • *n* капелю́х *(m)*, ша́пка *(f)*

hate • *v* ненави́діти

hatred • *n* нена́висть *(f)*

have • *v* мати */(máty)/*, у */(u)/*, в */(v)/*, мати, повинен */(-т, повинна - f, повинно - n, повинні - plural)/*

hawk • *n* я́струб *(m)*

hay • *n* сі́но *(n)*

hayloft • *n* синова́л *(m)*, сі́нник *(m)*

haystack • *n* стіг *(m)* /*(stih)*/, стіг сіна *(m)* /*(stih séna)*/

he • *pron* він

head • *n* голова́ *(f)*

headache • *n* головни́й біль *(m)*

headlight • *n* фа́ра *(f)*

headscarf • *n* хустка *(f)* /*(xústka)*/

heal • *v* лікува́ти, ви́лікувати, зцілюва́ти, зціли́ти

health • *n* здоро́в'я *(n)*

healthy • *adj* здоро́вий

heap • *n* ку́па *(f)*

hear • *v* чу́ти

hearing • *n* слух *(m)*

heart • *n* се́рце *(n)*

heating • *n* опалення *(n)* /*(opálennja)*/

heavens • *n* небеса́

heavy • *adj* важки́й

hectare • *n* гекта́р *(m)*, га *(m)*

hedgehog • *n* їжа́к *(m)*

heel • *n* п'я́тка *(f)*, п'ята́ *(f)*, каблу́к *(m)*

heir • *n* насліќдник *(m)*, насліќдниця *(f)*

helicopter • *n* вертолі́т *(m)*, гелікоќптер *(m)*

helium • *n* ге́лій *(m)*

hello • *interj* приві́т, до́брий день, алло́, слухати

helmet • *n* шоло́м *(m)*, ка́ска *(f)*

help • *n* допомо́га *(f)* • *v* допомага́ти, допомогти́, помага́ти, помогти́ • *interj* рятуйте

hemlock • *n* тсу́га *(f)*

hemp • *n* коно́плі

hen • *n* ку́рка *(f)*

heraldry • *n* геральдика *(f)* /*(herál dyka)*/

herbarium • *n* гербарій *(m)* /*(herbárij)*/

herd • *n* ста́до *(n)*, череда́ *(f)*, гурт *(m)*, табу́н *(m)*

here • *adv* тут, сюди́

heresy • *n* єресь *(f)* /*(jéres')*/

heretic • *n* єрети́к *(m)* • *adj* єретичний *(m)*

heretical • *adj* єретичний *(m)*

hermaphrodite • *n* гермафроди́т *(m)*

hero • *n* геро́й *(m)*, геро́їня *(f)*

heroine • *n* геро́їня *(f)* /*(herojínja)*/

heron • *n* ча́пля *(f)* /*(čáplja)*/

herring • *n* оселе́дець *(m)* /*(oselédec)*/

hers • *pron* її́ /*(jiji)*/

herself • *pron* вона́ сама́ *(f)*

hertz • *n* герц *(m)* /*(herc)*/

heterogeneity • *n* різнорі́дність *(f)* /*(riznoridnist)*/, гетероге́нність *(f)* /*(heterohennist)*/

hetman • *n* ге́тьман *(m)*

hey • *interj* гей /*(hej)*/, ей /*(ej)*/

hi • *interj* приві́т

hiccup • *v* гика́ти, іка́ти

hide • *v* хова́ти

high • *adj* висо́кий

hight • *v* називатися

highway • *n* шосе́ *(n)*, магістра́ль *(f)*, автошля́х *(m)*, автомагістра́ль *(f)*

hike • *n* похі́д *(m)*, екску́рсія *(f)*

hill • *n* па́горб *(m)*, паго́рок *(m)*

him • *pron* йому́ /*(jomú)*/, його́ /*(johó)*/

himself • *pron* він сам *(m)*

hinder • *adj* за́дній

hinny • *n* лоша́к *(m)*

hip • *n* стегно́ *(n)*, бедро́ *(n)*

hippodrome • *n* іподром *(m)* /*(ipodróm)*/

hippopotamus • *n* гіпопота́м *(m)*, бегемо́т *(m)*

hiss • *v* шипі́ти • *n* шипі́ння *(n)*

history • *n* істо́рія *(f)* /*(istórija)*/

hit • *v* вдаря́ти, вда́рити, би́ти

hither • *adv* сюди́

hobby • *n* хобі *(n)* /*(xóbi)*/

hockey • *n* гокей *(m)* /*(hokéj)*/, хокей *(m)* /*(xokéj)*/

hoe • *n* мотика *(f)* /*(motýka)*/

hog • *n* свиня *(f)* /*(svynjá)*/

hold • *v* трима́ти • *n* трюм *(m)*

hole • *n* ді́рка *(f)*

holiday • *n* свя́то *(n)*

holly • *n* па́дуб

holmium • *n* го́льмій *(m)*

holy • *adj* святи́й, свяще́нний

home • *n* дім *(m)*, батьківщина *(f)*, домі́вка *(f)* • *adv* вдо́ма, додо́му

hometown • *n* рі́дне мі́сто *(n)* /*(rídne místo)*/

homeward • *adv* додо́му /*(dodómu)*/

homework • *n* дома́шнє завда́ння *(n)*, дома́шня робо́та *(f)*

homophobia • *n* гомофо́бія *(f)* /*(homofóbija)*/

homosexual • *n* гомосексуалі́ст *(m)*, гей *(m)*, гей *(m)*, лесбія́нка *(f)*, лесбі́йка *(f)* • *adj* гомосексуа́льний

homosexuality • *n* гомосексуалі́зм /*(homoseksualízm)*/

honey • *n* мед *(m)*, мід *(m)*

honeycomb • *n* сті́льник *(m)*

honeymoon • *n* медо́вий мі́сяць *(m)*

honor • *n* честь *(f)*

hood • *n* ка́птур *(m)*, відло́га *(f)*, капюшо́н *(m)*

hoof • *n* копито *(n)* /*(kopýto)*/

hook • *n* гак *(m)* /*(hak)*/, гачок *(m)*

/(háčok)/

hooligan • *n* хуліган *(m)* */(xulihán)/*, хуліганка *(f)* */(xulihánka)/*

hoop • *n* обруч *(m)*

hoopoe • *n* одуд *(m)* */(ódud)/*

hope • *n* надія *(f)* */(nadíja)/* • *v* надіятися */(nadíjatysja)/*, сподіватися */(spodivátysja)/*, уповати */(upováty)/*

horizon • *n* горизонт *(m)*

horn • *n* ріг *(m)*, сирена *(f)*

horned • *adj* рогатий */(rohátyj)/*

hornet • *n* шершень *(m)* */(šéršen☐)/*

horror • *n* жах *(m)*, страх *(m)*

horse • *n* кінь *(m)*, коні

horsefly • *n* ґедзь *(m)* */(gedz')/*

horseradish • *n* хрін *(m)*

horseshoe • *n* підкова *(f)* */(pidkóva)/*

horsy • *n* коник *(m)* */(kónyk)/*

hose • *n* шланг *(m)*

hospital • *n* лікарня *(f)*, шпіталь *(m)*, болниця *(f)*

hospitality • *n* гостинність *(f)* */(hostýnnist')/*

hospitalization • *n* госпіталізація *(f)* */(hospitalizácija)/*

hostage • *n* заручник *(m)*

hostess • *n* господиня *(f)* */(hospodynja)/*

hot • *adj* гарячий, спекотний

hotel • *n* готель *(m)*

hour • *n* година *(f)*

house • *n* дім *(m)*, хата *(f)*

housewarming • *n* новосілля *(n)*

housewife • *n* домогосподарка *(f)*

how • *adv* як

however • *adv* однак, проте

howl • *v* вити */(výty)/*

hug • *v* обіймати */(obijmáty)/*, обійняти */(obijnjáty)/*, обнімати */(obnimáty)/*, обняти */(obnjáty)/* • *n* об'яття *(n)* */(ob☐játtja)/*, обійми */(obíjmy)/*, обіймання *(n)* */(obijmaánnja)/*

human • *n* людина *(f)*, люди

humanism • *n* гуманізм *(m)* */(humanízm)/*

humble • *adj* низький, скромний

humid • *adj* вологий

humidity • *n* вологість повітря

humiliate • *v* принижувати */(prynýžuvaty)/*, принизити */(prynýzyty)/*

hunger • *n* голод *(m)*

hungry • *adj* голодний

hunt • *v* полювати • *n* полювання *(n)*

hunter • *n* мисливець *(m)*

hurrah • *interj* ура */(urá)/*, слава */(sláva)/*

hurricane • *n* ураган *(m)*, ураган *(m)*

hurt • *v* боліти, хворіти, захворіти

husband • *n* чоловік *(m)* */(čolovík)/*, муж *(m)*

hydrate • *n* гідрат *(m)* */(hidrát)/*

hydrogen • *n* водень

hyena • *n* гієна *(f)* */(hijéna)/*

hygiene • *n* гігієна *(f)*

hygrometer • *n* гігрометр

hymn • *n* гімн *(m)*

hyperglycemia • *n* гіперглікемія */(hiperhlikemíya)/*

hyphen • *n* дефіс *(m)* */(defís)/*

hypotenuse • *n* гіпотенуза *(f)* */(gipotenúza)/*

I

ibex • *n* гірский альпійский цап */(girskij al'pijskij cap)/*, гірский альпійский козел */(girskij al'pijskij kozel)/*

ice • *n* лід *(m)*

iceberg • *n* айсберг *(m)* */(ájsberh)/*

icebreaker • *n* криголам *(m)* */(kryholám)/*

ichthyology • *n* іхтіологія *(f)* */(ixtiolóhija)/*

icicle • *n* бурулька *(f)*

idea • *n* ідея *(f)*, думка *(f)*

ideal • *n* ідеал *(m)* */(ideál)/*

idealism • *n* ідеалізм *(m)* */(idealízm)/*

idiosyncrasy • *n* ідіосинкразія *(f)*

if • *conj* якщо, коли

ignorance • *n* невігластво *(n)*, неуцтво

(n), незнання *(n)*

ill • *adj* хворий

illness • *n* хвороба *(f)* */(xvoróba)/*

ilmenite • *n* ільменіт */(îl☐menît)/*

image • *n* образ *(m)*, образ *(m)* */(óbraz)/*

imam • *n* імам *(m)*

immediately • *adv* зараз */(záraz)/*, негайно */(nehájno)/*

immigrant • *n* іммігрант *(m)*, іммігрантка *(f)*, переселенець *(m)*, переселенка *(f)*

immigration • *n* імміграція *(f)*

immolate • *v* приносити в жертву

immolation • *n* жертвоприношення *(n)*, жертва *(f)*

immortal • *adj* безсмертний *(m)*

impatiently • *adv* нетерпляче

impeachment • *n* імпічмент *(m)*

impenetrable • *adj* непроникний */(nepronyknyj)/*

imperfective • *adj* недоконаний

implore • *v* благати */(blagaty)/*

import • *v* імпортувати */(importuváty)/*, увозити */(uvózyty)/*, ввозити */(vvózyty)/*, увезти */(uveztý)/*, ввезти */(vveztý)/*

important • *adj* важливий, значний, важний

impressionist • *n* импресионист *(m)*

imprisonment • *n* ув'язнення *(n)* */(uv'jáznennja)/*

in • *prep* в, у

incest • *n* інцест *(m)*, кровозмішення *(n)*

inch • *n* дюйм *(m)*, цаль *(m)*

incinerate • *v* згоряти */(zhorjaty)/*

inconvenient • *adj* незручний

incredible • *adj* неймовірний

incursion • *n* вторгнення *(n)*

indefatigable • *adj* невтомний */(nevtomyj)/*, неослабний */(neoslabnyj)/*

independence • *n* незалежність

index • *n* індекс *(m)*

indigence • *n* біднота *(f)*

indium • *n* індій *(m)*

industrialization • *n* індустріалізація *(f)*

industry • *n* промисловість *(f)*, індустрія *(f)*

ineffable • *adj* невимовний

infanticide • *n* дітовбивство *(n)* */(ditovbývstvo)/*

infection • *n* інфекція *(f)* */(infékcija)/*, зараження *(n)* */(zaražénnja)/*, закаження *(n)* */(zakažénnja)/*, зараза *(f)* */(zaráza)/*

infinitive • *n* інфінітив *(m)*, дієйменник *(m)*, невизначена форма *(f)*

inflation • *n* інфляція *(f)*

inflorescence • *n* суцвіття *(n)*

influence • *n* вплив *(m)*, уплив *(m)*

influential • *adj* впливовий

influenza • *n* грип *(m)* */(hryp)/*

inform • *v* повідомляти, повідомити

information • *n* інформація *(f)*

inheritance • *n* спадок *(m)*, наслідування *(n)*

inhibit • *v* перешкоджати */(pereškodžaty)/*

injurious • *adj* небезпечний, шкідливий

injury • *n* пошкодження *(n)*, рана *(f)*, травма *(f)*

ink • *n* чорнило *(n)*

inkwell • *n* чорнильниця *(f)*, каламар *(m)*

inn • *n* трактир *(m)*, готель *(m)*, корчма *(f)*

inning • *n* інінг *(m)* */(íning)/*

innocuous • *adj* нешкідливий *(m)* */(neškidlyvyj)/*

insect • *n* комаха *(f)*, комашка *(f)*, хробак *(m)* */(xrobák)/*

insert • *v* вставляти, вставити

insomnia • *n* безсоння *(n)*

insufficiently • *adv* недостатньо

insulin • *n* інсулін *(m)*

insult • *v* ображати, образити • *n* образа *(f)*

insurgent • *n* повстанець *(m)*

insurrection • *n* повстання *(n)*

intelligence • *n* розвідка *(f)*

intelligentsia • *n* інтелігенція *(f)*

intend • *v* наміритись, планувати, збиратися

intentional • *adj* навмисний */(navmýsnyj)/*, умисний */(umýsnyj)/*

interest • *v* цікавити, інтересувати • *n* відсоток *(m)*, процент *(m)*, цікавість *(f)*, інтерес *(m)*

interesting • *adj* цікавий

interjection • *n* вигук *(m)*

international • *adj* міжнародний, інтернаціональний

interpreter • *n* перекладач *(m)*, перекладачка *(f)*

intersection • *n* перехресток *(m)*, перехрестя *(n)*, перетин множин */(peretyn mnóžyn)/*

intervention • *n* втручання *(n)*, інтервенція *(f)*, вторгнення *(n)*

interview • *n* інтерв'ю *(n)*, співбесіда *(f)*

intestine • *n* кишка *(f)*, кишечник *(m)*, черево *(n)*

intonation • *n* інтонація *(f)*

intransitive • *adj* неперехідний

inundation • *n* повінь *(f)* */(póvin□)/*, повідь *(f)* */(póvid□)/*, затоплення *(n)* */(zatóplennja)/*, потоп *(m)* */(potóp)/*

invader • *n* наїзник *(m)* */(najíznyk)/*, загарбник *(m)* */(zahárbnyk)/*

invasion • *n* вторгнення *(n)*

invention • *n* винахід *(m)* */(výnaxid)/*

invertebrate • *n* безхребетна тварина *(f)* */(bezkhrebetna tvaryna)/*

invitation • *n* запрошення *(n)*

invite • *v* запрошувати, запросити

iodine • *n* йод *(m)*

iridium • *n* іридій *(m)*

iron • *v* прасува́ти • *n* залі́зо *(n)*, пра́ска *(f)*, залі́зко *(n)* • *adj* залі́зний
irredentism • *n* іредентизм *(m)*
is • *v* є
island • *n* о́стрів *(m)*
isolation • *n* ізоля́ція *(f)*
isolationism • *n* ізоляціонізм *(m)*

/(izoljacionízm)/
isomorphism • *n* ізоморфізм *(m)*
isotope • *n* ізотоп *(m)* /(izotóp)/
isthmus • *n* перешийок *(m)*
it • *pron* воно́ *(n)*
itself • *pron* воно́ сам *(n)*

J

jack • *n* домкрат *(m)* /(domkrát)/
jackal • *n* шакал *(m)*
jackdaw • *n* га́лка *(f)*
jam • *n* джем *(m)*, варе́ння *(n)*, мармела́д *(m)*
janissary • *n* яничар *(m)*
jasmine • *n* жасми́н *(m)*
jasper • *n* яшма *(f)* /(jášma)/, яспис *(m)* /(jáspys)/
jaundice • *n* жовтяниця *(f)*
jaw • *n* щелепа *(f)*
jay • *n* сойка *(f)*
jazz • *n* джаз *(m)*
jealous • *adj* ревнивий /(revnývyj)/
jellyfish • *n* меду́за *(f)*
jihad • *n* джиха́д *(m)*
jinn • *n* джин *(m)* /(džyn)/
job • *n* робо́та *(f)*, пра́ця *(f)*
joint • *n* з'є́днання *(n)* /(zjédnannja)/, суглоб *(m)* /(suhlób)/ • *adj* сумісний /(sumísnyj)/, спільний /(spíl'nyj)/

joke • *v* жартува́ти • *n* жарт *(m)*
joule • *n* джоуль *(m)* /(džóul')/
journalism • *n* журналістика *(f)*
journalist • *n* журналі́ст *(m)*, журналі́стка *(f)* /(žurnalístka)/, репортер *(m)*, кореспонде́нт *(m)*
journey • *v* подорожувати • *n* подоро́ж *(f)* /(podoróž)/
joy • *n* ра́дість *(f)*
judge • *n* суддя́ *(m)*, рефері *(m)*, арбітр *(m)*
juggling • *n* жонглювання *(n)* /(žonhljuvánnja)/
juice • *n* сік *(m)*
jump • *v* стрибати, скака́ти
jungle • *n* джу́нглі
junior • *adj* молодший /(molódšyj)/
juniper • *n* яловець *(m)* /(jalovéc□')/, ялівець *(m)* /(jalivéc□)/
junta • *n* хунта *(f)* /(xúnta)/

K

kangaroo • *n* кенгуру́ *(m)*
karate • *n* карате́ *(n)*
kasha • *n* каша *(f)* /(káša)/
kerchief • *n* ху́стка *(f)*
kestrel • *n* сокіл *(m)* /(sokil)/, сапсан *(m)* /(sapsan)/, боривітер /(boriviter)/, постільга /(postil'ga)/
key • *n* ключ *(m)*
keyboard • *n* клавіату́ра *(f)*
khan • *n* хан *(m)*
kid • *n* козеня́ *(n)*, цапеня́ *(n)*
kidnap • *v* викрада́ти, ви́красти
kidney • *n* ни́рка *(f)*
killer • *n* уби́вця *(f)*, вбивця *(f)*
kilogram • *n* кілогра́м *(m)*
kimono • *n* кімоно́ *(n)*
kind • *adj* до́брий, серде́чний, люб'я́зний
kindergarten • *n* дитя́чий сад *(m)*, ди-

тя́чий садо́к *(m)*
king • *n* король *(m)*, цар *(m)*
kingdom • *n* королі́вство *(n)*, ца́рство *(n)*, світ *(m)*
kingfisher • *n* зимородок *(m)*
kiosk • *n* кіоск *(m)* /(kiósk)/
kiss • *v* цілува́ти, поцілува́ти, цілува́тися • *n* поцілу́нок *(m)*
kitchen • *n* ку́хня *(f)*
kite • *n* шуліка *(m)*, повітряний змій *(m)*, змій *(m)*
kitten • *n* кошеня *(n)* /(košenjá)/
knee • *n* колі́но *(n)*
knife • *n* ніж *(m)*, лезо *(n)* /(lézo)/
knight • *n* ли́цар *(m)*, ри́цар *(m)*, ві́тязь *(m)*, кінь *(m)*
knit • *v* в'яза́ти
knock • *v* сту́кати, сту́кнути
knockout • *n* нокаут *(m)* /(nokáut)/

knot • *n* вýзол *(m)*
know • *v* знáти, вíдати
knowledge • *n* знання *(n)*
known • *adj* відомий */(vidómyj)/*
kolkhoz • *n* колгóсп *(m)*

kopek • *n* копíйка *(f)* */(kopíjka)/*
koumiss • *n* кумíс *(m)*
krypton • *n* криптóн *(m)*
kvass • *n* квас *(m)* */(kvas)/*

L

lace • *n* шнурóк *(m)*
lack • *n* брак *(m)*, відсýтність *(f)*, недо-стáча *(f)*
lacrosse • *n* лакросс *(m)* */(lakróss)/*
lad • *n* хлопець *(m)* */(xlópec□)/*
ladder • *n* драбúна *(f)*
lake • *n* óзеро *(n)*
lamb • *n* ягня *(n)*, барáнчик *(m)*
lame • *adj* кульгавий */(kul□hávyj)/*
lamp • *n* лáмпа *(f)*, лáмпочка *(f)*
lampoon • *n* пáсквіль *(m)*
lamppost • *n* ліхтар *(m)* */(lixtár)/*
lampshade • *n* абажýр *(m)*
lancet • *n* ланцет *(m)*
land • *v* приземлятися, приземлúти-ся • *n* земля *(f)*
landing • *n* призéмлення *(n)*, посáдка *(f)*
lane • *n* провýлок *(m)*, алéя *(f)*
language • *n* мóва *(f)*, мова *(f)* */(móva)/*
languid • *adj* кволий */(kwolyj)/*
lantern • *n* ліхтар *(m)*
lanthanum • *n* лантáн *(m)*
lapwing • *n* чибис *(m)* */(čýbys)/*, чайка *(f)* */(čájka)/*
larch • *n* модрúна *(f)*, лúствениця *(f)*, модрúна
lard • *n* сало *(n)* */(sálo)/*, смалець *(m)* */(smálec□)/*
largess • *n* щедрість *(f)*
lark • *n* жáйворонок *(m)*
larva • *n* личинка *(f)* */(lyčýnka)/*
larynx • *n* гортáнь *(f)*, глóтка *(f)*
lascivious • *adj* хтивий */(xtývyj)/*
laser • *n* лáзер *(m)*
last • *adj* остáнній, минýлий
lat • *n* лат *(m)* */(lat)/*
late • *adj* пізній • *adv* пізно
latitude • *n* широтá *(f)*
laugh • *v* сміятися
laughter • *n* сміх *(m)*, рéгіт *(m)*
launcher • *n* гранатомéт
laundry • *n* прання *(n)*, прáльня *(f)*
lava • *n* лава *(f)* */(láva)/*
law • *n* закóн *(m)*
lawrencium • *n* лоуренсíй *(m)* */(lourénsij)/*

lawyer • *n* юрúст *(m)*, юрúстка *(f)*, адвокáт *(m)*
lazy • *adj* лінúвий, ледáчий
lazybones • *n* лéдар *(m)*
lead • *n* свинéць *(m)* • *v* водúти, по-водúти, вести, повести, провóдити, провестú
leaf • *n* лист *(m)*
leaflet • *n* листíвка *(f)*
league • *n* ліга *(f)* */(líha)/*
learn • *v* учúтися
leather • *n* шкíра *(f)*
leech • *n* п'явка *(f)*
left • *adj* лíвий • *adv* злíва, лівóруч, на-лíво
leg • *n* ногá *(f)*
legend • *n* легéнда *(f)*
legible • *adj* розбíрливий
legislation • *n* законодáвство *(n)* */(zakonodávstvo)/*, закон *(m)* */(zakón)/*
legislative • *adj* законодавчий */(zakonodávčyj)/*
legislator • *n* законодáвець *(m)*, зако-нодáвиця *(f)*
legislature • *n* законодавча влада *(f)* */(zakonodávča vláda)/*
leisure • *n* вільний час *(m)* */(víl′nyj čas)/*
lemon • *n* лимóн *(m)*
lend • *v* позичáти, позúчити
length • *n* довжинá *(f)*
leopard • *n* леопáрд *(m)*
lesbian • *n* лесбíйка *(f)*, лесбіянка *(f)* • *adj* лесбíйський */(lesbíjs□kyj)/*
lesson • *n* урóк *(m)*
letter • *n* бýква *(f)*, лíтера *(f)*, лист *(m)*
lettuce • *n* салáт *(m)*, салáт-латýк *(m)*
leu • *n* лей *(m)* */(lej)/*
lev • *n* лев *(m)* */(lev)/*
lever • *n* важіль *(m)* */(vážil′)/*
lewd • *adj* хтúвий
lexeme • *n* лексема *(f)* */(lekséma)/*
liar • *n* брехýн *(m)*, брехýха *(f)*, бреху-́нка *(f)*, брехлó *(n)*
liberate • *v* звільняти */(zvil□njáty)/*, звíльнити */(zvil□nýty)/*, визволяти */(vyzvoljáty)/*, визволити */(výzvolyty)/*

liberation • *n* визволення *(n)* /*(vyzvólennja)*/
librarian • *n* бібліотéкар *(m)*, бібліотé-карка *(f)*
library • *n* бібліотéка *(f)*
license • *n* ліцéнзія *(f)*
lichen • *n* лишáйник *(m)*
lid • *n* крúшка *(f)*
lie • *v* лежáти, лягтú, брехáти • *n* бре-хня́ *(f)*, непрáвда *(f)*
life • *n* життя́ *(n)*
lift • *n* ліфт *(m)*
ligament • *n* зв'язка *(f)* /*(zv'jázka)*/
light • *n* світлó *(n)* • *v* запáлювати, за-палúти • *adj* свíтлий, лéгкий
lighter • *n* запальнúчка *(f)*
lighthouse • *n* маяк *(m)*
lightning • *n* блúскавка *(f)*, перýн *(m)*
like • *v* подóбатися, любúти • *adv* як • *prep* як
lily • *n* лілéя *(f)*
lime • *n* лайм *(m)* • *adj* лáймовий
limestone • *n* вапняк *(m)* /*(vapnják)*/
limousine • *n* лімузин *(m)*
line • *n* чергá *(f)*
lingonberry • *n* брусниця *(f)* /*(brusnýcja)*/
linguistics • *n* мовознáвство *(n)*
lion • *n* лев *(m)*
lioness • *n* левúця *(f)*
lip • *n* губá *(f)*
lipstick • *n* губна помада
liqueur • *n* лікéр *(m)* /*(likér)*/
list • *n* спúсок *(m)*
listen • *v* слýхати, послýхати, слýха-тися, чýти
listener • *n* слухáч *(m)*, слухáчка *(f)*
literary • *adj* літератýрний *(m)* /*(literaturnyj)*/
literature • *n* літератýра *(f)*
lithium • *n* лíтій *(m)*
little • *adj* малéнький, малúй
liturgy • *n* літургíя
live • *v* жúти, проживáти, мéшкати •

adv нáживо
liver • *n* печíнка *(f)*
livery • *n* ліврея
livestock • *n* худоба *(f)* /*(xudóba)*/, ско-тина *(f)* /*(skotýna)*/
living • *adj* живúй /*(žyvýj)*/
lizard • *n* я́щірка *(f)*
lobster • *n* омáр *(m)*
location • *n* місцеполóження *(n)*, по-лóження *(n)*, розташувáння *(n)*
lock • *n* замóк *(m)*
locomotive • *n* локомотив *(m)* /*(lokomotýv)*/
locust • *n* саранá *(f)*
lodging • *n* житлó *(n)*
loess • *n* лес *(m)* /*(les)*/
log • *n* колода *(f)* /*(koloda)*/
long • *adj* довгий *(m)* /*(dóvhyj)*/, дóвгий
longitude • *n* довготá *(f)*
look • *v* дивúтися, подивúтися
loon • *n* гагара *(f)*
loop • *n* петля́ *(f)*
lose • *v* втрачáти, втрáтити, губúти, загубúти, програвáти, прогрáти
loser • *n* невдаха *(f)* /*(nevdáxa)*/
lottery • *n* лотерéя *(f)*
loud • *adj* голóсний, гýчний
loudly • *adv* гóлосно, гýчно
louse • *n* вóша *(f)*
love • *n* любóв *(f)*, кохáння *(n)*
lover • *n* кохáнець *(m)*, кохáнка *(f)*
low • *adj* нúзький
luggage • *n* багáж *(m)*
lullaby • *n* колискóва *(f)*
luminous • *adj* блискучий /*(blyskučyj)*/
lunch • *n* обíд *(m)* /*(obíd)*/, ланч *(m)*
lung • *n* легéня *(f)*, лéгке *(n)*
lust • *n* пóхіть *(f)* /*(póxit')*/
lustration • *n* люстрація
lute • *n* лю́тня *(f)*
lutetium • *n* лютецій *(m)* /*(ljutétsij)*/
lynx • *n* рись *(f)*
lysine • *n* лізин /*(lizyn)*/

M

ma • *n* мама *(f)* /*(máma)*/
macaroni • *n* макарони /*(makaróny)*/
machine • *n* машúна *(f)*
mackerel • *n* скýмбрія *(f)*
madam • *n* пáні *(f)*
mafia • *n* мафія *(f)* /*(máfija)*/
magazine • *n* журнáл *(m)*, часóпис *(m)*, магазúн *(m)*

magenta • *adj* пýрпурний
magic • *n* мáгія *(f)*, чарівнúцтво *(n)*, чаклýнство *(n)*, фóкус *(m)*
magician • *n* чарівнúк *(m)*, маг *(m)*
magma • *n* мáгма *(f)*
magnesium • *n* мáгній *(m)*
magnet • *n* магнíт *(m)*
magnitude • *n* величинá *(f)*

magpie • *n* сорока

maiden • *n* діва (*f*), дівчина (*f*), панна (*f*), незаймана (*f*)

mailbox • *n* поштова скринька (*f*) /(poštóva skrýn′ka)/

mailman • *n* листоноша (*m*) /(lystonóša)/, поштар (*m*) /(poštár)/

mainland • *n* материк (*m*)

mainly • *adv* головним чином /(holovným čýnom)/

make • *v* робити, зробити, виготовляти, виготовити

malaria • *n* малярія (*f*) /(maljaríja)/

malice • *n* злий умисел (*m*) /(zlyj úmysel)/

mall • *n* торговий центр (*m*)

mallard • *n* крижень /(križen′)/

mallow • *n* мальва (*f*)

mammal • *n* ссавець (*m*), звір (*m*)

mammoth • *n* мамонт (*m*), мамут (*m*)

man • *n* людина (*f*), люди, чоловік (*m*), муж (*m*)

man-of-war • *n* військовий корабель (*m*)

manage • *v* управляти /(upravljáty)/, керувати /(keruváty)/, вдаватися

mandrake • *n* мандрагора (*f*)

mane • *n* грива (*f*) /(hrýva)/

manganese • *n* марганець (*m*)

manger • *n* годівниця (*f*) /(hodivnýcja)/, ясла /(jásla)/

mango • *n* манго (*n*), манго (*n*)

manhole • *n* люк (*m*)

manicure • *n* манікюр (*m*)

mankind • *n* людство (*n*)

mantis • *n* богомол (*m*) /(bohomól)/

manual • *n* інструкція (*f*) /(instrúkcija)/

manul • *n* манул (*m*) /(manul)/

manure • *v* угноювати • *n* гній (*m*)

map • *n* карта (*f*), мапа (*f*)

maple • *n* клен (*m*)

marble • *n* мармур (*m*) /(mármur)/

march • *n* марш (*m*)

mare • *n* кобила (*f*)

margarine • *n* маргарин (*m*) /(marharýn)/

marijuana • *n* марихуана (*f*)

market • *n* ринок (*m*), базар (*m*)

marmalade • *n* джем (*m*) /(džem)/, повидло (*n*) /(povýdlo)/, мармеляда (*f*) /(marmeljáda)/

marmot • *n* бабак /(babak)/

marquess • *n* маркіз (*m*) /(markíz)/

marriage • *n* шлюб (*m*), одруження (*n*)

married • *adj* одружений (*m*), жона-тий (*m*), заміжня (*f*)

marry • *v* женитися /(ženýtysja)/

marshmallow • *n* зефір (*m*)

marten • *n* куниця (*f*)

mascara • *n* туш (*f*) /(tuš)/

masculine • *n* чоловічий рід (*m*) • *adj* чоловічий

mask • *n* маска (*f*)

mass • *n* маса (*f*) /(mása)/

massage • *n* масаж (*m*)

mast • *n* щогла (*f*) /(ščóhla)/, мачта (*f*) /(máčta)/

masterpiece • *n* шедевр (*m*)

match • *n* матч (*m*), сірник (*m*)

matchstick • *n* сірник (*m*)

material • *n* матеріал (*m*)

mathematics • *n* математика (*f*)

mattress • *n* матрас (*m*), матрац (*m*)

matzo • *n* маца (*f*)

mayonnaise • *n* майонез (*m*)

mayor • *n* мер (*f*) /(mer)/

me • *pron* мене /(mené)/, мені /(mení)/

meadow • *n* луг (*m*), поляна (*f*)

meal • *n* їжа (*f*), страва (*f*)

mean • *v* означати, значити

meaning • *n* значення (*n*)

measles • *n* кір (*m*) /(kir)/

measurement • *n* вимірювання

meat • *n* м′ясо (*n*)

mechanism • *n* механізм (*m*) /(mexanízm)/

medal • *n* медаль (*f*) /(medál′)/

medicine • *n* ліки, лік (*m*), лікарство (*n*), лікування (*n*), медицина (*f*)

meet • *v* зустрічати, зустріти

meeting • *n* збори, зустріч (*f*), засідання (*n*)

megalith • *n* мегаліт (*m*)

megalithic • *adj* мегалітичний

melodrama • *n* мелодрама (*f*) /(melodráma)/

melon • *n* диня (*f*)

membership • *n* членство (*n*) /(člénstvo)/

meme • *n* мем (*m*)

memoir • *n* мемуари

memorize • *v* запам′ятовувати /(zapam′jatóvuvaty)/, запам′ятати /(zapam′jatáty)/

memory • *n* пам′ять (*f*)

mendacious • *adj* брехливий

mendelevium • *n* менделевій (*m*)

menstruation • *n* менструація (*f*)

menu • *n* меню (*n*)

mercenary • *n* найманець (*m*), найманка (*f*), наймит (*m*), наймитка (*f*)

mercury • *n* ртуть (f)

merely • *adv* лишé, тíльки, прóсто

message • *n* повідóмлення (n), послáння (n)

metabolism • *n* обмін речовин

metal • *n* метáл (m)

metallic • *adj* металíчний, металевий

metallurgist • *n* металург (m) /(metallúrh)/

meteor • *n* метеор (m) /(meteór)/

meteorite • *n* метеорит (m)

methionine • *n* метіонін (m)

method • *n* мéтод (m), спóсіб (m), прийóм (m)

metro • *n* метро (n) /(metró)/

metropolis • *n* метрополія

microbe • *n* мікрóб (m)

micrometer • *n* мікрометр (m)

microphone • *n* мікрофóн (m)

microscope • *n* мікроскоп (m) /(mikroskop)/

microwave • *n* мікрохвиля (f)

midnight • *n* північ (f)

midwife • *n* акушéрка

mildew • *n* пліснява, цвіль (f), плíсень (f)

mile • *n* миля (f)

militant • *n* бойовик (m) • *adj* войовничий, бойовий

military • *adj* воéнний, військóвий

militia • *n* мілíція (f) /(milícija)/

militiaman • *n* міліціонéр (m), міліціянт (m), ополчéнець (m)

milkshake • *n* молóчний коктейль (m) /(molóčnyj koktéjl□)/

mill • *n* млин (m)

millennium • *n* тисячолíття (n)

millet • *n* прóсо (n), пшонó (n)

millionaire • *n* мільйонéр (m), мільйонéрка (f)

millipede • *n* багатоніжка (f) /(bahatonížka)/

millisecond • *n* мілісекунда (f) /(milisekúnda)/

millstone • *n* жорно /(žórno)/

minaret • *n* мінарéт (m)

mince • *n* фарш (m)

mind • *n* рóзум (m)

mine • *pron* мій (m) /(mij)/, моя (f), моє (n) • *n* шáхта (f), руднúк (m), міна (f)

miner • *n* шахтар (m) /(šaxtár)/, гірник (m) /(hirnyk)/

mineralogy • *n* мінералóгія (f) /(mineralóhija)/

minion • *n* фаворит (m)

minister • *n* мінíстр (m) /(minístr)/

ministry • *n* міністéрство (m)

mint • *n* м'ята (f)

minute • *n* хвилина (f) /(xvylýna)/

miracle • *n* чýдо (n), дúво (n)

mirage • *n* мірáж (m), мáрево (n)

mirror • *n* дзéркало (n)

miscarriage • *n* викидень (m)

misery • *n* нещастя (n) /(neščástja)/, бідá (f) /(bidá)/, горе (n) /(hóre)/

miss • *n* пáнна (f)

missile • *n* ракéта (f)

mission • *n* місія (f) /(mísija)/

missionary • *n* місіонéр (m), місіонéрка (f)

mist • *n* туман (m), серпанок (m)

mistake • *n* помúлка (f)

mister • *n* пан (m) /(pan)/

mistletoe • *n* омела (f) /(oméla)/

mite • *n* кліщ (m)

mitochondrion • *n* мітохондрія (f) /(mitoxondrija)/

mitosis • *n* мітоз (m) /(mitóz)/

mobilization • *n* мобілізáція (f)

modem • *n* модéм (m)

modern • *adj* сучасний /(sučásnyj)/

modified • *adj* змінений (m)

mold • *n* пліснява, цвіль (f), плíсень (f)

mole • *n* родúмка (f), кріт (m)

molecule • *n* молéкула (f)

molybdenum • *n* молібдéн (m)

monarchy • *n* монáрхія (f)

money • *n* грóші

mongoose • *n* мангýст (m)

monk • *n* монáх (m)

monkey • *n* мáвпа (f)

monotheism • *n* монотеїзм (m)

monsoon • *n* мусон

monstrosity • *n* жахливість

month • *n* мíсяць (m)

monument • *n* пáм'ятник (m), монумéнт (m)

moon • *n* мíсяць (m)

moonlight • *n* мíсячне світлó (n)

moonshine • *n* самогóн (m)

moose • *n* лось (m)

moot • *v* піднімати питання /(pidnimáty pytánnja)/ • *adj* спірний /(spírnyj)/

mop • *n* швабра (f) /(švábra)/

moped • *n* мопед (m) /(mopéd)/

morgue • *n* морг (m)

morning • *n* рáнок (m)

morpheme • *n* морфема (f) /(morféma)/

mortal • *adj* смéртний (m)

mortgage • *n* іпотéка

mosaic • *n* мозаїка (f)

mosque • *n* мечéть
mosquito • *n* комáр *(m)*
moss • *n* мох *(m)*
motel • *n* мотéль *(m)*
moth • *n* міль *(f)* /(mil□)/
mother • *n* мáти *(f)*, мáма *(f)*, мáтір *(f)*, неня, матуся, мамця *(f)*
mother-in-law • *n* свекрýха *(f)*, тéща *(f)*
mother-of-pearl • *n* перламýтр *(m)*
motor • *n* мотóр *(m)*, двигýн *(m)*
motorcycle • *n* мотоци́кл *(m)*
motto • *n* девіз *(m)* /(devíz)/
mouflon • *n* муфлон /(muflon)/
mountain • *n* горá *(f)*
mourn • *v* оплáкувати, скорбóти
mouse • *n* ми́ша *(f)*, ми́шка *(f)*
moustache • *n* вýса, вýси
mouth • *n* рот *(m)* /(rot)/
movable • *n* вільний /(vil'nyi)/ • *adj* мобільний *(m)* /(mobil'nyi)/, рухомий *(m)* /(rukhomyi)/, рухливий /(rukhlyvyi)/, рухомий /(rukhomyi)/, перехідний /(perekhidnyi)/
movie • *n* фільм *(m)*, кінó *(n)*, кінофі́льм *(m)*
mow • *v* коси́ти, сікти́
mucus • *n* слиз *(m)*
mud • *n* грязь *(f)*
muezzin • *n* муедзи́н *(m)*
muffin • *n* мáфін *(m)*
muffler • *n* глушни́к *(m)*
mufti • *n* мýфтій *(m)*
mug • *n* гýртка *(f)*, кýхоль *(m)*
mugwort • *n* полин *(m)*, чорнобиль

(m)
mulberry • *n* шовковиця *(f)*
mullah • *n* муллá *(m)*
mullet • *n* кефáль *(f)*
multiplication • *n* множення *(n)* /(mnóžennja)/
mum • *n* мáма *(f)*, матýся *(f)*, мáтінка *(f)*, нéнька *(f)*, нéня *(f)*
mummy • *n* мýмія *(f)*, мама *(f)* /(máma)/
murder • *n* вби́вство *(n)*
murderer • *n* вби́вця *(f)*, уби́вця *(f)*, душогýб *(m)*
muscle • *n* м'яз *(m)*, мýскул *(m)*
museum • *n* музéй *(m)*
mushroom • *n* гриб *(m)*
music • *n* музи́ка *(f)*
musical • *n* м'юзикл *(m)* /(mjúzykl)/ • *adj* музичний /(muzýčnyj)/
musician • *n* музикант *(m)* /(muzykánt)/
muskrat • *n* ондáтра *(f)*
must • *v* мýсити, повинен
mustard • *n* гірчи́ця *(f)*, муштáрда *(f)*
mute • *n* німи́й *(m)* • *adj* німи́й
muteness • *n* німотá *(f)* /(nimotá)/
mutton • *n* баранина *(f)* /(barányna)/
myself • *pron* себé, собí, собóю, -ся, я сам *(m)*, я сам *(f)*
mysterious • *adj* таємни́чий
mystery • *n* таємни́ця *(f)*, загáдка *(f)*
myth • *n* міф *(m)*, повір'я *(n)* /(povírja)/, легенда *(f)* /(lehénda)/
mythology • *n* міфологія *(f)* /(mifolóhija)/

N

nail • *n* ні́готь *(m)*, цвях *(m)*
naked • *adj* гóлий, наги́й
name • *n* ім'я *(n)*, нáзва *(f)*, репутáція *(f)*
nanny • *n* нянька *(f)* /(nján□ka)/, няня *(f)* /(njánja)/
napalm • *n* напáлм *(m)*
nape • *n* поти́лиця *(f)*, зашийок *(m)*
napkin • *n* сервéтка *(f)*
narcolepsy • *n* нарколепсія
narrow • *adj* вузький
narrowed • *v* звужений
narrowly • *adv* вузько /(vúz□ko)/
narwhal • *n* нарвáл *(m)*
nasalization • *n* назалізáція *(f)*
nation • *n* нáція *(f)*, нарóд *(m)*, держа́ва *(f)*

nationalism • *n* націоналізм *(m)* /(nacionalízm)/
nationality • *n* нарóдність *(f)*, громадянство *(n)*, національність *(f)*, нарóд *(m)*, нáція *(f)*, люд *(m)*, éтнос *(m)*, плем'я *(n)*, незалéжність *(f)*, самостій́ність *(f)*, автонóмія *(f)*
nature • *n* прирóда *(f)*
navel • *n* пупóк *(m)*, пуп *(m)*
navy • *n* флот *(m)*, військóво-морськи́й флот *(m)*, ВМФ *(m)*, темно-синій колір *(m)* • *adj* темно-синій, флотський
near • *adj* бли́зький, бли́жній • *adv* бли́зько • *prep* біля́
nearly • *adv* мáйже, сливé
nebula • *n* тумáнність *(f)*

neck • *n* шúя (*f*)

necklace • *n* намúсто (*n*), монúсто (*n*), нашúйник (*m*)

necktie • *n* кравáтка (*f*), гáлстук (*m*)

necromancy • *n* некромантíя (*f*) /(*nekromantija*)/

need • *n* нуждá (*f*), потрéба (*f*), необхí-́дність (*f*)

needle • *n* гóлка (*f*), стрíлка (*f*)

needlefish • *n* сарган (*m*) /(*sarhán*)/, гóлка-рúба (*f*)

negress • *n* муринка (*f*) /(*múrynka*)/, не-гритянка (*f*) /(*nehrytjánka*)/

neigh • *v* іржати /(*iržáty*)/

neighborhood • *n* сусíдство (*n*) /(*susídstvo*)/, округа (*f*) /(*okrúha*)/, околиці /(*okólyci*)/

neither • *pron* жоден (*m*)

nematode • *n* нематода /(*nematóda*)/

neodymium • *n* неодúм (*m*)

neon • *n* неóн (*m*)

nephew • *n* племíнник (*m*)

neptunium • *n* нептунíй (*m*) /(*neptúnij*)/

nerve • *n* нерв (*m*)

nest • *n* гніздó (*n*)

nestling • *n* пташеня (*n*) /(*ptašenjá*)/

nettle • *n* кропивá (*f*)

network • *n* сіть (*f*), мерéжа (*f*)

neuralgic • *adj* невралгíчний /(*nevralhíčnyj*)/

neurological • *adj* неврологíчний /(*nevrolohíčnyj*)/

neuroscience • *n* нейробіологія (*f*) /(*néjrobiolóhija*)/

neurosis • *n* неврóз (*m*)

neuter • *n* середнíй рід (*m*) • *adj* серед-нíй

neutron • *n* нейтрон (*m*) /(*neytron*)/

never • *adv* ніколи

new • *adj* нóвий (*m*)

news • *n* новúни, вíсті

newspaper • *n* газéта (*f*)

newt • *n* тритóн (*m*)

nexus • *n* зв'язок (*m*) /(*zvjazók*)/

nickel • *n* нікель (*m*)

nickname • *v* прозивáти, прозвáти • *n* прíзвисько (*n*), клúчка (*f*)

niece • *n* племíнниця (*f*)

night • *n* ніч (*f*)

nightgown • *n* нічнá сорóчка (*f*)

nightingale • *n* соловéйко (*m*), солове-́й (*m*)

nihilism • *n* нігілíзм

nineteenth • *adj* дев'ятнáдцятий (*m*)

ninetieth • *adj* дев'яностих

ninth • *adj* дев'ятий (*m*)

niobium • *n* ніóбій (*m*)

nipple • *n* сосóк (*m*)

nirvana • *n* нірвáна (*f*)

nit • *n* гнида (*f*) /(*hnýda*)/

nitrogen • *n* азот (*m*)

no • *n* не

nobelium • *n* нобéлій (*m*)

nobility • *n* дворя́нство (*n*)

nocturnal • *adj* нічнúй

node • *n* точка перетин (*f*) /(*tóčka peretýny orbít*)/, вузол (*m*) /(*vúzol*)/, вершина (*f*) /(*veršýna*)/

noise • *n* шум (*m*) /(*šum*)/

nomenclature • *n* номенклатýра (*f*)

nonaligned • *adj* неприéднаний, поза-блóковий

noodle • *n* лóкшина (*f*)

noon • *n* пóлудень (*m*), південь (*m*)

noose • *n* петля́ (*f*)

norm • *n* нóрма (*f*)

north • *n* північ (*f*) /(*pívnič*)/ • *adj* півні-́чний (*m*) • *adv* на північ

northeast • *n* північний схід (*m*)

northerly • *adj* півнíчний (*m*)

northern • *adj* півнíчний (*m*)

northwest • *n* півнíчний зáхід (*m*)

nose • *n* ніс (*m*)

nostril • *n* нíздря (*f*)

not • *adv* не

notary • *n* нотáріус (*m*)

notebook • *n* блокнóт (*m*), зóшит (*m*), записнá кнúжка (*f*)

nothing • *pron* ніщо /(*niščó*)/, нічого /(*ničóho*)/

notification • *n* сповіщення (*f*) /(*spovishchennya*)/

notion • *n* поняття (*n*) /(*ponjáttja*)/

noun • *n* імéнник (*m*)

novel • *n* ромáн (*m*), новéла (*f*), пóвість (*m*)

now • *adv* тепéр, нúні

nowadays • *adv* тепер /(*tepér*)/, нині /(*nýni*)/

nowhere • *adv* ніде /(*nidé*)/, нікуди /(*nikudý*)/

nuclear • *adj* ядерний /(*jádernyj*)/

nucleolus • *n* ядерце

nude • *adj* голий

nudity • *n* наготá (*f*)

number • *n* число (*n*) /(*čysló*)/, числíв-ник (*m*), цúфра (*f*), числó (*n*), нóмер (*m*)

numerator • *n* чисéльник (*m*)

nurse • *n* нáня (*f*), медсестрá (*f*), сестрá (*f*)

nut • *n* горіх *(m)*, гáйка *(f)*
nutcracker • *n* лускунчик */(luskunčyk)/*
nuthatch • *n* повзик *(m)*
nutrition • *n* харчування *(n)* */(xarčuvánnja)/*
nylon • *n* нейлон *(m)* */(nejlón)/*

O

o • *interj* о */(o)/*
o'clock • *adv* година *(f)* */(hodýna)/*, перша *(f)* */(pérša)/*, у годину */(u hodýnu)/*, о першій */(o péršij)/*
oak • *n* дуб *(m)*
oar • *n* весло́ *(n)*
oat • *n* овéс *(m)*
oath • *n* прися́га *(f)*, кля́тва *(f)*
obedience • *n* покі́рність *(f)*, послу́шність *(f)*, покóра *(f)*
obedient • *adj* слухня́ний, покі́рний
obesity • *n* ожирі́нння
obey • *v* підкорятися */(pidkoriatysia, pokoriatysia)/*
object • *n* предмéт *(m)*, об'єкт *(m)*
obligation • *n* зобов'язання *(n)* */(zobov'jázannja)/*
oboe • *n* гобой *(m)* */(hobój)/*
observatory • *n* обсерватóрія *(f)*
obvious • *adj* очеви́дний *(m)*, я́вний *(m)*
occupant • *n* окупáнт *(m)*, окупáнтка *(f)*
occupation • *n* окупáція *(f)*
occupier • *n* окупáнт *(m)*, окупáнтка *(f)*
occupy • *v* окупувáти, займáти, зайня́ти
ocean • *n* океáн *(m)*
octopus • *n* восьминíг *(m)*
offensive • *n* нáступ *(m)*, атáка *(f)* • *adj* обрáзливий *(m)*
office • *n* óфіс *(m)*, контóра *(f)*, бюрó *(n)*
officer • *n* офіцéр *(m)*
official • *n* службóва особа *(f)*, урядóва особа *(f)*, службóвець *(m)*, службóвка *(f)*, чинóвник *(m)*
offshoot • *n* відгалуження *(n)*, бічний паросток *(m)*
offspring • *n* нащадок *(m)*, потомство *(n)*, нащадки, плід *(m)*, дітище *(n)*
often • *adv* чáсто
oil • *n* олíя *(f)*, нáфта *(f)*
old • *adj* старий
olive • *n* оли́вка *(f)*, масли́на *(f)*
ominous • *adj* провісницький */(provísnyc☐kyj)/*, пророчий */(proróčyj)/*,

зловíщий */(zlovíščyj)/*
on • *prep* на
once • *adv* раз, оди́н раз
oncology • *n* онкологíя *(f)*
onion • *n* лук *(m)*, цибýля *(f)*, лýковиця *(f)*, цибýлина *(f)*
only • *adj* єди́ний • *adv* тíльки, лише́ • *conj* алé, однáк, протé
onomastics • *n* ономастика *(f)* */(onomastyka)/*
opera • *n* óпера *(f)*
operetta • *n* оперéта *(f)*
opportunity • *n* можли́вість *(f)*, шанс *(m)*
opposite • *adj* протилéжний
or • *conj* чи, абó
orange • *n* апельси́н *(m)*, оранжевий • *adj* орáнжевий, помарáнчевий
orangutan • *n* орангутан *(m)*
orator • *n* промóвець *(m)*
oratorio • *n* ораторíя
orchard • *n* фруктóвий сад *(m)*, сад *(m)*
orchestra • *n* оркестр *(m)* */(orkéstr)/*
order • *n* поря́док *(m)*, óрден *(m)*
ore • *n* руда
oregano • *n* материнка *(f)* */(materinka)/*
organelle • *n* органéла *(f)*, органóїд *(m)*
organic • *adj* органíчний
organism • *n* організм *(m)*
organization • *n* організáція *(f)*
orgasm • *v* відчувáти оргáзм *(m)* • *n* оргáзм *(m)*
orphan • *n* сиротá *(f)*
orphanage • *n* дитя́чий буди́нок *(m)*
orthography • *n* правóпис *(m)*, орфогрáфія *(f)*
oscillate • *v* осцилювати
osmium • *n* óсмíй *(m)*
ostrich • *n* стрáус *(m)*
other • *adj* íнший
otter • *n* ви́дра *(f)*
ours • *pron* наш */(naš)/*
ourselves • *pron* ми самí, ми самí
ovary • *n* яєчник *(m)* */(jajéčnyk)/*
oven • *n* піч *(f)*, пíчка *(f)*
overgrown • *adj* зарослий, порослий,

заріс, без догляду, запущений, на-
дмірно вирослий, перерослий, перерісший
owl • *n* сова (*f*), сич (*m*)
own • *v* володіти, мати • *adj* свій, вла-

´сний
owner • *n* власник (*m*), хазяїн (*m*)
ox • *n* віл (*m*) /(*vil*)/, бик (*m*) /(*byk*)/
oxygen • *n* кисень
ozone • *n* озон (*m*)

P

pace • *n* крок (*m*)
pacifism • *n* пацифізм (*m*)
package • *n* пакунок (*m*)
packet • *n* пакет (*m*)
page • *n* сторінка (*f*)
pagoda • *n* пагода (*f*) /(*páhoda*)/
pain • *n* біль (*m*)
painter • *n* художник (*m*)
pair • *n* пара (*f*) /(*pára*)/
pajamas • *n* піжама (*f*)
palace • *n* палац (*m*)
palate • *n* піднебіння (*n*), небо (*n*)
palladium • *n* паладій (*m*) /(*paládij*)/
palm • *n* долонь (*f*)
pancake • *n* млинець (*m*), блін (*m*)
pancreas • *n* підшлункова залоза (*f*)
panhandle • *n* виступ (*m*) /(*vystup*)/
panic • *v* панікувати /(*panikuváty*)/
pants • *n* брюки, штани, труси
papaya • *n* папайя (*f*)
paper • *n* папір (*m*), документ (*m*) • *adj*
паперовий
parachute • *n* парашут (*m*)
parade • *n* парад (*m*)
paradise • *n* рай (*m*), небеса
paradox • *n* парадокс (*m*) /(*paradóks*)/
paralyze • *v* паралізувати
parent • *n* родитель (*m*), батько (*m*)
park • *n* парк (*m*)
parliament • *n* парламент (*m*)
parrot • *v* наслідувати, мавпувати • *n*
папуга (*f*)
parsley • *n* петрушка (*f*)
part • *n* частина (*f*)
participate • *v* брати участь, взяти
участь
participation • *n* участь (*f*) /(*účast*□)/
particle • *n* частинка (*f*), частка (*f*), частиця (*f*)
partisan • *adj* партизанський
partridge • *n* куріпка сіра (*f*) /(*kuripka sira*)/, сіра куріпка (*f*) /(*sira kuripka*)/
parturition • *n* роди /(*ródy*)/
party • *n* партія (*f*), вечірка (*f*)
pasha • *n* паша /(*pašá*)/

passenger • *n* пасажир (*m*), пасажир-
ка (*f*)
passion • *n* страсть (*f*)
passport • *n* паспорт (*m*)
password • *n* пароль (*m*)
past • *n* минуле (*n*)
pasta • *n* макаронні вироби
/(*makaronni vyroby*)/
patch • *n* латка (*f*) /(*látka*)/, лата (*f*)
/(*láta*)/
patient • *adj* терплячий, терпеливий
patriot • *n* патріот (*m*) /(*patriót*)/, патріотка (*f*) /(*patriótka*)/
patronymic • *n* по батькові (*n*) /(*po bát'kovi*)/, патронім (*m*) /(*patrónim*)/
pavement • *n* тротуар (*m*) /(*trotuár*)/
paw • *n* лапа (*f*)
pawnbroker • *n* лихвар (*m*)
pawnshop • *n* ломбард (*m*)
pay • *v* платити, заплатити
pea • *n* горох (*m*), горошок (*m*)
peace • *n* спокій (*m*), мир (*m*)
peacekeeper • *n* замирювач (*m*)
/(*zamýrjuvač*)/
peacemaker • *n* миротворець (*m*)
peach • *n* персик (*m*)
peacock • *n* павич (*m*)
peanut • *n* арахіс (*m*)
pear • *n* груша (*f*)
pearl • *n* перла (*f*), перлина (*f*)
peasant • *n* селянин (*m*), селянка (*f*)
peasantry • *n* селянство (*n*)
/(*seljánstvo*)/
peat • *n* торф (*m*) /(*torf*)/
pedal • *n* педаль (*f*) /(*pedál*□)/
pederast • *n* педераст (*m*) /(*pederást*)/
pedicel • *n* квітконіжка (*f*)
pedigree • *n* родовід (*m*) /(*rodovíd*)/
pelican • *n* пелікан (*m*)
pelvis • *n* таз (*m*) /(*taz*)/
pen • *n* ручка (*f*), перо (*n*)
pencil • *n* олівець (*m*)
pendant • *n* кулон (*m*)
penguin • *n* пінгвін (*m*)
penicillin • *n* пеніцилін (*m*)
/(*penicylín*)/

peninsula • *n* півóстрів *(m)*

penis • *n* пéніс *(m)*, статéвий член *(m)*, хуй *(m)*

penury • *n* біднотá *(f)*

peony • *n* півóнія *(f)*

people • *n* лю́ди, нарóд *(m)*, нáція *(f)*

pepper • *n* пéрець *(m)*

perch • *n* óкунь *(m)* /*(ókun□)*/

perfective • *adj* докóнаний

perfectly • *adv* бездогáнно, цілкóм, цілковíто, абсолю́тно

perfume • *n* аромáт *(m)*, духи́, парфу́м *(m)*

perhaps • *adv* мáбуть, мóже бýти, мóжливо, мóже

perianth • *n* оцвíтина *(f)*

perineum • *n* промежина *(f)* /*(proméžyna)*/

peristalsis • *n* перистáльтика

periwinkle • *n* барвíнок *(m)*

persecute • *v* переслíдувати

persimmon • *n* хурмá *(f)*

person • *n* осóба *(f)*, персóна *(f)*, люди́на *(f)*, чоловíк *(m)*

perspicacity • *n* проникливість /*(proniklivist')*/

petiole • *n* черешóк *(m)*

phalanx • *n* фалáнга *(f)* /*(falánha)*/

pharaoh • *n* фараóн *(m)*

pharmaceutical • *adj* фармацевти́чний

pharmacist • *n* аптéкар *(m)*, аптéкарка *(f)*

pharmacy • *n* аптéка *(f)*

phase • *n* фáза *(f)*

pheasant • *n* фазáн *(m)* /*(fazán)*/

philately • *n* філателíя *(f)*

philology • *n* філолóгія *(f)*

philosopher • *n* філóсоф *(m)*

philosophy • *n* філосóфія *(f)*

phlogiston • *n* флогістóн /*(flohiston)*/

phobia • *n* фóбія *(f)*

phone • *v* дзвони́ти, подзвони́ти • *n* телефóн *(m)*

phosphate • *n* фосфáт *(m)*

phosphorus • *n* фóсфор *(m)*

photo • *n* фотогрáфія *(f)*, фотознíмок *(m)*, знíмок *(m)*, фóто *(n)*, фóтка *(f)*

photocopy • *n* ксерокóпія *(f)*

photograph • *v* фотографувáти, сфотографувáти, зніма́ти • *n* фотогрáфія *(f)*, фотознíмок *(m)*, знíмок *(m)*, фóто *(n)*

photographer • *n* фотóграф *(m)* /*(fotóhraf)*/

photography • *n* фотогрáфія *(f)*

photon • *n* фотóн *(m)*

phylum • *n* тип *(m)* /*(typ)*/, віддíл *(m)* /*(víddil)*/

physicist • *n* фíзик *(m)*

piano • *n* фортепіáно *(n)*

pickle • *v* квáсити • *n* квáшений огірóк *(m)*, рупá *(f)*, квас *(m)*

pickpocket • *n* кишенькóвий злóдій *(m)*

picnic • *n* пікнíк *(m)*

picture • *n* картúна *(f)*

pie • *n* пирíг *(m)*

pier • *n* прúстань *(f)*, пірс *(m)*

pig • *n* свиня́ *(f)*

pigeon • *n* гóлуб *(m)*

piglet • *n* поросá *(n)*, порося́тко *(n)*

pike • *n* щýка *(f)*

pilgrim • *n* прочáнин *(m)*, палóмник *(m)*

pill • *n* пігýлка *(f)* /*(pigulka)*/

pillow • *n* подýшка *(f)*

pilot • *n* льóтчик *(m)*, льóтчиця *(f)*, пілóт *(m)*

pimp • *n* сутенер *(m)* /*(sutenér)*/

pimple • *n* прищ *(m)*, вугóр *(m)*

pine • *n* соснá *(f)*

pineapple • *n* ананáс *(m)*

pink • *n* рожевий • *adj* рожéвий

pinna • *n* вушнá рáковина *(f)*

pioneer • *n* піонéр *(m)*, піонéрка *(f)*

piracy • *n* піратство *(n)* /*(piratstvo)*/

piranha • *n* піра́нья *(f)*

pirate • *n* пірáт *(m)*

pistol • *n* пістолет *(m)* /*(pistolét)*/

pit • *n* я́ма *(f)*

pitchfork • *n* вила /*(výla)*/, габлі /*(gábli)*/, габлі /*(hábli)*/

pixel • *n* піксель *(m)* /*(píksel')*/

pizza • *n* піца *(f)*

place • *n* мíсце *(n)*

plain • *n* рівнина *(f)* /*(rivnýna)*/

plait • *n* коса *(f)* /*(kosá)*/

plane • *n* літак

planet • *n* планéта *(f)* /*(planéta)*/, планéта *(f)*, планета *(f)*

plant • *n* рослúна *(f)*

plasma • *n* плáзма *(f)*

plate • *n* тарíлка *(f)*, мúска *(f)*

platform • *n* платфóрма *(f)*, перóн *(m)*

platinum • *n* плáтина *(f)*

platypus • *n* качкодзьóб *(m)*

play • *v* грáти • *n* гра *(f)*

plaza • *n* плóща *(f)*, майдáн *(m)*

please • *adv* будь лáска

pleasure • *n* задоволення *(f)* /*(zadovólennja)*/

plenary • *adj* пленарний /*(plenarnij)*/

plenty • *n* достáток (*m*)

plough • *v* орáти • *n* плуг (*m*)

plum • *n* слива (*f*) /*(slýva)*/

plunder • *v* плюндрувáти /*(pl'undruváty)*/

plural • *n* множинá (*f*) • *adj* чисельний /*(chyselny)*/

plush • *n* плюш (*m*) /*(pljuš)*/

plutonium • *n* плутóній (*m*)

pneumonia • *n* пневмонія (*f*) /*(pnevmoníja)*/

pocket • *n* кишéня (*f*)

poem • *n* вірш (*m*), поéма (*f*)

poet • *n* поéт (*m*)

poetess • *n* поетéса (*f*)

poetry • *n* поéзія (*f*)

pogrom • *n* погрóм (*m*)

point • *v* покáзувати, показáти, вкáзувати, укáзувати, вказáти, указáти

poison • *v* отрýювати, трýїти, отрýїти • *n* отрýта (*f*), яд (*m*)

poisoning • *n* отруєння (*f*)

poisonous • *adj* отрýйний (*m*)

poker • *n* кочергá (*f*) /*(kočerhá)*/

polecat • *n* тхір лісовий (*m*) /*(txir lisovýj)*/, тхір чóрний (*m*) /*(txir čórnyj)*/

polemic • *n* полемíка (*f*) /*(polémika)*/

police • *n* полíція (*f*), мілíція (*f*)

policeman • *n* поліціянт (*m*), поліцéйський (*m*), міліціонéр (*m*)

politburo • *n* Політбюрó (*n*), політбюрó (*n*)

polite • *adj* ввíчливий /*(vvíčlyvyj)*/, чемний /*(čémnyj)*/

politician • *n* полíтик (*m*)

politics • *n* полíтика (*f*)

polonium • *n* полóній (*m*)

poltergeist • *n* полтергéйст (*m*) /*(polterhéjst)*/

polyethylene • *n* поліетилен (*m*)

polyglot • *n* поліглóт (*m*)

polygon • *n* багатокутник

polytheism • *n* політеїзм (*m*) /*(politejízm)*/, багатобожжя (*n*) /*(bahatobóžžja)*/

pomegranate • *n* гранатове дéрево (*n*) /*(hranátove dérevo)*/, гранáт (*m*) /*(hranát)*/

pomelo • *n* помело (*n*)

pond • *n* став

pony • *n* пóні (*m*)

poodle • *n* пýдель (*m*)

pool • *n* калюжа (*f*)

poor • *adj* бíдний /*(bídnyj)*/

popcorn • *n* попкóрн (*m*)

pope • *n* папа римський (*m*), папа (*m*),

поп (*m*) /*(pop)*/

poplar • *n* тóполя (*f*)

poppy • *n* мак (*m*) /*(mak)*/

population • *n* насéлення (*n*)

porcelain • *n* фарфóр (*m*), порцеля́на (*f*)

porcupine • *n* дикобрáз (*m*) /*(dykobráz)*/

pork • *n* свини́на (*f*)

pornographic • *adj* порнографíчний /*(pornohrafíčnyj)*/

pornography • *n* порнографíя (*f*) /*(pornohráfija)*/

porpoise • *n* морськá свиня́ (*f*)

porridge • *n* кáша (*f*)

port • *n* порт (*m*), гáвань (*f*)

portrait • *n* портрéт (*m*)

positron • *n* позитрóн (*m*) /*(pozytrón)*/

possibility • *n* можли́вість (*f*)

post • *n* стовп (*m*) /*(stovp)*/

postcard • *n* листíвка (*f*), поштóва листíвка (*f*)

postmodernism • *n* постмодернíзм (*m*) /*(postmodernízm)*/

postscript • *n* постскриптум (*m*) /*(postskríptum)*/

potable • *adj* питни́й

potassium • *n* кáлій (*m*)

potato • *n* картóпля (*f*), бýльба (*f*), барабóля (*f*)

potter • *n* гончáр (*m*)

pour • *v* лити (*m*) /*(lýty)*/, наливáти /*(naliváty)*/, налити /*(nalýty)*/

poverty • *n* біднотá (*f*)

powder • *n* порошóк (*m*)

power • *n* влáда (*f*)

powerful • *adj* могýтній, мíцний

praseodymium • *n* празеоди́м (*m*) /*(prazeodým)*/

prawn • *n* кревéтка (*f*)

pray • *v* моли́тися, помоли́тися

prayer • *n* моли́тва (*f*)

precious • *adj* дорогоцíнний, коштóвний, дороги́й

precise • *adj* тóчний /*(tóčnyj)*/, доклáдний /*(dokládnyj)*/

predicate • *n* прис́удок (*m*), предикáт (*m*)

preface • *n* передмóва (*f*) /*(peredmóva)*/

prefix • *n* префíкс (*m*) /*(préfiks)*/

pregnancy • *n* вагíтність (*f*)

pregnant • *adj* вагíтна (*f*)

prelate • *n* прелáт (*m*) /*(prelát)*/

prepare • *v* готувáти, підготувáти, приготувáти

preposition • *n* приймéнник (*m*)

prepuce • *n* крáйня плоть (*f*) /*(krájnja*

plot')/, препуцій *(m)* /*prepúcij*/
prescription • *n* реце́пт *(m)*
present • *n* спра́вжнє *(n)*, тепе́рішній час *(m)*
president • *n* президе́нт *(m)*
pretend • *v* удавати /*udaváty*/, вдавати /*vdaváty*/
pretty • *adj* гарний *(m)* /*hárnyj*/
previous • *adj* до, Перш, перед
price • *n* ціна́ *(f)*, кошт *(m)*
prick • *n* хуй *(m)* /*xuj*/, пісюн *(m)* /*pisjún*/, прутень *(m)* /*prúten'*/
priest • *n* свяще́ник *(m)*, свяще́нник *(m)*, ксьондз *(m)*, оте́ць *(m)*, піп *(m)*, іере́й *(m)*, жрець *(m)*
prince • *n* князь *(m)*, принц *(m)*, царе́вич *(m)*, короле́вич *(m)*
princess • *n* принце́са *(f)*, царі́вна *(f)*, королі́вна *(f)*
principality • *n* князівство *(n)* /*knjazívstvo*/
printer • *n* при́нтер *(m)*
prison • *n* в'язни́ця *(f)*, тюрма́ *(f)*, темни́ця *(f)*, остро́г *(m)*
prisoner • *n* в'я́зень *(m)*, арешта́нт *(m)*
probable • *adj* правдоподі́бний, імові́рний, ймові́рний
probably • *adv* певно /*pévno*/, імовірно /*imovírno*/, ймовірно /*jmovírno*/
processor • *n* проце́сор *(m)*
profession • *n* профе́сія *(f)*, фах *(m)*
professor • *n* профе́сор *(m)*
program • *n* програ́ма *(f)*, переда́ча *(f)*
progress • *n* прогрес *(m)* /*prohrés*/
prohibit • *v* забороня́ти, заборони́ти
prohibition • *n* заборо́на *(f)*
project • *n* проект *(m)* /*proékt*/
promethium • *n* проме́тій *(m)*
pronoun • *n* займе́нник *(m)*
pronounce • *v* вимовля́ти, ви́мовити
pronunciation • *n* вимо́ва *(f)*, вимовля́ння
proof • *n* до́каз *(m)*, до́від *(m)*
propaganda • *n* пропага́нда *(f)*
propane • *n* пропа́н *(m)*
property • *n* вла́сність *(f)*, майно́ *(n)*, власність *(f)*, власти́вість *(f)*, я́кість *(f)*, властивість *(f)*, реквізит *(m)*
prophet • *n* проро́к *(m)*, проро́чиця *(f)*
prophetess • *n* проро́чиця *(f)*
prostitute • *n* проститу́тка *(f)*, повія *(f)*, шлюха *(f)*, ку́рва *(f)*
prostitution • *n* проституція *(f)* /*prostytúcija*/

protactinium • *n* протакти́ній *(m)*
protect • *v* захища́ти, захисти́ти
protection • *n* захист *(f)*, охорона *(f)*, заступництво *(f)*, оборона *(f)*, протекціонізм *(f)*, прикриття *(f)*, забезпека *(f)*, заслона *(f)*, заступа *(f)*, оберега *(f)*
protest • *n* проте́ст *(m)*
protist • *n* найпрості́ш *(m)*
proud • *adj* го́рдий
province • *n* о́бласть *(f)*, прові́нція *(f)*
provocateur • *n* провокатор *(m)* /*provokátor*/
prurient • *adj* хтивий
psychology • *n* психоло́гія *(f)*
pub • *n* кна́йпа *(f)*, бар *(m)*, пивна́ *(f)*, пивни́ця *(f)*, паб *(m)*, тракти́р *(m)*, корчма́ *(f)*, ши́нок *(m)*
publish • *v* публікува́ти, видавати /*vydaváty*/
puddle • *n* калю́жа *(f)*
pull • *v* тяга́ти, потяга́ти, тягти́, потягти́, тягну́ти, потягну́ти
pulsar • *n* пульса́р *(m)*
pumice • *n* пемза *(f)*
pump • *n* насо́с *(m)*, по́мпа *(f)*
pumpkin • *n* гарбу́з *(m)*
punch • *n* удар *(m)*
punctuation • *n* пунктуа́ція *(f)* /*punktuácija*/
punish • *v* кара́ти, покара́ти, нака́зувати, наказа́ти
punishment • *n* покара́ння *(n)*, ка́ра *(f)*
punitive • *adj* кара́льний
pupil • *n* учень *(m)* /*účen'*/, учениця *(f)* /*učenýcja*/, зіниця *(f)* /*zinýcja*/
puppy • *n* цуценя *(n)* /*cucenjá*/, щеня *(n)* /*ščenjá*/
puppyish • *adj* щеня́чий
purgatory • *n* чистилище *(n)* /*čystýlyšče*/
purge • *n* чистка *(f)* /*čýstka*/
purple • *adj* фіоле́товий
purse • *n* гаманець *(m)* /*hamanéc□*/
pus • *n* гній *(m)*
push • *v* штовхати /*štovxáty*/
pussy • *n* пизда́ *(f)*, манда́ *(f)*, піська *(f)*, табака *(f)*
put • *v* кла́сти
puzzle • *n* головоломка *(f)* /*holovolómka*/, пазл *(m)* /*pazl*/, загадка *(f)* /*zahádka*/
pyrotechnics • *n* піроте́хніка *(f)*
python • *n* пітон *(m)* /*pitón*/

Q

quagmire • *n* трясовина *(f)* /(trjasovýna)/, болото *(n)* /(bolóto)/
quail • *n* перепел *(m)* /(perepel)/
quality • *n* якість *(f)* /(jákist')/, надійність *(f)* /(nadíjnist')/ • *adj* якісний /(jákisnyj)/
quantity • *n* кількість *(f)* /(kíl□kist□)/
quark • *n* кварк *(m)*, творóг *(m)*, сир *(m)*
quarrel • *v* свáритися • *n* свáрка *(f)*, болт *(m)*
quart • *n* кварта *(f)* /(kvárta)/
quarter • *n* чверть *(f)*
quartz • *n* кварц *(m)* /(kvarc)/

quasar • *n* квазар *(m)* /(kvazár)/
quay • *n* набережна *(f)* /(náberežna)/
queen • *n* королéва *(f)*, царúця *(f)*
question • *n* питáння *(n)*
queue • *n* чéргá *(f)*
quick • *adj* швидкий /(švydkýj)/, скорий /(skóryj)/
quickly • *adv* швидко /(švýdko)/
quiet • *adj* тúхий
quietly • *adv* тúхо
quill • *n* перó *(n)*
quiver • *n* сагайдáк *(m)*

R

rabbi • *n* рабúн *(m)* /(rabyn)/, равúн *(m)*, рáбі *(m)*, рéбе *(m)*
rabbit • *n* кріль *(m)*, кролик *(m)* /(królyk)/
raccoon • *n* єнот *(m)* /(jenót)/
racism • *n* расúзм *(m)*
radiator • *n* радіáтор *(m)*
radio • *n* рáдіо *(n)*
radioactive • *adj* радіоактивний /(radioaktývnyj)/
radish • *n* редиска *(f)* /(redýska)/, редис *(m)* /(redýs)/
radius • *n* променева кістка *(f)*
radon • *n* радóн *(m)*
raft • *n* пліт *(m)*
railway • *n* залізниця *(f)*, колія *(f)*
rain • *n* дощ *(m)*
rainbow • *n* весéлка *(f)*, рáйдуга *(f)*
raincoat • *n* плащ *(m)*, дощовúк *(m)*
rainy • *adj* дощовий /(doščovýj)/
rajah • *n* раджа *(m)* /(radžá)/
rake • *n* грáблі
rally • *n* мітинг *(m)* /(mítynh)/
rape • *v* гвалтувáти, згвалтувáти, гвалтувáти, згвалтувáти • *n* згвалтувáння *(n)*, згвалтувáння *(n)*
rare • *adj* рідкий
raspberry • *n* малúна *(f)*
raven • *n* вóрон *(m)*, крук *(m)*
ravine • *n* яр *(m)* /(jar)/, ущелина *(f)* /(uščélyna)/
ray • *n* промінь *(m)* /(prómin□)/, скат *(m)* /(skat)/
razor • *n* брúтва *(f)*

reach • *v* доходити, дійтú, доїжджáти, доїхати
reaction • *n* реакція *(f)* /(reákcija)/
read • *v* читáти, прочитáти
reader • *n* читáч *(m)*
ready • *adj* готóвий
reap • *v* жати /(žáty)/, пожинати /(požynáty)/
rearmament • *n* переозбрóєння *(n)*
rebel • *n* бунтівник *(m)*, повстанець *(m)*, бунтар *(m)*
rebellion • *n* повстання *(n)* /(povstánnja)/, непокора *(f)* /(nepokóra)/, бунт *(m)* /(bunt)/
rebus • *n* ребус
receive • *v* отрúмувати, отрúмати
recent • *adj* остáнній
receptacle • *n* квітколóже *(n)*
recipe • *n* рецепт *(m)* /(recépt)/
reconnoiter • *v* розвідувати /(rozviduvaty)/, рекогносцирувати /(rekohnoscyruvaty)/, пластувати /(plastuvaty)/ • *n* розвідка *(f)* /(rozvidka)/, рекогнозцировка *(f)* /(rekohnoscyrovka)/, пласт *(m)* /(plast)/, пластування *(n)* /(plastuvannja)/
rectangle • *n* прямокутник
red • *adj* червóний
reef • *n* риф *(m)*
reek • *n* сморíд *(m)* /(smoríd)/, вонь *(f)* /(von□)/
referee • *n* суддя *(m)* /(suddjá)/, реферí *(m)* /(referí)/, арбітр *(m)* /(arbítr)/
referendum • *n* референдум *(m)*
refrigerator • *n* холодúльник *(m)*

refuge • *n* притулок *(m)* /*(prytúlok)*/

refugee • *n* біженець *(m)*

refuse • *v* відмовляти, відмовлятися

rein • *n* повід *(m)*, віжка *(f)*

reindeer • *n* північний олень *(m)*

reliability • *n* надійність *(f)* /*(nadíjnist')*/, точність *(f)* /*(tóčnist')*/

relief • *n* барельєф *(n)*

religion • *n* релігія *(f)*

remember • *v* пам'ятати

remote • *adj* далекий /*(dalékyj)*/

remove • *v* відносити, віднести

rentier • *n* рантьє *(f)*

repeat • *v* повторювати

repertoire • *n* репертуáр *(m)*

reply • *v* розповідати /*(rozpovidáty)*/, розповісти /*(rozpovísty)*/

reporter • *n* репортéр *(m)*, кореспондéнт *(m)*, журналíст *(m)*

reptile • *n* плазýн *(m)*, рептíлія *(f)*

republic • *n* респýбліка *(f)*

rescind • *v* анулювати /*(anuljuváty)*/, скасувати /*(skasuváty)*/

rescue • *v* рятувати /*(rjatuváty)*/ • *n* порятунок *(m)* /*(porjatúnok)*/

reside • *v* мéшкати, жити, проживати

resident • *n* житель *(m)* /*(žýtel')*/, мешканець *(m)* /*(meškánec')*/

resistance • *n* опір *(m)*

rest • *n* відпочинок *(m)*, рéшта *(f)* • *v* відпочивáти

restaurant • *n* ресторан *(m)* /*(restorán)*/

restrictive • *adj* обмежувальний /*(obméžuval□nyj)*/

result • *n* результáт *(m)*

retina • *n* сіткíвка *(f)*, ретíна *(f)*

retort • *n* реторта

retreat • *v* відступáти, відступíти • *n* відступ *(m)*

revenge • *n* пóмста *(f)*

reverse • *v* касувати /*(kasuváty)*/, скасувати /*(skasuváty)*/

revise • *v* повторювати

revolution • *n* револю́ція *(f)*

rhenium • *n* рéній *(m)*

rhetoric • *n* ретóрика *(f)*

rhinoceros • *n* носорíг *(m)*

rhodium • *n* рóдій *(m)*

rhombus • *n* ромб *(m)*

rhubarb • *n* ревíнь /*(revín')*/

rhythm • *n* ритм *(m)*

rib • *n* ребрó *(n)*

ribbon • *n* стрíчка *(f)*

rice • *n* рис *(m)*, риж *(m)*

rich • *adj* багáтий

rickshaw • *n* рикша *(m)*

rider • *n* вершник *(m)* /*(veršnýk)*/

rifle • *n* гвинтíвка *(f)*, рушниця *(f)*

right • *adj* прямий, прáвильний, вíрний, прáвий • *adv* зпрáва, напрáво

ring • *n* кільцé *(n)*, пéрстень *(m)* • *v* дзвонíти, подзвонíти

ripen • *v* зріти /*(zríty)*/, дозрівати /*(dozriváty)*/

rite • *n* обряд *(m)* /*(obrjád)*/, ритуал *(m)* /*(rytuál)*/

ritual • *n* ритуал *(m)* /*(rytuál)*/, обряд *(m)* /*(obrjád)*/

river • *n* рікá *(f)*, рíчка *(f)*

road • *n* дорóга *(f)*, шлях *(m)*

roe • *n* ікра *(f)* /*(ikrá)*/

roger • *interj* зрозуміти /*(vas zrozumív)*/

role • *n* роль *(f)*

roof • *n* дах *(m)*

rook • *n* грак *(m)*, гáйворон *(m)*, тура

room • *n* кімнáта *(f)*, пóкій *(m)*, хáта *(f)*

roomy • *adj* просторий /*(prostóryj)*/

rooster • *n* пíвень *(m)*, кóгут *(m)*

root • *n* кóрінь *(m)*, корíння *(n)*

rope • *n* вірьóвка *(f)*

rosary • *n* чотки /*(čótky)*/, розарій *(m)* /*(rozárij)*/

rose • *n* троянда *(f)*, шипшина *(f)*, рóза *(f)* • *adj* рожéвий

rotor • *n* ротор *(m)* /*(rótor)*/

round • *n* круг *(m)* /*(kruh)*/, коло *(n)* /*(kólo)*/ • *adj* круглий /*(krúhlyj)*/

rowan • *n* горобина звичайна *(f)* /*(horobýna zvyčájna)*/, горобина *(f)* /*(horobýna)*/

rubber • *n* гýма *(f)*, каучýк *(m)*

rubidium • *n* рубíдій *(m)*

ruble • *n* карбóванець *(m)*, рубль *(m)*

ruby • *n* рубíн *(m)*

rudd • *n* краснопíрка *(f)* /*(krasnopírka)*/, червонопíрка *(f)* /*(červonopírka)*/

rule • *n* прáвило *(n)*

ruler • *n* правитель *(m)*, правителька *(f)*

rum • *n* ром *(m)* /*(rom)*/

run • *v* бíгати, бíгти

ruthenium • *n* рутéній *(m)*

rutherfordium • *n* резерфóрдій *(m)*

rye • *n* жито *(f)*

S

sack • *n* мішóк *(m)* /(mišók)/, мішóк *(m)*
sacred • *adj* святий /(svjatýj)/, священний /(svjaščénnyj)/
sacrifice • *v* жертвувати /(žértvuvaty)/
• *n* жертва *(f)* /(žértva)/
sad • *adj* смýтний
saddle • *n* сідло *(n)* /(sidló)/
sadness • *n* печáль *(f)*, смýток *(m)*
safe • *n* сейф *(m)* • *adj* безпéчний
safety • *n* безпéка *(f)*
sage • *n* мудрець, шавлія • *adj* мудрий
saiga • *n* сайгак
sail • *n* вітрúло *(n)*, пáрус *(m)*
sailboat • *n* вітрúльник *(m)*
sailor • *n* матрос *(m)* /(matrós)/
saint • *n* святий *(m)* /(svjatýj)/, свята *(f)* /(svjatá)/
sake • *n* сакé *(n)*
salacious • *adj* хтивий /(xtývyj)/, похітливий /(poxitlývyj)/
salad • *n* салáт *(m)*
salamander • *n* саламáндра *(f)*
salami • *n* салямі *(f)* /(saljámi)/
salesperson • *n* продавець *(m)* /(prodavéc□)/
saliva • *n* слúна *(f)*
salmon • *n* лосось *(m)* /(losós□)/
salt • *n* сіль *(f)*
salty • *adj* солóний /(solónyj)/
salvation • *n* спасíння *(n)*, порятýнок *(m)*
salve • *n* мазь *(f)*, піна *(f)*, бальзáм *(m)*
samara • *n* крилáтка *(f)*
samarium • *n* самáрій *(m)*
same • *adj* одноманітний
samovar • *n* самовáр *(m)*
samurai • *n* самурáй *(m)*
sanatorium • *n* санатóрій *(m)*
sanction • *n* сáнкція *(f)*
sand • *n* пісóк *(m)*
sandy • *adj* піщаний
sap • *n* сік *(m)* /(sik)/
sapwood • *n* óболонь *(f)*
sarcasm • *n* сарказм *(m)*
sarcophagus • *n* саркофаг *(m)* /(sarkofáh)/
sardine • *n* сардинка *(f)*
sashimi • *n* сашімі *(n)*
satellite • *n* супýтник *(m)*
satire • *n* сатúра *(f)*
satirize • *v* висмíювати /(vysmíjuvaty)/
sauce • *n* сóус *(m)*, підлúва *(f)*
sauerkraut • *n* квашена капуста *(f)* /(kvášena kapústa)/

sauna • *n* сауна *(f)* /(sáuna)/
sausage • *n* ковбасá *(f)*, сосíска *(f)*
save • *v* рятувáти
saw • *n* пилá *(f)*
say • *v* говорúти, казáти, сказáти
scaffold • *n* риштування /(ryshtuvannia)/
scales • *n* вага *(f)* /(váha)/
scandium • *n* скандій *(m)* /(skándij)/
scanner • *n* скáнер *(m)*
scapegoat • *n* козел відпýщення *(m)* /(kozél vidpúščennja)/
scar • *n* шрам *(m)*, рубéць *(m)*
scare • *v* лякати
scarf • *n* шарф *(m)*
scenery • *n* краєвúд *(m)*, пейзáж *(m)*, ландшáфт *(m)*, вид *(m)*
scent • *n* зáпах *(m)*
schedule • *n* рóзклад *(m)*, грáфік *(m)*
schizophrenia • *n* шизофренія *(f)*
schnapps • *n* шнапс *(m)* /(šnaps)/
schnitzel • *n* шніцель *(m)*
school • *n* зграя *(f)*, шкóла *(f)*, учúлище *(n)*, вúща шкóла *(f)*, вúщий навчáльний зáклад *(m)*, університéт *(m)*, акадéмія *(f)*, інститýт *(m)*, консерватóрія *(f)*, колéдж *(m)*, технікум *(m)*, факультéт *(m)*, відділення *(f)* • *v* навчáти
science • *n* наýка *(f)*, дисциплíна *(f)*, знання *(n)*
scientific • *adj* науковий /(naukóvyj)/
scientist • *n* вчéний *(m)*, учéний *(m)*
scion • *n* нащáдок *(m)*
scissors • *n* нóжиці
scorpion • *n* скорпіон *(m)*
scouting • *n* розвідка *(f)* /(rozvidka)/, рекогносцировка *(f)* /(rekohnoscyrovka)/, пласт *(m)* /(plast)/, пластування *(n)* /(plastuvannja)/, скаутінг *(m)* /(skauting)/
scrap • *n* металобрýхт *(m)*
scrape • *v* скребти /(skrebtý)/
scratch • *v* шкрябати /(škrjábaty)/
screen • *n* екрáн *(m)*
screw • *n* гвинт *(m)*, шурýп *(m)*
screwdriver • *n* викрутка *(f)* /(výkrutka)/, завертка *(f)* /(zavértka)/
scroll • *n* сувій *(m)* /(suvíj)/
scrotum • *n* мошóнка *(f)*, калúтка *(f)*
scythe • *v* косити /(kosýty)/ • *n* коса *(f)* /(kosá)/
sea • *n* мóре *(n)*
seal • *n* тюлень *(m)*, печáть *(f)*
search • *v* шукáти • *n* пóшук *(m)*

seashell • *n* му́шля (f), ра́ковина (f), черепа́шка (f)

season • *n* пора́ ро́ку (f)

seasoning • *n* приправа (f) /(pryprava)/

secession • *n* відді́лення (n), сецéсія (f)

second • *adj* другий /(drúhyj)/ • *n* секунда (f) /(sekúnda)/

secret • *n* таéмниця (f), секрéт (m)

secretly • *adv* таємно /(tajémno)/

sect • *n* секта (f) /(sékta)/

security • *n* безпéка (f)

see • *v* ба́чити, ви́діти

seed • *n* сíм'я (n), насíнина (f), насíння (n), сíм'я

seek • *v* шука́ти

seismology • *n* сейсмологія (f) /(sejsmolóhija)/

seldom • *adv* рíдко, зрíдка

selenium • *n* селéн (m)

self-service • *n* самообслуговування (n) /(samoobsluhóvuvannja)/, самообслуга (f) /(samoobslúha)/

sell • *v* продава́ти, прода́ти

semen • *n* спéрма (f), сíм'я (f), еякуля́т (m), насíння (n)

senate • *n* сенат (m) /(senát)/

send • *v* посила́ти, сла́ти, посла́ти

sentence • *n* рéчення (n), фра́за (f)

sepal • *n* чашолисто́к (m)

separatist • *n* сепарати́ст (m), сепарати́стка (f) • *adj* сепарати́стський

serious • *adj* серйозний /(serjóznyj)/

seriously • *adv* серйозно /(serjózno)/

servant • *n* слуга́ (m), служни́ця (f)

service • *n* слу́жба (f) /(slúžba)/

serviceman • *n* військовослужбо́вець (m), військови́к (m)

seventh • *adj* сьо́мий (m)

sew • *v* ши́ти

sex • *n* лю́бощі, секс (m), статéві зно́сини, стать (f)

sexism • *n* сексизм (m) /(seksýzm)/

shabbiness • *n* убогість, занéдбаність, зно́шеність, нікчéмність

shack • *n* хала́па (f) /(xalúpa)/, хатинка (f) /(xatýnka)/

shadow • *n* тінь (f)

shaft • *n* шахта (f) /(šáxta)/

shah • *n* шах (m) /(šax)/, шаг (m) /(šah)/

shaitan • *n* шайта́н (m)

shallow • *n* мілина (f) /(milyná)/ • *adj* мілки́й /(milkýj)/, неглибо́кий /(nehlybókyj)/, поверхнéвий /(poverxnévyj)/

shamanism • *n* шаманíзм (m)

shampoo • *n* шампу́нь (m)

shark • *n* акула (f) /(akúla)/

sharp • *adj* го́стрий

shave • *v* голи́ти, голи́тися

she • *pron* вона́

sheaf • *n* сніп (m), в'яза́нка (f)

shearwater • *n* буревісник (m)

sheik • *n* шейх (m)

shelduck • *n* галагаз (m)

shelf • *n* полиця (f)

shepherd • *n* пасту́х (m), па́стир (m)

sheriff • *n* шериф (m) /(šerýf)/

shield • *n* щит (m)

shin • *n* гомíлка (f) /(homílka)/

shine • *v* світи́ти, ся́яти

ship • *n* корабéль (m), судно́ (n)

shipbuilder • *n* корабéл (m) /(korabél)/, суднобудíвник (m) /(sudnbudivnýk)/

shipyard • *n* верф (f)

shirt • *n* соро́чка (f), кошу́ля (f)

shit • *n* гімно́ (n), дерьмо́ (n), лайно́ (n) • *v* сра́ти

shoe • *n* черевúк (m)

shoehorn • *n* рíжок (m) /(rižók)/

shoelace • *n* шнуро́к (m)

shogun • *n* сьо́гун (m)

shoot • *v* стріля́ти, ви́стрелити

shooting • *n* стрільба́ (f), стріляни́на (f)

shop • *v* ходити до крамни́ць /(xodýty do kramnýс□)/ • *n* крамни́ця (f), магазúн (m)

shore • *n* бéріг (m), бéрег (m)

short • *adj* коро́ткий, ни́зький

shorten • *v* скоро́чувати, скороти́ти

shorts • *n* шо́рти

shot • *n* по́стріл (m)

shotgun • *n* рушниця (f) /(rušnýcja)/

shoulder • *n* плечé (n)

shout • *v* крича́ти

shovel • *n* лопа́та (f)

show • *v* пока́зувати, показа́ти

shower • *v* бризкати, прийняти душ • *n* до́щик (m), душ (m)

shrew • *n* землерúйка (f) /(zemlerýjka)/

shrimp • *n* кревéтка (f)

shrine • *n* ра́ка (f), святи́ня (f), храм (m)

shut • *v* зачиня́ти, зачини́ти, закрива́ти, закри́ти

shuttlecock • *n* волан (m) /(volán)/

sibling • *n* суро́дженець (m) /(suródženeć)/, роджéнство (n) /(rodžénstvo)/

sic • *adv* так /(tak)/

sich • *n* Січ (f) /(Sich)/

sickle • *v* жати /(žáty)/ • *n* серп (m)

sidewalk • *n* тротуар (m) /(trotuár)/

sieve • *n* рéшето (n) /(réšeto)/, сито (n)

/(sýto)/

sign • *v* підпи́сувати, підписа́ти, під-
пи́суватися, підписа́тися

signature • *n* пі́дпис (*m*)

silence • *n* ти́ша (*f*), мовча́ння (*n*)

silencer • *n* глушни́к (*m*)

silicon • *n* кре́мній (*m*)

silique • *n* стручок (*m*) /(struchok)/

silk • *n* шовк (*m*)

silver • *n* срі́бло, срібля́стий (*m*) • *adj*
срі́бний

similarity • *n* схо́жість (*f*) /(sxóžist□)/,
подібність (*f*) /(podíbnist□)/

simony • *n* симонія (*f*) /(symonija)/

simoom • *n* самум (*m*)

simple • *adj* про́стий, ле́гкий

sin • *v* гріши́ти • *n* гріх (*m*)

since • *prep* з /(z)/, від /(vid)/

sing • *v* співа́ти, заспіва́ти

singer • *n* співа́к (*m*), співа́чка (*f*)

singlet • *n* ма́йка (*f*)

singular • *n* однина́ (*f*)

sink • *v* опуска́тися, зни́жуватися, па-
да́ти, впада́ти, запада́ти, заходи́ти,
тону́ти, зану́рюватися, іти́ на дно, по-
тупа́ти, осіда́ти, запа́сти в па́м'ять,
врі́затися в па́м'ять, слабша́ти, ги́ну-
ти, зубожі́ти, занепа́сти ду́хом, топи́-
ти, копа́ти колодя́зь, ри́ти колодя́зь,
невда́ло покла́сти, затопи́ти, всади́ти,
вколо́ти • *n* кухо́нний злив, ра́ковина
для стіка́ння во́ди

sinker • *n* грузило (*n*) /(hruzýlo)/

sinless • *adj* безгрі́шний

sinner • *n* грі́шник (*m*) /(hríšnyk)/, грі-
шниця (*f*) /(hríšnycja)/

sir • *n* пан (*m*)

siskin • *n* чиж (*m*) /(čyž)/

sister • *n* сестра́ (*f*)

sit • *v* сиді́ти, сі́сти

situation • *n* ситуа́ція (*f*), місцеполо-
́ження (*n*), положення (*n*), розташува́-
ння (*n*), стан (*m*), обстано́вка (*f*), поса́-
да (*f*)

sixth • *n* шостий (*m*) • *adj* шо́стий

sixtieth • *adj* шестидеся́тих

size • *n* ро́змір (*m*)

skate • *n* ковза́н (*m*), ли́жва (*f*)

skateboard • *n* скейтбо́рд (*m*)

skeleton • *n* скеле́т (*m*)

skepticism • *n* скептицизм (*m*)
/(skeptycýzm)/, скептицизм

skewer • *n* рожен (*m*), шампу́р (*m*)

ski • *n* ли́жа (*f*)

skin • *n* шкі́ра (*f*), шку́ра (*f*)

skinhead • *n* скінхе́д (*f*), скін (*f*)

skinny • *adj* худи́й

skirt • *n* спідниця (*f*)

skull • *n* че́реп (*m*)

sky • *n* не́бо (*n*), небеса́

skylark • *n* жа́йворонок (*m*)

skyscraper • *n* хмарочос (*m*)
/(xmaročós)/

slave • *n* раб (*m*), раби́ня (*f*)

sledge • *n* са́ни, са́нки

sleep • *v* спа́ти • *n* сон (*m*)

sleeve • *n* рука́в (*m*)

slime • *n* слиз (*m*), іл (*m*), шлам (*m*)

slipper • *n* пантофля (*f*) /(pantóflja)/

slivovitz • *n* сливовиця (*f*)
/(slyvóvytsja)/

sloop • *n* шлюп (*m*) /(šljup)/

sloth • *n* лінь (*f*), ледарство (*n*), лінощі
(*f*), лінивець (*m*)

slow • *adj* пові́льний, нудни́й

slowly • *adv* пові́льно

slug • *n* слимак (*m*) /(slymák)/, слизняк
(*m*) /(slyznják)/, слизень (*m*) /(slýzen□)/

sluice • *n* шлюз (*m*) /(šljuz)/

slum • *n* трущо́ба (*f*)

slut • *n* шлю́ха (*f*), шльо́ндра (*f*), ку́рва
(*f*)

small • *adj* мале́нький, мали́й, моло-
ди́й

smart • *adj* розу́мний

smell • *n* за́пах (*m*)

smile • *v* посміха́тися, посміхну́тися
• *n* посмішка (*f*)

smith • *n* коваль (*m*)

smoke • *v* кури́ти, палити • *n* дим (*m*)

smoked • *adj* вуджений /(vúdženyj)/

smoking • *n* палі́ння (*n*), курі́ння (*n*)

smolder • *v* тлі́ти /(tlíty)/

smooth • *adj* гладки́й

snail • *n* ра́влик (*m*)

snake • *n* змія́ (*f*)

sneeze • *v* чха́ти, чхну́ти, чиха́ти, чи-
хну́ти

sniper • *n* сна́йпер (*m*)

snooker • *n* сну́кер (*m*)

snore • *v* хропі́ти • *n* храп (*m*)

snot • *n* смарка́ль (*m*), со́плі, шма́рклі

snow • *n* сніг (*m*)

snowball • *n* сніжок (*m*) /(snižók)/

snowflake • *n* сніжи́нка (*f*)

snowman • *n* снігова баба (*f*) /(snihová
bába)/, сніговик (*m*) /(snihovýk)/

so • *adv* так

soap • *n* ми́ло (*n*)

soccer • *n* футбо́л (*m*), ко́паний м'яч
(*m*)

socialism • *n* соціалізм /(socializm)/

socialist • *n* соціаліст *(m)*, соціалістка *(f)*

society • *n* суспільство *(n)*

sock • *n* носок *(m)*, шкарпетка *(f)*

sodium • *n* натрій *(m)*

sofa • *n* софа *(f)*, диван *(m)*

soft • *adj* м'який /(m'jákyj)/

softly • *adv* м'яко, тихо

software • *n* програмне забезпечення *(n)*, ПЗ *(n)*

soil • *n* земля *(f)*, ґрунт *(m)*, грунт *(m)*

soldier • *n* солдат *(m)*, воїн *(m)*, жовнір *(m)*, вояк *(m)*, військовий *(m)*

sole • *n* підошва *(f)*, підметка *(f)*

some • *pron* деякий, кілька, трохи

somebody • *pron* хтось *(m)*

something • *pron* щось /(ščos☐)/, дещо /(déščo)/, що-небудь /(ščo-nebúd☐)/, чого-небудь /(čohó-nebúd☐)/, деякий /(déjakyj)/, дехто /(déxto)/, певний /(pévnyj)/, досить /(dósyt')/, сякий-такий /(sjakýj-takýj)/, проклятий /(prokljátyj)/

sometime • *adv* колись, коли-небудь

sometimes • *adv* іноді, часом

somewhere • *adv* десь /(des☐)/, кудись /(kudýs☐)/, десь

son • *n* син *(m)*

son-in-law • *n* зять *(m)*

song • *n* пісня *(f)*

sonnet • *n* сонет *(m)*

soon • *adv* скоро, незабаром

soothe • *v* полегшувати /(polehshuvaty)/

sorceress • *n* чарівниця *(f)*

sorrel • *n* щавель *(m)*

sorrow • *n* печаль *(f)*, горе *(n)*, смуток *(m)*

sorry • *interj* пробачте, пробач, перепрошую

soul • *n* душа *(f)*

sound • *n* звук *(m)*

sour • *adj* кислий

south • *n* південь *(m)* /(pívden')/

southeast • *n* південний схід *(m)*

southward • *adv* на південь

southwest • *n* південний захід *(m)*

soviet • *n* рада *(f)*, совєт *(m)*

sow • *n* свиня *(f)* /(svynjá)/, льоха *(f)* /(l'óxa)/ • *v* сіяти

spaceship • *n* космічний корабель *(m)* /(kosmičnyї korabel')/

spade • *n* лопата *(f)*, заступ *(m)*

spark • *n* іскра *(f)* /(ískra)/

speak • *v* говорити, сказати, розмовляти

spear • *n* спис *(m)* /(spys)/

spectacles • *n* окуляри

speech • *n* мова *(f)*, говір *(m)*, промова *(f)*

spell • *n* заклинання *(n)*, закляття *(n)*, чари

spellbound • *adj* зачарований

spelling • *n* правопис *(m)*

sperm • *n* сперма *(f)* /(spérma)/

sphere • *n* сфера *(f)* /(sféra)/

sphincter • *n* сфінктер *(m)* /(sfínkter)/

spider • *n* павук *(m)*

spin • *v* прясти /(prjastý)/

spinach • *n* шпинат *(m)* /(špynát)/

spindle • *n* веретено *(n)* /(veretenó)/

spinster • *n* стара діва *(f)* /(stará díva)/

spit • *n* рожен *(m)*, шампур *(m)*, коса *(f)*, слина *(f)*, плювок *(m)* • *v* плювати, наплювати, плюнути

spleen • *n* селезінка *(f)*, сум *(m)*

spoil • *v* псувати /(psuváty)/

spoiler • *n* спойлер *(m)*

sponge • *n* губка *(f)*

spool • *n* намотувати *(f)* /(namotuvaty)/

spoon • *n* ложка *(f)*

spoonbill • *n* косар *(m)*

spore • *n* спора *(f)*

sport • *n* спорт *(m)* /(sport)/

spring • *n* весна *(f)*

spruce • *n* ялиця *(f)*, смерека *(f)*, ялина *(f)*

sputnik • *n* супутник *(m)*, спутнік *(m)*

spy • *n* шпигун *(m)* /(špyhún)/

square • *n* квадрат *(m)* /(kvadrat)/, площа *(f)*, майдан *(m)*

squat • *n* присідання *(n)*

squiggle • *v* шкрябати /(škrjábaty)/

squirrel • *n* білка *(f)* /(bílka)/

stab • *n* спроба *(f)*, критика *(f)*

stadium • *n* стадіон *(m)*

staircase • *n* сходи, сходова клітка *(f)*

stairs • *n* сходи

stake • *n* кіл *(m)*

stallion • *n* жеребець *(m)*

stamen • *n* тичинка *(f)*

stand • *v* стояти

standpoint • *n* точка зору *(f)*

star • *n* зірка *(f)*, звізда *(f)*

starfish • *n* морська зірка *(f)* /(mors☐ká zírka)/

starling • *n* шпак /(špak)/

start • *n* початок *(m)* /(počátok)/ • *v* починати /(počynáty)/, почати /(počáty)/, починатися /(počynátysja)/, початися /(počátysja)/

starve • *v* голодувати

state • *n* держава *(f)*, стан *(m)*, стано-

ʹвище *(n)*

station • *n* ста́нція *(f)*, вокза́л *(m)*

statue • *n* ста́туя *(f)*

stay • *v* затримуватися */(zatrýmuvatysja)/*

steak • *n* біфштекс *(m)* */(bifštéks)/*

steal • *v* кра́сти, укра́сти

steam • *n* па́ра *(f)*, пар *(m)*

steamboat • *n* пароплав *(m)* */(paropláv)/*

steamer • *n* пароплав *(m)* */(paropláv)/*

steamship • *n* пароплав *(m)* */(paropláv)/*

steel • *n* сталь *(f)*, кри́ця *(f)*

stench • *n* сморі́д *(m)* */(smoríd)/*, вонь *(f)* */(von□)/*

step • *n* крок *(m)* */(krok)/*, щабель *(m)* */(ščabél')/*, сходинка *(f)* */(sxódynka)/*, хо́да *(f)* */(xodá)/*

stepdaughter • *n* падчерка *(f)* */(pádčerka)/*, пасербиця *(f)* */(páserbycja)/*

stepfather • *n* ві́тчим *(m)*

stepmother • *n* ма́чуха *(f)* */(máčuxa)/*

steppe • *n* степ *(f)*

stepson • *n* пасинок *(m)* */(pásynok)/*, пасерб *(m)* */(páserb)/*

stethoscope • *n* стетоско́п *(m)*

stick • *n* палиця *(f)* */(palítsja)/*

stigmatize • *v* таврува́ти

sting • *v* жалити */(žályty)/*, ужалити */(užályty)/*, кусати */(kusáty)/*, укусити */(ukusýty)/*

stinger • *n* жало *(n)* */(žálo)/*

stink • *v* смерді́ти

stirrup • *n* стре́мено *(n)*

stocking • *n* панчо́ха *(f)*

stomach • *n* шлу́нок *(m)*, живі́т *(m)* */(žyvít)/*, черево *(n)* */(čérevo)/*

stone • *n* ка́мінь *(m)*, камінець *(m)*

stop • *v* зупиня́тися, зупини́тися • *n* зупи́нка *(f)*

stork • *n* лелека *(m)* */(leléka)/*, чорногуз *(m)* */(čornohúz)/*, бусел *(m)* */(búsel)/*

storm • *n* бу́ря *(f)*

story • *n* оповідь *(f)* */(ópovid')/*

stove • *n* піч *(f)*, пі́чка *(f)*, плита́ *(f)*, плитка *(f)*

strait • *n* прото́ка *(f)*, проли́в *(m)*

strange • *adj* ди́вний

straw • *n* соло́ма *(f)*

strawberry • *n* суни́ця *(f)*, полуни́ця *(f)* • *adj* суничний *(f)* */(sunýčnyj)/*, полуничний *(f)* */(polunýčnyj)/*

stream • *n* струмок *(m)* */(strumók)/*, рі́чка *(f)* */(ríčka)/*, потік *(m)* */(potík)/*

street • *n* ву́лиця *(f)*

strength • *n* сила *(f)* */(syla)/*, міць *(f)* */(meets')/*, дієвість *(f)* */(diyevist')/*, авторитет *(m)* */(avtorytet)/*

streptococcus • *n* стрептокок */(streptokok)/*

strike • *n* страйк *(m)* */(strajk)/*, забастовка *(f)* */(zabastóvka)/*

strong • *adj* си́льний, мі́цний

strontium • *n* стро́нцій *(m)*

structure • *n* структура *(f)* */(struktúra)/*

struggle • *v* боротися */(borótysja)/*, битися */(býtysja)/* • *n* боротьба *(f)* */(borot□bá)/*, бій *(m)* */(bij)/*, битва *(f)* */(býtva)/*

stubborn • *adj* впе́ртий

student • *n* студент *(m)* */(studént)/*, студентка *(f)* */(studéntka)/*

study • *v* вчити */(včýty)/*, учити */(učýty)/*, вчитися */(včýtysja)/*, учитися */(učýtysja)/*, навчатися */(navčátysja)/*

stump • *n* пень *(m)* */(pen□)/*

stupid • *adj* дурний */(durnýj)/*, тупий

stupor • *n* ступор *(m)* */(stúpor)/*

sturgeon • *n* осетер *(m)*

stutter • *n* заїкання

subject • *n* пі́дмет *(m)*

submarine • *n* підво́дний чо́вен *(m)*

submissive • *adj* покірний

subset • *n* підмножина *(f)* */(pidmnožyná)/*

substrate • *n* субстрат *(m)* */(substrát)/*

substratum • *n* субстра́т *(m)*

subterranean • *adj* підземний */(pidzémnyj)/*

suburb • *n* передмі́стя *(n)*, при́город *(m)*

subway • *n* метро *(n)* */(metró)/*

success • *n* успіх *(m)* */(úspix)/*

successful • *adj* успі́шний, вда́тний

suck • *v* смоктати */(smoktáty)/*, ссати */(ssáty)/*

sudden • *adj* раптовий, несподіваний */(nespodívanyj)/*, наглий */(náhlyj)/*

suddenly • *adv* раптово */(raptovo)/*, несподівано */(nespodivano)/*

suffering • *n* страждання *(n)*, му́ка *(f)* • *adj* страждаючий

suffix • *n* суфікс *(m)* */(súfiks)/*

sugar • *n* цу́кор *(m)*

suggestion • *n* пропозиція *(f)* */(propozýcija)/*

suicide • *n* самогу́бство *(n)*, суїци́д *(m)*

suit • *n* масть *(f)*

suite • *n* сюї́та *(f)*

sulfur • *n* сі́рка *(f)*

sultan • *n* султа́н *(m)*

sum • *n* су́ма *(f)*

summary • *n* пі́дсумок *(m)* */(pídsumok)/*

summer • *n* лі́то *(n)*

summit • *n* верши́на *(f)*, пік *(m)*, верхі́вка *(f)*, са́міт *(m)*, зу́стріч *(f)*

sun • *n* со́нце *(n)*

sundial • *n* сонячний годинник *(m)* /(*sónjačnyj hodýnnyk*)/

sunfish • *n* риба-місяць

sunflower • *n* соняшник *(m)* /(*sónjašnyk*)/, соняx *(m)* /(*sónjax*)/, жовтогарячий /(*žóvto-har'áčyj*)/

sunny • *adj* сонячний /(*sónjačnyj*)/

supermarket • *n* супермаркет *(m)* /(*supermárket*)/

supernova • *n* наднова зірка *(f)* /(*nadnová zírka*)/, наднова *(f)* /(*nadnová*)/

superstition • *n* забобон

supper • *n* вече́ря *(f)*, вечеря *(f)* /(*večerja*)/

supreme • *adj* верховний /(*verxóvnyj*)/, найвищий /(*najvýščyj*)/

surface • *n* поверхня *(f)* /(*povérxnja*)/

surface-to-air • *adj* земля-повітря

surgeon • *n* хірург *(m)*

surname • *n* прізвище *(n)*

survive • *v* переживати /(*perežyváty*)/, пережити /(*perežýty*)/

sushi • *n* су́ші *(n)*

suslik • *n* ховрáх *(m)* /(*xovráx*)/, ховрашо́к *(m)*

swallow • *v* ковтати /(*kovtáty*)/ • *n* ла́стівка *(f)*

swamp • *n* боло́то *(n)*

swan • *n* ле́бідь *(m)*

swarm • *v* киши́ти • *n* рій *(m)*, на́товп *(m)*, юрбá *(f)*

swastika • *n* свастика *(f)* /(*svástyka*)/

sweat • *n* піт *(m)* • *v* поті́ти

sweater • *n* светр *(m)*, пуло́вер *(m)*

sweep • *v* підмітати /(*pidmitáty*)/, мести /(*mestý*)/, підмести /(*pidmestý*)/

sweet • *adj* соло́дкий

swim • *v* плáвати, поплáвати, плисти́, поплисти́

swimming • *n* плавання *(n)* /(*plávannja*)/

sword • *n* меч *(m)*

syllabus • *n* програма *(f)* /(*prohráma*)/, навчальна програма *(f)* /(*navčál□na prohráma*)/

symbol • *n* символ *(m)* /(*sýmvol*)/, знак *(m)* /(*znak*)/

symmetry • *n* симе́трія *(f)*

symphony • *n* симфонія *(f)* /(*symfónija*)/

synagogue • *n* синагога *(f)* /(*synahóha*)/

synclinal • *n* синкліна́ль

synonym • *n* синóнім *(m)*

syringe • *n* шприц *(m)*

syrup • *n* сироп *(m)* /(*syróp*)/

system • *n* система *(f)* /(*sistéma*)/

T

table • *n* стіл *(m)* /(*stil*)/, таблиця *(f)* /(*tablýts'a*)/, таблиця *(f)*

tablecloth • *n* скатерть *(f)* /(*skátert□*)/, скатерка *(f)* /(*skatérka*)/

tabular • *adj* табличний /(*tablíčnyj*)/

tadpole • *n* пу́головок *(m)*

taiga • *n* тайгá *(f)*

tail • *n* хвіст *(m)*

take • *v* брáти, взя́ти, узя́ти

talent • *n* талант *(m)*, талант *(m)* /(*talánt*)/, дар *(m)* /(*dar*)/

talk • *v* розмовляти /(*rozmovljáty*)/, говорити /(*hovorýty*)/

tall • *adj* високий

tallow • *n* сало *(n)* /(*sálo*)/

talon • *n* кіготь *(m)* /(*kíhot□*)/

tampon • *n* тампон *(m)* /(*tampón*)/

tan • *n* смага *(f)* /(*smága, smagá*)/, загар *(m)* /(*zagár*)/

tangerine • *n* мандари́н *(m)*

tank • *n* бак *(m)*, танк *(m)*

tanker • *n* тáнкер *(m)*, бензово́з *(m)*,

танкíст *(m)*, танкíстка *(f)*

tantalum • *n* тантал *(m)* /(*tantál*)/

tape • *n* стрічка *(f)* /(*stríčka*)/

tapeworm • *n* стьожкóвий черв *(m)*, стьожак широкий *(m)*

tapioca • *n* тапіока *(f)* /(*tapioka*)/

tar • *n* дьóготь *(m)*, смолá *(f)*

target • *n* мішень *(f)* /(*mišén'*)/

taste • *n* смак *(m)*

tax • *n* подáток *(m)*

taxi • *n* таксі *(n)* /(*taksí*)/, таксівка *(f)* /(*taksívka*)/

tea • *n* чай *(m)*, чáшка чай *(f)*

teach • *v* вчи́ти, виклада́ти

teacher • *n* учитель *(m)* /(*učýtel□*)/, вчитель *(m)* /(*včýtel□*)/, учителька *(f)* /(*učýtel□ka*)/, вчителька *(f)* /(*včýtel□ka*)/, викладач *(m)* /(*vykladáč*)/, викладачка *(f)* /(*vykladáčka*)/

teak • *n* тик /(*tyk*)/, дерево тика /(*derevo tyka*)/

teakettle • *n* чайник *(m)* /(*čájnyk*)/

teapot • *n* чайник *(m)* /*čájnyk*/

tear • *n* сльоза *(f)*

technetium • *n* технецій *(m)* /*(tekhnétsij)*/

technology • *n* технологія *(f)*, техніка *(f)*

telegram • *n* телеграма *(f)*

telegraph • *n* телеграф *(m)*

telepathy • *n* телепатія *(f)* /*(telepátija)*/

telephone • *v* дзвонити /*(dzvonýty)*/, подзвонити /*(podzvonýty)*/, телефонувати /*(telefonuváty)*/ • *n* телефон *(m)*

telescope • *n* телескоп *(m)*

television • *n* телебачення *(n)*, телевізор *(m)*

tellurium • *n* телур *(m)* /*(telúr)*/

temperature • *n* температура *(f)* /*(temperatúra)*/

template • *n* шаблон *(m)* /*(šablón)*/

temple • *n* храм *(m)*, скроня *(f)*, висок *(m)*

tempura • *n* темпура *(f)*

tench • *n* лин /*(lyn)*/

tendon • *n* сухожилля *(n)*

tennis • *n* теніс *(m)*

tent • *n* палатка *(f)*, намет *(m)*, шатро *(n)*

tentacle • *n* щупальце *(n)* /*(ščúpal ce)*/

tenth • *adj* десятий *(m)*

terbium • *n* тербій *(m)* /*(térbij)*/

termite • *n* терміт *(m)*

tern • *n* крячок *(m)* /*(kryáčok)*/

terrible • *adj* жахливий /*(žaxlývyj)*/, страшний /*(strášnyj)*/, грізний /*(hríznyj)*/

territory • *n* територія *(f)*

terrorism • *n* тероризм *(m)*

terrorist • *n* терорист *(m)*, терорист *(f)* • *adj* терористичний

text • *n* текст *(m)*

textbook • *n* підручник *(m)*

thallium • *n* талій *(m)* /*(tálij)*/

than • *prep* ніж

thank • *v* дякувати, подякувати

thankful • *adj* вдячний /*(vdjáčnyj)*/

thanks • *interj* дякую /*(djákuju)*/, спасибі /*(spasýbi)*/

that • *conj* що /*(ščo)*/

theater • *n* театр *(m)* /*(teátr)*/

theft • *n* крадіжка *(f)* /*(kradížka)*/, покража *(f)* /*(pokráža)*/, крадіж *(m)* /*(krádiž)*/

theirs • *pron* їх /*(jix)*/

themselves • *pron* вони самі, вони самі

then • *adv* тоді /*(todí)*/, потім /*(pótim)*/

theorbo • *n* теорбо *(n)*

theorem • *n* теорема *(f)* /*(teoréma)*/

theoretical • *adj* теоретичний *(m)*

theosophy • *n* теософія *(f)*

there • *adv* там /*(tam)*/, туди

therefore • *adv* тому /*(tomú)*/, затим /*(zatým)*/

thermos • *n* термос *(m)* /*(térmos)*/

theta • *n* тета *(f)* /*(téta)*/

they • *pron* вони /*(voný)*/

thick • *adj* товстий /*(tóvstyj)*/

thicket • *n* хаща *(f)* /*(xášča)*/

thief • *n* злодій *(m)*, злодійка *(f)*

thigh • *n* стегно *(n)*

thin • *adj* тонкий

thine • *pron* твій /*(tvij)*/

thing • *n* річ *(f)* /*(rič)*/

think • *v* думати /*(dúmaty)*/, мислити /*(mýslyty)*/

third • *n* терція *(f)* /*(tércija)*/ • *adj* третій /*(trétij)*/

thirst • *n* спрага /*(spráha)*/, жага *(f)* /*(žága)*/, смага *(f)* /*(smáha)*/

thirsty • *adj* спраглий

thirteenth • *adj* тринадцятий *(m)*

thirtieth • *adj* тридцятий

this • *pron* цей *(m)*, це

thistle • *n* осот *(m)* /*(osót)*/, чортополох *(m)* /*(čortopolóx)*/

thither • *adv* туди /*(tudý)*/

thong • *n* в'єтнамки

thorium • *n* торій *(m)* /*(tórij)*/

thou • *pron* ти /*(ty)*/

though • *adv* тим не менш /*(tym ne mensh)*/

thought • *n* думка *(f)* /*(dúmka)*/

thread • *n* нитка *(f)*

threat • *n* погроза *(f)*, загроза *(f)*, небезпека *(f)*

three • *n* трійка *(f)*

threshold • *n* поріг *(m)* /*(poríh)*/

thrice • *adv* тричі

throat • *n* горло *(n)* /*(hórlo)*/

throne • *n* трон *(m)* /*(tron)*/

throng • *n* натовп *(m)* /*(nátovp)*/

throw • *v* кидати

thrush • *n* дрізд *(m)*

thulium • *n* тулій *(m)* /*(túlij)*/

thumb • *n* великий палець *(m)*, полекс *(m)*

thunder • *n* грім *(m)* /*(hrim)*/

thunderstorm • *n* гроза *(f)*, буря *(f)*

tick • *n* кліщ *(m)*

ticket • *n* квиток *(m)*, білет *(m)*

tide • *n* прилив *(m)* /*(prylýv)*/, відлив *(m)* /*(vidlýv)*/

tiger • *n* тигр *(m)*

tigress • *n* тигриця *(f)* /(tyhrýcja)/

time • *n* час *(m)*, строк *(m)*, термін *(m)*, година *(f)*, раз *(m)*

timetable • *n* розклад *(m)*, графік *(m)*, розклад *(m)*

tin • *n* олово *(n)* /(ólovo)/

tiny • *adj* крихітний /(krýxitnyj)/

tissue • *n* серветка *(f)*

tit • *n* цицька *(f)*

titanium • *n* титан *(m)* /(titán)/

toad • *n* ропуха *(f)*, жаба *(f)*

toast • *n* грінка *(f)*, тост *(m)*

tobacco • *n* тютюн *(m)* /(tjutjún)/

today • *n* сьогодні /(siohodni)/ • *adv* сьогодні

toe • *n* палець *(m)*, палець нога *(m)*

together • *adv* разом, спільно

toilet • *n* туалет *(m)*, вбиральня *(f)*, унітаз *(m)*

tom • *n* кіт *(m)* /(kit)/

tomahawk • *n* томагавк

tomato • *n* помідор *(m)*, томат *(m)*

tomorrow • *n* завтра *(n)* • *adv* завтра

ton • *n* тонна *(f)* /(tónna)/

tongue • *n* язик *(m)*

tonsil • *n* мигдалик *(m)*

too • *adv* теж /(tež)/, також /(takóž)/

tooth • *n* зуб *(m)*

toothbrush • *n* зубна щітка *(f)* /(zubná ščítka)/

toothpaste • *n* зубна паста *(f)*

toothpick • *n* зубочистка *(f)* /(zubočýstka)/

topknot • *n* чуб *(m)* /(čub)/, оселедець *(m)* /(oselédec☐)/

torch • *n* смолоскип *(m)*

tortoise • *n* черепаха *(f)* /(čerepáxa)/

torture • *n* тортура *(f)* /(tortúra)/

touch • *v* доторкатися, доторкнутися, зворушуватися • *n* дотик *(m)*

touchdown • *n* приземлення *(n)*

tourism • *n* туризм *(m)* /(turýzm)/

tourniquet • *n* джгут *(m)*

towel • *n* рушник *(n)* /(rušnýk)/

tower • *n* башта *(f)*, вежа *(f)*, вишка *(f)*

town • *n* місто *(n)*

toy • *n* іграшка *(f)*

tractor • *n* трактор *(m)*

trade • *n* торгівля *(f)*

tradition • *n* традиція *(f)* /(tradýcija)/

traditional • *adj* традиційний /(tradycíjnyj)/

traffic • *n* рух *(m)*

tragedy • *n* трагедія *(f)*, нещастя *(n)*, горе *(n)*, біда *(f)*

train • *n* поїзд *(m)*

trainer • *n* тренер *(m)*

traitor • *n* зрадник *(m)*, зрадниця *(f)*

tram • *n* трамвай *(m)* /(tramváj)/

transitive • *adj* перехідний, образний, перехідне дієслово, форма перехідного дієслова

translate • *v* перекладати, перекласти, переводити, перевести

translation • *n* переклад *(m)*

translator • *n* перекладач *(m)* /(perekladáč)/

transliteration • *n* транслітерація *(f)* /(transliterácija)/

trauma • *n* травма *(m)* /(trávma)/

travel • *v* подорожувати /(podoróžuvaty)/, мандрувати /(mandruváty)/, їздити /(jízdyty)/ • *n* подорож *(f)* /(pódorož)/, поїздка *(f)* /(pojízdka)/

tray • *n* піднос *(m)* /(pidnós)/

treason • *n* зрада *(f)* /(zráda)/

tree • *n* дерево *(n)*

trefoil • *n* трилисник *(m)* /(trylýsnyk)/

tribe • *n* плем'я *(n)*, рід *(m)*

tribunal • *n* трибунал *(m)*, суд *(m)*

trident • *n* тризубець *(m)* /(tryzubets)/

triennial • *adj* трирічний

triennium • *n* триріччя *(n)*

trimester • *n* триместр *(m)* /(tryméstr)/

tripe • *n* рубець *(m)*, тельбух *(m)*, требух *(m)*

troika • *n* трійка *(f)*

troll • *n* троль *(m)*

trombone • *n* тромбон *(m)* /(trombón)/

troop • *n* військо

trophy • *n* трофей *(m)*

trouble • *n* халепа

trough • *n* корито *(m)*

trout • *n* форель *(f)* /(forel☐)/

truce • *n* перемир'я *(n)*

truck • *n* грузовик *(m)*, вантажівка *(f)*

trumpet • *n* труба /(truba)/

trunk • *n* скриня *(f)* /(skrýnja)/, куфер *(m)* /(kúfer)/, хобот *(m)* /(xóbot)/, багажник *(m)* /(bahážnyk)/

trust • *v* довіряти /(dovirjaty)/

truth • *n* вірність *(f)* /(vírnist☐)/, правда *(f)* /(právda)/, істина *(f)* /(ístyna)/

try • *v* пробувати, старатися, намагатися

tsar • *n* цар *(m)*

tugboat • *n* буксир *(m)* /(buksýr)/

tulip • *n* тюльпан *(m)* /(tjul☐pán)/

tulle • *n* тюль *(m)* /(t́úl̇)/

tundra • *n* тундра *(f)*

tungsten • *n* вольфрам *(m)* /(vol☐frám)/

tunnel • *n* тунель *(m)* /(tunél☐)/

turban • *n* чалма́ *(f)*, тюрба́н *(m)*
turkey • *n* інди́к *(m)*, інди́чка *(f)*
turnip • *n* рі́па *(f)*, рі́пка *(f)*
turquoise • *n* туркус *(m)* /*(turkus)*/, піруза *(f)* /*(piruza)*/, фіруза *(f)* /*(firuza)*/, бірюза *(f)* /*(biriuza)*/, туркусова *(f)* /*(turkusova)*/, туркусовий *(m)* /*(turkusovyj)*/, пірузовий *(m)* /*(piruzovyj)*/
turtle • *n* черепаха *(f)* /*(čerepáxa)*/
tuxedo • *n* смокінг *(m)* /*(smókinh)*/
twelfth • *adj* двана́дцятий *(m)*
twentieth • *adj* двадця́тий
twice • *adv* дві́чі /*(dvichi)*/

twig • *n* гі́лка *(f)*, гі́лочка *(f)*, галу́зка *(f)*
twilight • *n* сутінки /*(sútinki)*/, присмерк *(m)* /*(prýsmerk)*/
twin • *n* близню́к *(m)*
twist • *v* кривити /*(kryvýty)*/
two • *n* дві́йка *(f)*
type • *n* тип *(m)*, вид *(m)*, рід *(m)*
typewriter • *n* друка́рська маши́нка *(f)*
typhoon • *n* тайфу́н *(m)*
tyrannize • *v* тиранити
tyre • *n* ши́на *(f)*, автоши́на *(f)*

U

udder • *n* ви́м'я *(n)*
ugly • *adj* потво́рний
umbrella • *n* парасо́лька *(f)* /*(parasól□ka)*/
umlaut • *n* умла́ут *(m)*
unavailable • *adj* недосту́пний /*(nedostúpnyj)*/
unbelieving • *adj* невірую́чий /*(nevírujučyj)*/
uncle • *n* дя́дько *(m)*
unclear • *adj* нея́сний /*(nejásnyj)*/
uncomfortable • *adj* незру́чний
under • *prep* під /*(pid)*/
underpants • *n* труси /*(trusý)*/
understand • *v* розумі́ти /*(rozumíty)*/
underwear • *n* нижня білизна *(f)* /*(nýžnja bilýzna)*/
unearthly • *adj* неземний
unemployed • *adj* безробітний /*(bezrobítnyj)*/
unemployment • *n* безробі́ття *(n)*
unicameral • *adj* однопала́тний /*(odnopalátnyj)*/
unicorn • *n* єдиноріг *(m)* /*(jedynoríh)*/
uniform • *n* форма *(f)* /*(fórma)*/

union • *n* сою́з *(m)* /*(sojúz)*/
unit • *n* одиниця *(f)* /*(odynýcja)*/
universe • *n* всéсвіт *(m)*, Всéсвіт *(m)*
university • *n* університéт *(m)*
unless • *conj* якщо не /*(yákshcho ne)*/
unmarried • *adj* нежона́тий *(m)*, незамі́жня *(f)*
up • *adv* вгору /*(vhóru)*/, догори /*(dohorý)*/, вгорі /*(vhorí)*/
uplift • *v* піднімати вгору
uprising • *n* повста́ння *(n)*
upstairs • *adv* вгорі́, вго́ру
uranium • *n* уран *(m)* /*(urán)*/
ureter • *n* сечовід *(m)* /*(sečovíd)*/
urine • *n* сеча́ *(f)*
us • *pron* нас /*(nas)*/
use • *n* вжива́ння *(n)* • *v* ужива́ти, вжива́ти, ужи́ти, вжи́ти, використо́вувати, ви́користати
useful • *adj* корисний /*(korýsnyj)*/
user • *n* кори́стувач *(m)*, користува́ч
utter • *adj* абсолю́тний *(m)*, по́вний, цілкови́тий *(m)*
uvula • *n* язичок *(m)* /*(jazyčók)*/

V

vacant • *adj* вакантний /*(vakántnyj)*/
vaccine • *n* вакцина *(f)* /*(vakcýna)*/
vacuole • *n* вакуо́ля *(f)*
vagina • *n* піхва *(f)* /*(píxva)*/
valise • *n* чемодан *(m)* /*(chemodan)*/
valkyrie • *n* валькірія *(f)* /*(val'kyrija)*/
valley • *n* доли́на *(f)*
value • *n* ці́нність *(f)* /*(cínnist□)*/,

ва́ртість *(f)* /*(vártist□)*/, значення *(n)* /*(znáčennja)*/, ціна *(f)* /*(ciná)*/
vampire • *n* упи́р *(m)*, вампі́р *(m)*
van • *n* фурго́н *(m)*, ваго́н *(m)*
vanadinite • *n* ванадиніт
vanadium • *n* ванадій *(m)* /*(vanádij)*/
vandalism • *n* вандалізм *(m)* /*(vandalízm)*/

vanish • *v* зникати /*(znikáty)*/

vapor • *n* па́ра (f), пар (m)

variegated • *adj* строка́тий, пістри́й

vase • *n* ваза (f) /*(váza)*/

vegetable • *n* о́воч (m)

vegetarianism • *n* вегетаріа́нство (n)

vehicle • *n* тра́нспортний засі́б (m)

vein • *n* ве́на (f), жи́ла (f)

velocity • *n* швидкість (f)

veranda • *n* веранда (f)

verb • *n* дієслово (n) /*(dijeslóvo)*/

verse • *n* вірш (m)

version • *n* перекла́д (m)

verst • *n* верста́ (f)

vertex • *n* тім'я (n) /*(tím'ja)*/, маківка (f) /*(mákivka)*/

very • *adv* ду́же

vest • *n* жиле́т (m)

veterinarian • *n* ветеринар, лі́кар

veto • *n* ве́то (n), запре́т (m)

viburnum • *n* калина (f) /*(kalýna)*/

victim • *n* же́ртва (f), потерпі́лий (m)

victory • *n* перемога (f) /*(peremóha)*/

videocassette • *n* відеокасета (f) /*(videokaséta)*/

vigilance • *n* пильність (f)

villa • *n* ві́лла (f) /*(vílla)*/, дача (f) /*(dáča)*/

village • *n* село (n) /*(seló)*/

vinaigrette • *n* вінігрет (m) /*(vinihrét)*/

vinegar • *n* оцет (m) /*(ócet)*/

violin • *n* скрипка (f) /*(skrýpka)*/

viper • *n* гадюка (f) /*(hadjúka)*/

virgin • *n* незайманець (m), незаймана (f), ді́ва (f)

virginity • *n* цнота (f), незайманість (f), цнотли́вість (f)

virtual • *adj* як би /*(ják by)*/, віртуальний /*(virtuál'nyj)*/

virtue • *n* цнотливість (f) /*(cnotlývist□)*/,

доброчесність (f) /*(dobročésnist□)*/

virus • *n* ві́рус (m), комп'ютерний ві́рус (m)

visa • *n* ві́за (f)

vise • *n* лещата

vision • *n* зір (m)

visit • *v* відві́дувати, відві́дати • *n* візи́т (m), візи́та (f), відві́дування (n)

visor • *n* забра́ло (n), козиро́к (m)

vitalism • *n* віталі́зм (m) /*(vitalízm)*/

vitamin • *n* вітамі́н (m) /*(vitamín)*/

vixen • *n* лисиця (f)

vodka • *n* горі́лка (f), во́дка (f)

voice • *n* го́лос (m)

voivode • *n* воєво́да (m)

volcano • *n* вулкан

volleyball • *n* волейбол (m) /*(volejból)*/, відбиванка (f) /*(vidbývanka)*/, волейбольний м'яч (m) /*(volejból'nyj m"jač)*/, м'яч до відбиванки (m) /*(m"jač do vidbývanky)*/

volt • *n* вольт (m) /*(vol't)*/

voluntarily • *adv* добровільно

volunteer • *n* доброво́лець (m), волонтер (m)

vomit • *v* блюва́ти, рва́ти, ригати • *n* блювота (f) /*(bljuvóta)*/, блювотиння (n) /*(bljuvotýnnja)*/

vote • *v* голосува́ти, проголосува́ти • *n* го́лос (m)

vowel • *n* голосний (m) /*(holósnyj)*/

vulcanization • *n* вулканізація (f) /*(vulkanizácija)*/

vulgarian • *adj* вульга́рний

vulture • *n* гриф (m) /*(hryf)*/, падальник (m) /*(pádal□nyk)*/

vulva • *n* вульва (f) /*(vúl□va)*/

W

wage • *n* заробі́тна пла́та (f), зарпла́та (f)

wagtail • *n* плі́ска (f)

waistcoat • *n* жиле́т (m)

wait • *v* чека́ти, жда́ти

waiter • *n* офіціа́нт (m), офіціа́нтка (f), ке́льнер (m)

waitress • *n* офіціантка (f) /*(oficiántka)*/, кельнерка (f) /*(kél'nerka)*/

walk • *v* ходи́ти, іти́, іти́ кро́ком, гуля́ти, іти́ пі́шки • *n* прогулянка (f) /*(prohaljánka)*/

wall • *n* стіна́ (f), мур (m)

wallet • *n* гамане́ць (m)

wallpaper • *n* шпалери /*(špaléry)*/

walrus • *n* морж (m)

want • *v* хоті́ти, бажа́ти

war • *n* війна́ (f)

wardrobe • *n* ша́фа (f)

warhead • *n* боєголо́вка (f)

warlock • *n* чаклу́н (m), чарівни́к (m), маг (m), чорнокни́жник (m), чарнакні́жнік (m)

warm • *adj* те́плий

warn • *v* попередити /*(poperedýty)*/

warning • *n* попере́дження (n)

warrior • *n* вояк *(m)* /*(voják)*/, воїн *(m)* /*(vójin)*/, боєць *(m)* /*(bojéc')*/

warship • *n* військо́вий кора́бель *(m)*

wart • *n* борода́вка *(f)*

wash • *v* мити /*(mýty)*/, прати /*(práty)*/, ми́тися

washer • *n* праля *(f)* /*(prálja)*/

wasp • *n* оса́ *(f)*

watch • *n* годи́нник *(m)*, нару́чний годи́нник *(m)* • *v* дивитися /*(dyvýtysja)*/

watchfulness • *n* насторо́женість *(f)*

water • *n* вода́ *(f)*

waterfall • *n* водоспа́д *(m)*

waterfowl • *n* водопла́вні птахи *(m)*

watermelon • *n* каву́н *(m)*

watt • *n* ват *(m)* /*(vat)*/

wattle • *n* пліт *(m)* /*(plit)*/, борі́дка *(f)*, австралійська акація *(f)*

wavelength • *n* довжина́ хвилі *(f)* /*(dovžyná xvýli)*/

we • *pron* ми

weak • *adj* слабки́й, сла́бий

wealth • *n* бага́тство *(n)*

weapon • *n* збро́я *(f)*

wear • *v* носи́ти, надяга́ти, наді́ти

weasel • *n* ласка *(f)* /*(láska)*/

weather • *n* пого́да *(f)*

weave • *v* тка́ти, плести́

wedding • *n* весі́лля *(n)*

wedge • *n* клин *(m)*

week • *n* ти́ждень *(m)*

weekend • *n* вихідні́, уїк-е́нд *(m)*

weep • *v* плакати /*(plákaty)*/

weevil • *n* довгоносик *(m)*, слоник *(m)*

weigh • *v* зва́жувати, зва́жити, ва́жити

weight • *n* ва́га *(f)*

welcome • *n* віта́ння *(n)* • *interj* ласка́во про́симо!

well • *adv* до́бре /*(dóbre)*/, га́рно /*(hárno)*/ • *interj* ну • *n* колодязь *(m)* /*(kolódjaz')*/

west • *n* за́хід *(m)* • *adj* за́хідний *(m)*

westerly • *adj* за́хідний *(m)*

western • *adj* за́хідний /*(záxidnyj)*/

westernization • *n* вестернізація *(f)*

westward • *adv* на за́хід

wet • *v* мочи́ти /*(močýty)*/, змочува́ти /*(zmóčuvaty)*/, мокну́ти /*(móknuty)*/, змокнути /*(zmóknuty)*/ • *adj* мо́крий, воло́гий, дощови́тий, дощови́й

whale • *n* кит *(m)*

wharf • *n* при́стань *(f)*

what • *pron* що, яки́й

whatchamacallit • *n* як його́ *(n)*, як її *(f)*, як їх

wheat • *n* пшени́ця *(f)*

wheel • *n* ко́лесо *(n)* /*(kóleso)*/, ко́ло *(n)* /*(kólo)*/

wheelbarrow • *n* та́чка *(f)*

wheelchair • *n* інвалі́дний візо́к *(m)* /*(invalídnyj vizók)*/, крі́сло-ката́лка *(n)* /*(kríslo-katálka)*/

when • *adv* коли́ • *conj* коли́

where • *adv* де, куди́, звідки́ • *conj* де, звідки́, куди́

whether • *conj* чи

whey • *n* сирова́тка *(f)*

which • *pron* котрий /*(kotrýj)*/, який /*(jakýj)*/

whip • *n* батіг *(m)* /*(batíh)*/

whirlwind • *n* вихор *(m)* /*(výxor)*/

whiskey • *n* віскі *(m)* /*(víski)*/

whisper • *v* шепта́ти, шепну́ти • *n* ше́піт *(m)*

whistle • *v* свисті́ти, сюрча́ти • *n* свист *(m)*, свисто́к *(m)*, сюрчо́к *(m)*, свисто *(m)*

white • *n* бі́лий • *adj* бі́лий

whither • *adv* куди́ /*(kudý)*/

who • *pron* хто

whole • *adj* ці́лий /*(cílyj)*/, повний /*(póvnyj)*/

whore • *n* ку́рва *(f)*, блудни́ця *(f)*, пові́я *(f)*, шльо́ндра *(f)*, ля́рва *(f)*

whose • *pron* чий /*(čyj)*/

why • *adv* чому́

wide • *adj* широкий /*(šyrókyj)*/

widely • *adv* широко /*(šýroko)*/, далеко /*(daléko)*/

widow • *n* вдова́ *(f)* /*(vdová)*/

widower • *n* вдіве́ць *(m)* /*(vdivéc□)*/

width • *n* ширина *(f)* /*(šyryná)*/

wife • *n* дружи́на *(f)*, жі́нка *(f)*

wig • *n* перука *(f)* /*(perúka)*/

wild • *adj* дикий /*(dýkyj)*/

wildfowl • *n* водопла́вні птахи

willow • *n* верба *(f)*

wind • *n* вітер *(m)*

window • *n* вікно́ *(n)*

windowsill • *n* підвіко́ння *(n)* /*(pidvikónnja)*/

windpipe • *n* трахея *(f)* /*(traxéja)*/, дихальне горло *(n)* /*(dyxál□ne hórlo)*/

wine • *n* вино́ *(n)*

wing • *n* крило́ *(n)*

winner • *n* переможець /*(peremóžec□)*/

winter • *n* зима́ *(f)*

wintry • *adj* зимо́вий *(m)*

wipe • *v* витира́ти, ви́терти

wire • *n* про́від *(m)*, дріт *(m)*

wisdom • *n* му́дрість *(f)*

wise • *adj* мудрий /*(múdryj)*/

wisent • *n* зубр *(m)* /(zubr)/
wish • *v* бажа́ти, побажа́ти
witch • *n* ві́дьма *(f)*
with • *prep* з /(z)/
without • *prep* без /(bez)/
wizard • *n* чарівник *(m)*
wolf • *n* вовк *(m)*
wolverine • *n* росома́ха *(f)*
woman • *n* жі́нка *(f)*, жона́ *(f)*
womb • *n* ма́тка *(f)*, утро́ба *(f)*, чре́во *(n)*
wonder • *v* дивуватися /(dyvuvátysja)/, цікавитися /(cikávytysja)/ • *n* чудо *(n)* /(čúdo)/, диво *(n)* /(dývo)/
woodcut • *n* дереворит *(m)* /(derevorýt)/
woodlouse • *n* мокри́ця *(f)*
woodpecker • *n* дя́тел *(m)*
wool • *n* во́вна *(f)*, шерсть *(f)*, пря́жа *(f)*
woolen • *adj* вовняний, шерстяний
word • *n* сло́во *(n)*
work • *n* робо́та *(f)*, пра́ця *(f)* • *v* працювати /(pracjuváty)/, трудитися /(trudýtysja)/, робити /(robýty)/
worker • *n* робі́тник *(m)* /(robítnyk)/, робітниця *(f)* /(robítnycja)/, пра́цівник *(m)* /(pracivnýk)/, працівниця *(f)* /(pracivnýcja)/, трудящий *(m)* /(trudjáščyj)/, трудящий *(f)* /(trudjášča)/
workshop • *n* майсте́рня *(f)*
world • *n* світ *(m)*
worldwide • *adj* світовий
worm • *n* черв'як *(m)*, черв *(m)*, хробак *(m)*, негідник *(m)*
wormwood • *n* поли́н *(m)*
wound • *n* ра́на *(f)*
wreath • *n* вінок *(m)* /(vinók)/, вінець *(m)* /(vinéc□)/
wrinkle • *n* зморшка *(f)* /(zmórška)/
wrist • *n* зап'ястя *(f)*
write • *v* писа́ти, написа́ти
writer • *n* письме́нник *(m)*
writing • *n* писемність *(f)* /(pysémnist')/, письмо *(n)* /(pys□mó)/, твір *(m)* /(tvir)/, почерк *(m)* /(pôčerk)/
wrong • *adj* непра́вильний

X

xenon • *n* ксенон *(m)*
xenophobia • *n* ксенофобія *(f)*

Y

yard • *n* двір *(m)* /(dvir)/, дворик *(m)* /(dvóryk)/, ярд *(m)*
yarmulke • *n* ярмулка *(f)* /(jarmúlka)/
yarn • *n* пряжа *(f)* /(prjáža)/
yataghan • *n* ятаган *(m)* /(jatahán)/
yawn • *v* позіха́ти, позіхну́ти, зіва́ти, зівну́ти
year • *n* рік *(m)* /(rik)/, рік *(m)*, клас *(m)*, курс *(m)*
yearly • *adj* щорічний *(m)* /(shchorichny)/ • *adv* щорічно /(shchorichno)/
yeast • *n* дрі́жджі
yellow • *adj* жо́втий *(m)*
yesterday • *n* учо́ра, вчо́ра • *adv* учо́ра, вчо́ра
yew • *n* тис *(m)* /(tys)/
yo-yo • *n* йо-йо *(n)* /(jo-jó, jó-jo)/
yoga • *n* йо́га *(f)*
yogurt • *n* йо́гурт *(m)*, йо́гурт *(m)*, югу-
рт *(m)*
yoke • *n* ярмо́ *(n)*, хому́т *(m)*, і́го *(n)*, коромисло *(n)*
yolk • *n* жовток *(m)* /(žovtók)/
you • *pron* вас, ви /(vy)/, ти, ви
young • *adj* молоди́й *(m)*, ю́ний
younger • *adj* молодший /(molódšyj)/
yours • *pron* твій /(tvij)/, ваш /(vaš)/
yourself • *pron* ти сам *(m)*, ти сама́ *(f)*, ви самі́, ви самі́
youth • *n* мо́лодість *(f)*, ю́ність *(f)*, юна́цтво *(n)*, молода́ люди́на *(f)*, юна́к *(m)*, па́рубок *(m)*, хло́пець *(m)*, мо́лодіж *(f)*, мо́лодь *(f)*
ytterbium • *n* ітербій *(m)* /(itérbij)/
yttrium • *n* ітрій *(m)* /(ítrij)/
yuan • *n* юа́нь *(m)*
yurt • *n* ю́рта *(f)*

Z

zebra • *n* зе́бра *(f)*

zest • *n* запал *(m)*, завзяття *(n)*, потяг *(m)*, цедра *(f)*

zinc • *n* цинк *(m)*

zirconium • *n* цирконій *(m)*

zloty • *n* злотий *(m)*

zoo • *n* зоопа́рк *(m)*

UKRAINIAN-ENGLISH

а • *conj* and, but
аб'юра́ція • *n* abjuration
абажу́р • *n* lampshade
абак • *n* abacus
абандон • *n* abandonment
абандо́н • *n* abandonment
аба́т • *n* abbot
абати́са • *n* abbess
абе́тка • *n* alphabet
абіогенез • *n* abiogenesis
або́ • *conj* or
аболіціоніст • *n* abolitionist
абориге́н • *n* aborigine
аборигенський • *adj* aboriginal
абревіату́ра • *n* abbreviation
абрикос • *n* apricot
абсент • *n* absinthe
абсолютний • *adj* absolute
абсолю́тний • *adj* utter
абсолю́тно • *adv* perfectly
абстракціонізм • *n* abstractionism
авантюри́зм • *n* adventurism
ава́рія • *n* accident, crash
авіакомпа́нія • *n* airline
авіала́йнер • *n* airliner
авіалі́нії • *n* airline
авіапо́шта • *n* airmail
авто́ • *n* automobile, car
автобіографія • *n* autobiography
автобус • *n* bus
автомагістра́ль • *n* highway
автомаши́на • *n* automobile, car
автомобі́ль • *n* automobile, car
автоно́мія • *n* nationality
автопіло́т • *n* autopilot
а́втор • *n* author
авторитет • *n* strength
автострада • *n* freeway
автотомія • *n* autotomy
автохтонний • *adj* aboriginal
автоши́на • *n* tyre
автошля́х • *n* highway
ага́ • *interj* aha
агава • *n* agave
агреси́вний • *adj* aggressive
агре́сія • *n* aggression
агре́сор • *n* aggressor
агрикульту́ра • *n* agriculture
агрус • *n* gooseberry
агуті • *n* agouti
адвока́т • *n* lawyer
а́дже • *conj* because
адреналі́н • *n* adrenaline

адреса • *n* address
адюльте́р • *n* adultery
аероліт • *n* aerolite
аеропла́п • *n* airplane
аеропо́рт • *n* airport
аероскопія • *n* aeroscopy
а́збука • *n* alphabet
азот • *n* nitrogen
ай-ай • *n* aye-aye
айсберг • *n* iceberg
айстедфед • *n* eisteddfod
академі́чний • *adj* academical
акаде́мія • *n* school
ака́ція • *n* acacia
аква́ріум • *n* aquarium
аколада • *n* accolade
акордео́н • *n* accordion
акробатика • *n* acrobatics
акробати́чний • *adj* acrobatic
акромега́лія • *n* acromegaly
акт • *n* act
активі́ст • *n* activist
активі́стка • *n* activist
актиній • *n* actinium
актинометр • *n* actinometer
акто́р • *n* actor
актри́са • *n* actor, actress
акула • *n* shark
акумуля́тор • *n* battery
акупункту́ра • *n* acupuncture
акуше́рка • *n* midwife
алі́гатор • *n* alligator
а́лгебра • *n* algebra
алгори́тм • *n* algorithm
але • *conj* but
але́ • *conj* but, only
алергі́я • *n* allergy
алея • *n* alley, lane
алилу́я • *interj* hallelujah
аліл́уя • *interj* hallelujah
алкоголі́зм • *n* alcoholism
алкого́ль • *n* alcohol
алло́ • *interj* hello
алма́з • *n* diamond
алое • *n* aloe
алотропічний • *adj* allotropic
алфаві́т • *n* alphabet
альдегі́д • *n* aldehyde
альтруї́ст • *n* altruist
альтруї́стка • *n* altruist
альфа • *n* alpha
альфабе́т • *n* alphabet
амбіці́йний • *adj* ambitious

áмбра • *n* ambergris
амбразýра • *n* embrasure
америцій • *n* americium
амілаза • *n* amylase
ампер-годúна • *n* ampere-hour
амфíбія • *n* amphibian
анагрáма • *n* anagram
анакóнда • *n* anaconda
анальгéтик • *n* analgesic
ананáс • *n* pineapple
анáрхія • *n* anarchy
анахронíзм • *n* anachronism
áнгел • *n* angel
англіцúзм • *n* anglicism
анéксія • *n* annexation
анексувáти • *v* annex
анóд • *n* anode
анóнс • *n* advertisement
антéна • *n* aerial
антибіóтик • *n* antibiotic
антидепресáнт • *n* antidepressant
антихрист • *n* antichrist
антресóль • *n* entresol
антрополóгія • *n* anthropology
анулювати • *v* rescind
áнус • *n* anus
áншлюс • *n* annexation
аорист • *n* aorist
аóрта • *n* aorta
апартамéнт • *n* apartment
апатит • *n* apatite
апельсúн • *n* orange
апетúт • *n* appetite
апострóф • *n* apostrophe

апофтéгма • *n* apothegm
аптéка • *n* pharmacy
аптéкар • *n* pharmacist
аптéкарка • *n* pharmacist
арахíс • *n* peanut
арбá • *n* araba
арбалéт • *n* crossbow
арбíтр • *n* referee
арбíтр • *n* judge
аргінíн • *n* arginine
аргóн • *n* argon
арéшт • *n* arrest
арештáнт • *n* prisoner
арештóвувати • *v* arrest
арештувáти • *v* arrest
áрмія • *n* army
арнíка • *n* arnica
аромáт • *n* fragrance, perfume
артилéрія • *n* artillery
артúст • *n* artist
артишóк • *n* artichoke
áрфа • *n* harp
архієпúскоп • *n* archbishop
архіпелáг • *n* archipelago
архітéктор • *n* architect
архітектýра • *n* architecture
архітектýрний • *adj* architectural
аскетúзм • *n* asceticism
аскетúчно • *adv* ascetically
астáт • *n* astatine
астерóїд • *n* asteroid
áстма • *n* asthma
астронáвт • *n* astronaut

Астронóмія • *n* astronomy

атáка • *n* attack, offensive
атакувáти • *v* attack
атеїзм • *n* atheism
ательє́ • *n* atelier
атмосфéра • *n* atmosphere
атóл • *n* atoll

áтом • *n* atom
атрибýт • *n* attribute
аукціóн • *n* auction
афорúзм • *n* aphorism
ацетóн • *n* acetone

ба́ба • *n* grandmother
бабак • *n* marmot
ба́бка • *n* dragonfly
бабуня • *n* granny
бабуся • *n* granny
бабу́ся • *n* grandmother
бавовна • *n* cotton
бавовник • *n* cotton
бавовня́ний • *adj* cotton
баво́вняний • *adj* cotton
багаж • *n* erudition
бага́ж • *n* luggage
багажник • *n* trunk
бага́тий • *adj* rich
багатобожжя • *n* polytheism
багатокутник • *n* polygon
багатоніжка • *n* millipede
багатство • *n* wealth
бага́тство • *n* capital
бага́ття • *n* bonfire
багне́т • *n* bayonet
бадмінто́н • *n* badminton
бажа́ння • *n* desire
бажати • *v* fancy
бажа́ти • *v* desire, want, wish
база́льт • *n* basalt
база́р • *n* bazaar, market
ба́йка • *n* fable
байт • *n* byte
бак • *n* tank
баккара • *n* baccarat
баклава́ • *n* baklava
баклажан • *n* eggplant
баклан • *n* cormorant
бактерицид • *n* bactericide
бала́кати • *v* chat
балала́йка • *n* balalaika
балери́на • *n* ballerina
бале́т • *n* ballet
балка • *n* beam
балко́н • *n* balcony
балон • *n* balloon
бальза́м • *n* salve
балюстра́да • *n* balustrade
баля́сина • *n* baluster
банан • *n* banana
ба́нда • *n* gang
ба́нджо • *n* banjo
банди́т • *n* bandit
банк • *n* bank
банке́т • *n* banquet
ба́ня • *n* bathhouse
бар • *n* bar, pub
ба́рій • *n* barium
барабан • *n* drum
барабо́ля • *n* potato
бара́к • *n* barrack

баран • *n* ram
баранина • *n* mutton
бара́нчик • *n* lamb
барельє́ф • *n* relief
ба́ржа • *n* barge
барха́н • *n* dune
басе́йн • *n* basin
баскетбо́л • *n* basketball
батаре́йка • *n* battery
батарея • *n* battery
батаре́я • *n* battery
батик • *n* batik
батискаф • *n* bathyscaphe
баті́г • *n* whip
батьківщина • *n* fatherland, home
ба́тько • *n* father, parent
баци́ла • *n* bacillus
ба́чити • *v* see
ба́шта • *n* tower
бджільни́цтво • *n* beekeeping
бджола • *n* bee
бегемо́т • *n* hippopotamus
бегонія • *n* begonia
бедро́ • *n* hip
бедуї́н • *n* bedouin
без • *prep* without
безбо́жний • *adj* godless
безволо́сий • *adj* hairless
безгрі́шний • *adj* sinless
бездога́нно • *adv* perfectly
безза́хисний • *adj* defenseless
безпе́ка • *n* safety, security
безпе́чний • *adj* safe
безпіло́тник • *n* drone
безробі́тний • *adj* unemployed
безробі́ття • *n* unemployment
безсме́ртний • *adj* immortal
безсо́ння • *n* insomnia
безсторо́нність • *n* detachment
безстрасність • *n* detachment
бейсбо́л • *n* baseball
беко́н • *n* bacon
бел • *n* bel
белетри́стика • *n* belles-lettres
бензи́н • *n* gasoline
бензово́з • *n* tanker
бензо́л • *n* benzene
бе́рег • *n* bank, beach, shore
бере́за • *n* birch
берил • *n* beryl
бери́лій • *n* beryllium
бе́ріг • *n* bank, shore
берке́лій • *n* berkelium
бесі́да • *n* chat, conversation, dialogue
бето́н • *n* concrete
би́дло • *n* cattle

бик • *n* bull, cattle, ox
битва • *n* struggle
бúтва • *n* battle, fight
бúти • *v* beat, hit
битися • *v* struggle
бúтися • *v* fight
біб • *n* bean
бібліотéка • *n* library
бібліотéкар • *n* librarian
бібліотéкарка • *n* librarian
бігамія • *n* bigamy
бíгати • *v* run
бíгти • *v* run
біда • *n* misery
бідá • *n* disaster, tragedy
бідний • *adj* poor
біднотá • *n* indigence, penury, poverty
біженець • *n* refugee
бíзнес • *n* business
бізнесмéн • *n* businessman
бізóн • *n* bison, buffalo
бій • *n* battle, fight, struggle
бíйка • *n* fight
бікíні • *n* bikini
білéт • *n* ticket
бíлий • *n* white • *adj* white
білка • *n* squirrel
білóк • *n* albumen
біль • *n* ache, pain
більярд • *n* billiards
біля • *prep* at, near
бíнго • *n* bingo
бінóкль • *n* binoculars
біогрáфія • *n* biography
біологія • *n* biology
біохíмія • *n* biochemistry
бірюза • *n* turquoise
біс • *n* demon, devil
бісексуáльність • *n* bisexuality
бíстро • *n* bistro
біфштекс • *n* steak
біфштéкс • *n* beefsteak
біхевіоризм • *n* behaviorism
благати • *v* implore
благотворний • *adj* beneficial
блаженство • *n* bliss
блакитний • *n* blue • *adj* blue
блейзер • *n* blazer
блешня • *n* fly
блúжній • *adj* close, near
близнюк • *n* twin
блúзький • *adj* close, near
близько • *adv* closely
блúзько • *adv* near
блиск • *n* glitter

блúскавка • *n* lightning
блискучий • *adj* luminous
блищати • *v* glitter
блін • *n* pancake
блокáда • *n* blockade
блокбастер • *n* blockbuster
блокнóт • *n* notebook
блохá • *n* flea
блудницля • *n* whore
блювáти • *v* vomit
блювота • *n* vomit
блювотиння • *n* vomit
блюз • *n* blues
блюзнíрство • *n* blasphemy
бо • *conj* because
бобéр • *n* beaver
бог • *n* god
богиня • *n* goddess
богомол • *n* mantis
богохýльство • *n* blasphemy
бод • *n* baud
боєголóвка • *n* warhead
боєць • *n* warrior
божевілля • *n* alienation
божественність • *n* deity, divinity
бойкот • *n* boycott
бóйня • *n* abattoir
бойовúй • *adj* militant
бойовúк • *n* militant
бокс • *n* boxing
болíти • *v* ache, hurt
болнúця • *n* hospital
болото • *n* quagmire
болóто • *n* bog, swamp
болт • *n* bolt, quarrel
бóмба • *n* bomb
бомбардувáння • *n* bombardment
бомбардувáти • *v* bombard
бомбувáння • *n* bombardment
бор • *n* boron
борг • *n* debt, duty
бордéль • *n* brothel
бордовий • *adj* burgundy
борець • *n* aconite
боривітер • *n* kestrel
борідка • *n* wattle
бородá • *n* beard, chin
борóдавка • *n* wart
борознá • *n* furrow
боронá • *n* harrow
боротися • *v* struggle
борóтися • *v* fight
боротьба • *n* struggle
боротьбá • *n* fight
бóрошно • *n* flour
борсýк • *n* badger
борт • *n* cushion

борщ • *n* borscht
босо́ніж • *adv* barefoot
ботанізірова́ть • *v* botanize
бота́ніка • *n* botany
ботулі́зм • *n* botulism
бо́чка • *n* barrel
боягу́з • *n* coward
боягу́зка • *n* coward
боя́рин • *n* boyar
брак • *n* lack
бра́ма • *n* gate
бра́нець • *n* captive
брасле́т • *n* bracelet
брат • *n* brother
бра́ти • *v* take
бред • *n* delirium
бре́нді • *n* brandy
бреха́ти • *v* bark, lie
брехли́вий • *adj* mendacious
брехло́ • *n* liar
брехня́ • *n* lie
бреху́н • *n* liar
бреху́нка • *n* liar
бреху́ха • *n* liar
бриз • *n* breeze
бризкати • *v* shower
бри́тва • *n* razor
брі • *n* brie
брід • *n* ford
брідж • *n* bridge
бро́ва • *n* eyebrow
брова́рня • *n* brewery
бром • *n* bromine
бро́шка • *n* brooch
бруд • *n* dirt, filth
бру́дний • *adj* dirty
брукува́ти • *v* flag
брусниця • *n* lingonberry
бру́хо • *n* belly
брю́ки • *n* pants
буга́й • *n* cattle
бугай • *n* bittern

буга́й • *n* bull
бугенвілія • *n* bougainvillea
буди́нок • *n* building
будівни́цтво • *n* building
будува́ти • *v* construct
буду́вати • *v* build
будьмо • *interj* cheers
бузина • *n* elder
бузина́ • *n* elder, elderberry
буй • *n* boyar, buoy
бу́йвол • *n* buffalo
бук • *n* beech
бу́ква • *n* letter
буке́т • *n* bouquet
буксир • *n* tugboat
бу́лочка • *n* bun
бу́льба • *n* potato
бульдо́зер • *n* bulldozer
бу́лькати • *v* gluck
бу́нкер • *n* bunker
бунт • *n* rebellion
бунтар • *n* rebel
бунтівник • *n* rebel
буреві́сник • *n* shearwater
бу́рий • *adj* brown
буру́лька • *n* icicle
буршти́н • *n* amber
бу́ря • *n* storm, thunderstorm
буря́к • *n* beet, beetroot
бусел • *n* stork
бусо́ля • *n* compass
бу́ти • *v* be
буття́ • *n* being, existence
буфер • *n* cushion
буфет • *n* cupboard
бухга́лтер • *n* accountant
бухга́лтерка • *n* accountant
бу́хта • *n* bay
бюро́ • *n* office
бюрокра́тія • *n* bureaucracy
бюстга́льтер • *n* bra

в • *prep* at, in • *v* have
ве́тна́мки • *n* flip-flop, thong
ві́зд • *n* entrance
вю́ро́к • *n* brambling
в'яза́нка • *n* sheaf
в'яза́ти • *v* knit
в'язень • *n* prisoner
в'язни́ця • *n* prison
вага • *n* scales
ва́га • *n* weight

вагі́тна • *adj* pregnant
вагі́тність • *n* pregnancy
ваго́н • *n* car, carriage, van
ва́жити • *v* weigh
важіль • *n* lever
ва́жка • *n* dragonfly
важки́й • *adj* difficult, heavy
важли́вий • *adj* important
важни́й • *adj* important
ваза • *n* vase

вакантний • *adj* vacant
вакуо́ля • *n* vacuole
вакцина • *n* vaccine
валькирія • *n* valkyrie
вампі́р • *n* vampire
ванадій • *n* vanadium
ванадині́т • *n* vanadinite
вандалізм • *n* vandalism
ва́нна • *n* bath, bathroom, bathtub
ванта́ж • *n* cargo
вантажі́вка • *n* truck
вапняк • *n* limestone
ва́рвар • *n* barbarian
варваризм • *n* barbarism
ва́рварка • *n* barbarian
варварський • *adj* barbarian
варе́ння • *n* jam
вари́ти • *v* boil, cook
ва́рта • *n* guard
вартість • *n* value
вас • *pron* you
ват • *n* watt
ваш • *pron* yours
вби́вство • *n* murder
вбивця • *n* murderer
вби́вця • *n* killer
вбира́льня • *n* toilet
ввезти • *v* import
ввійти́ • *v* enter
ввічливий • *adj* courteous, polite
ввозити • *v* import
вгада́ти • *v* guess
вга́дувати • *v* guess
вго́лос • *adv* aloud
вгорі • *adv* up
вгорі́ • *adv* upstairs
вгору • *adv* up
вго́ру • *adv* upstairs
вдавати • *v* pretend
вдаватися • *v* manage
вда́рити • *v* beat, hit
вдаря́ти • *v* beat, hit
вда́тний • *adj* successful
вдівець • *n* widower
вдова • *n* widow
вдо́ма • *adv* home
вдячний • *adj* grateful, thankful
вегетаріа́нство • *n* vegetarianism
ведмі́дь • *n* bear
ве́жа • *n* tower
везти́ • *v* carry
вели́кий • *adj* great
велич • *n* glory
величина́ • *n* magnitude
велосипе́д • *n* bicycle
ве́на • *n* vein

вентиля́тор • *n* fan
веранда • *n* veranda
верба́ • *n* willow
верблю́д • *n* camel
веретено • *n* spindle
верста́ • *n* verst
вертолі́т • *n* helicopter
верф • *n* shipyard
верхі́вка • *n* summit
верховний • *adj* supreme
верхово́дка • *n* bleak
вершина • *n* node
верши́на • *n* summit
вершки́ • *n* cream
вершник • *n* rider
весе́лка • *n* rainbow
весі́лля • *n* wedding
весло́ • *n* oar
весна́ • *n* spring
весня́нка • *n* freckle
вестерніза́ція • *n* westernization
вести́ • *v* guide, lead
весь • *adj* entire
ветеринар • *n* veterinarian
ве́то • *n* veto
вечеря • *n* supper
вече́ря • *n* dinner, supper
вечеряти • *v* dine
ве́чір • *n* evening
вечі́рка • *n* party
вже́ • *adv* already
вжива́ння • *n* use
вжива́ти • *v* use
вжи́ти • *v* use
взуття́ • *n* footwear
взяти • *v* take
ви • *pron* you
вибача́тися • *v* apologize
ви́бачення • *n* apology
ви́бачитися • *v* apologize
вибира́ти • *v* choose
вибор • *n* election
ви́брати • *v* choose
виважено • *adv* deliberately
виводити • *v* exterminate
виганя́ти • *v* banish
вигі́дний • *adj* advantageous, beneficial
ви́гнати • *v* banish
ви́года • *n* advantage
виго́нити • *v* banish
вигото́вити • *v* make
виготовля́ти • *v* make
вигук • *n* exclamation
ви́гук • *n* interjection
вид • *n* scenery, type

видавати • *v* publish
виде́лка • *n* fork
ви́діти • *v* see
ви́дра • *n* otter
визволення • *n* liberation
визволити • *v* liberate
визволяти • *v* liberate
ви́значення • *n* definition
ви́їзд • *n* departure, exit
викидень • *n* miscarriage
виклада́ти • *v* teach
викладач • *n* teacher
викладачка • *n* teacher
ви́користати • *v* use
використо́вувати • *v* use
викрада́ти • *v* kidnap
ви́красти • *v* kidnap
викрутка • *n* screwdriver
вила • *n* pitchfork
ви́лікувати • *v* heal
виліт • *n* departure
ви́лка • *n* fork
ви́мя́ • *n* udder
вимага́ння • *n* blackmail
вимі́рювання • *n* measurement
вимо́ва • *n* pronunciation
ви́мовити • *v* pronounce
вимовля́ння • *n* pronunciation
вимовля́ти • *v* pronounce
вина́ • *n* guilt
винахід • *n* invention
винищувати • *v* exterminate
вино́ • *n* wine
виногра́д • *n* grape
винятковий • *adj* exceptional
ви́падок • *n* accident
ви́пити • *v* drink
випіка́ти • *v* bake
ви́порожнення • *n* excrement, feces
виправля́ти • *v* correct
виража́ти • *v* express
вираз • *n* expression
ви́разити • *v* express
ви́рішити • *v* decide
виріша́ти • *v* decide
ви́рости • *v* grow
висила́ти • *v* banish, deport, exile
ви́силка • *n* deportation
висі́ти • *v* hang
ви́слати • *v* banish, deport, exile
вислів • *n* expression
висмі́ювати • *v* satirize
виснажливий • *adj* consumptive
висна́жувати • *v* drain
висок • *n* temple
висо́кий • *adj* high, tall

вистила́ти • *v* flag
ви́стрелити • *v* shoot
виступ • *n* panhandle
вису́шувати • *v* drain
ви́терти • *v* wipe
вити • *v* howl
витира́ти • *v* wipe
вихваля́ння • *n* eulogy
ви́хід • *n* exit
вихідні́ • *n* weekend
вихор • *n* whirlwind
ви́шка • *n* tower
вишневий • *adj* burgundy
ви́шня • *n* cherry
вівсянка • *n* bunting
вівта́р • *n* altar
вівця́ • *n* ewe
від • *prep* from, since
віді́зд • *n* departure
ві́дати • *v* know
відбиванка • *n* volleyball
відва́га • *n* bravery, courage
відва́жний • *adj* brave
відві́дати • *v* visit
відві́дування • *n* call, visit
відві́дувати • *v* visit
відгалуження • *n* offshoot
відго́мін • *n* echo
відгук • *n* echo
віддалення • *n* alienation, estrangement
відда́лення • *n* distance
ві́ддаль • *n* distance
відданий • *adj* faithful
відділ • *n* faculty, phylum
відділення • *n* detachment
відді́лення • *n* school, secession
відеока́мера • *n* camera
відеокасета • *n* videocassette
відірваність • *n* detachment
відкриття • *n* discovery
відлив • *n* tide
відло́га • *n* hood
відмі́нний • *adj* excellent, exceptional
відмі́нний • *adj* different
відмова • *n* denial
відмо́ва • *n* abandonment
відмовля́ти • *v* refuse
відмовля́тися • *v* refuse
віднести́ • *v* remove
відноси́ти • *v* remove
відокремлення • *n* detachment
відомий • *adj* known
відо́мий • *adj* familiar
відомість • *n* fame
відповіда́ти • *v* answer

відповідь • *n* answer
відповісти • *v* answer
відпочивати • *v* rest
відпочинок • *n* rest
відправитися • *v* depart
відправлення • *n* departure
відправлятися • *v* depart
відраза • *n* disgust
відрижка • *n* burp
відро • *n* bucket
відсоток • *n* interest
відстань • *n* distance
відступ • *n* retreat
відступати • *v* retreat
відступити • *v* retreat
відсутній • *adj* absent
відсутність • *n* lack
відхилення • *n* departure
відхід • *n* departure
відхідник • *n* anus
відчувати • *v* feel
відчуженість • *n* alienation, aloofness, detachment, estrangement
відчуження • *n* alienation, detachment, estrangement
відчужування • *n* alienation
відчути • *v* feel
відьма • *n* witch
віжка • *n* rein
віза • *n* visa
візит • *n* call, visit
візита • *n* call, visit
війна • *n* war
військо • *n* troop
військо • *n* army
військовий • *adj* military • *n* soldier
військовик • *n* serviceman
військовослужбовець • *n* serviceman
вік • *n* age
вікно • *n* window
віко • *n* eyelid
віл • *n* bullock, ox
вілла • *n* villa
вільний • *n* movable
вільний • *adj* free
вільність • *n* freedom
він • *pron* he
вінець • *n* wreath
віник • *n* broom
вінігрет • *n* vinaigrette
вінок • *n* wreath

віночок • *n* corolla
віолончель • *n* cello
віра • *n* belief, faith
вірити • *v* believe
вірний • *adj* faithful
вірний • *adj* right
вірність • *n* truth
віртуальний • *adj* virtual
вірус • *n* virus
віруюча • *n* believer
віруючий • *adj* faithful
віруючий • *n* believer
вірш • *n* poem, verse
вірьовка • *n* rope
вісімка • *n* eight
вісімнадцятий • *adj* eighteenth
віскі • *n* whiskey
віслюк • *n* donkey
вісмут • *n* bismuth
вісті • *n* news
віталізм • *n* vitalism
вітамін • *n* vitamin
вітання • *n* welcome
вітати • *interj* congratulations
вітер • *n* wind
вітерець • *n* breeze
вітка • *n* branch
вітрило • *n* sail
вітрильник • *n* sailboat
вітчим • *n* stepfather
вітязь • *n* knight
вічність • *n* eternity
вічно • *adv* forever
вішати • *v* hang
вія • *n* eyelash
віяти • *v* blow
вказати • *v* point
вказувати • *v* point
вколоти • *v* sink
вкривати • *v* cover
вкрити • *v* cover
влада • *n* authority, power
власний • *adj* own
власник • *n* owner
власність • *n* property
власність • *n* property
властивість • *n* property
властивість • *n* property
вміти • *v* can

внаслі́док • *conj* because
вниз • *adv* down
внизу́ • *adv* down
внук • *n* grandson
внутрощі • *n* entrails
вну́чка • *n* granddaughter
вовк • *n* wolf
во́вна • *n* fleece, wool
вовняний • *adj* woolen
вогнеме́т • *n* flamethrower
во́гнище • *n* bonfire
вого́нь • *n* fire
вода́ • *n* water
во́день • *n* hydrogen
води́ти • *v* lead
во́дій • *n* chauffeur, driver
во́дка • *n* vodka
во́дний • *adj* aquatic
водогра́й • *n* fountain
водозбір • *n* columbine
во́дорость • *n* alga
водоспа́д • *n* waterfall
воєво́да • *n* voivode
воє́нний • *adj* military
вози́ти • *v* carry
воїн • *n* warrior
воїн • *n* soldier
войовни́чий • *adj* militant
вокза́л • *n* station
волан • *n* shuttlecock
волейбол • *n* volleyball
волинка • *n* bagpipes
вологий • *adj* humid
воло́гий • *adj* wet
володі́ти • *v* own
волонте́р • *n* volunteer

волос • *n* hair
волоса́тий • *adj* hairy
волоси • *n* hair
волосина • *n* hair
волосся • *n* hair
вольт • *n* volt
вольфрам • *n* tungsten
вона́ • *pron* she
вони • *pron* they
воно́ • *pron* it
вонь • *n* reek, stench
во́рог • *n* enemy
воро́жість • *n* animosity
во́рон • *n* raven
воро́на • *n* crow
воро́нка • *n* funnel
ворота • *n* goal
воро́та • *n* gate
воротар • *n* goalkeeper
восьмий • *adj* eighth
восьмині́г • *n* octopus
во́ша • *n* louse
вояк • *n* warrior
воя́к • *n* soldier
впада́ти • *v* sink
впе́ртий • *adj* stubborn
вплив • *n* influence
впливовий • *adj* influential
вправа • *n* exercise
вро́да • *n* beauty
вродли́вий • *adj* beautiful
всади́ти • *v* sink
все • *pron* everything
всéсвіт • *n* cosmos, universe

Всéсвіт • *n* universe

всі • *pron* everybody, everyone
встава́ти • *v* arise
вста́вити • *v* insert
вставля́ти • *v* insert
вступ • *n* accession

вто́ргнення • *n* incursion, intervention, invasion
втра́тити • *v* lose
втрача́ти • *v* lose
втруча́ння • *n* intervention

вугілля • *n* coal
вуглець • *n* carbon
вугол • *n* angle
вугор • *n* eel, pimple
вуджений • *adj* smoked
вуздечка • *n* bridle
вузол • *n* node
вузол • *n* knot
вузький • *adj* narrow
вузько • *adv* narrowly
вулик • *n* beehive
вулиця • *n* street
вулкан • *n* volcano
вулканізація • *n* vulcanization
вульва • *n* vulva
вульгарний • *adj* vulgarian

вуса • *n* moustache
вуси • *n* moustache
вухо • *n* ear
вушко • *n* eye
вхід • *n* entrance
входити • *v* enter
вчений • *n* scientist
вчинок • *n* act
вчитель • *n* teacher
вчителька • *n* teacher
вчити • *v* study
вчити • *v* teach
вчитися • *v* study
вчора • *n* yesterday • *adv* yesterday

га • *n* hectare
ґаблі • *n* pitchfork

ґаблі • *n* pitchfork

ґава • *n* crow

ґава • *n* crow

ґавань • *n* port
ґавкати • *v* bark
ґаґа • *n* eider
ґаґара • *n* diver, loon
ґад • *n* asshole
ґадоліній • *n* gadolinium
ґадюка • *n* viper
ґадюка • *n* adder
ґаз • *n* gas
ґазета • *n* newspaper
ґай • *n* grove
ґайворон • *n* rook
ґайка • *n* nut

ґак • *n* hook
ґал • *n* gall
ґалій • *n* gallium
ґалаґаз • *n* shelduck
ґалактика • *n* galaxy
ґалерея • *n* gallery
ґаліон • *n* galleon
ґалка • *n* jackdaw
ґалліцизм • *n* gallicism
ґалстук • *n* necktie
ґалузка • *n* branch, twig
ґалузь • *n* branch
ґалушка • *n* dumpling

гальмо́ • *n* brake
гальмува́ти • *v* brake
гамак • *n* hammock
гаманець • *n* purse
гамане́ць • *n* wallet
га́мбургер • *n* hamburger
гангре́на • *n* gangrene
гандбол • *n* handball
гантель • *n* dumbbell
ганьба́ • *n* disgrace
ганя́ти • *v* chase, drive
гара́ж • *n* garage
гарбу́з • *n* pumpkin
гарма́та • *n* cannon

гармо́нія • *n* accordion
гарний • *adj* pretty
га́рний • *adj* beautiful, good
гарно • *adv* well
гарпун • *n* harpoon
гаря́чий • *adj* hot
гастрит • *n* gastritis
га́учо • *n* gaucho
га́фній • *n* hafnium
гачок • *n* hook
гашиш • *n* hashish
ґвалтува́ти • *v* rape

гвалтува́ти • *v* rape

гва́рдія • *n* guard
гвинт • *n* screw

гвинті́вка • *n* rifle

ґедзь • *n* horsefly

гей • *n* gay, homosexual • *interj* hey

ґей • *n* gay, homosexual

гейзер • *n* geyser
ге́йша • *n* geisha
геко́н • *n* gecko
екта́р • *n* hectare
ге́лій • *n* helium
геліко́птер • *n* helicopter
геноцид • *n* genocide
геогра́фія • *n* geography
геоло́гія • *n* geology

геоме́трія • *n* geometry
геофі́зика • *n* geophysics
гепа́рд • *n* cheetah
гера́льдика • *n* heraldry
гербарій • *n* herbarium
герма́ній • *n* germanium
гермафроди́т • *n* hermaphrodite
героїня • *n* heroine
героїня • *n* hero

герóй • *n* hero
герц • *n* hertz
гéрцог • *n* duke
герцогиня • *n* duchess
герцогство • *n* duchy
гетерогéнність • *n* heterogeneity
гéтто • *n* ghetto
геть • *adv* away
гéтьман • *n* hetman
гикáти • *v* hiccup
гúнути • *v* sink
гівнюк • *n* asshole
гігієна • *n* hygiene
гігрометр • *n* hygrometer
гíдний • *adj* dignified
гíдність • *n* dignity
гідрат • *n* hydrate
гієна • *n* hyena
гíлка • *n* bough, branch, twig
гíлочка • *n* branch, twig
гімн • *n* anthem, hymn
гімнастика • *n* gymnastics
гімнó • *n* shit
гінекологія • *n* gynecology
гіперглікемія • *n* hyperglycemia
гіпопотáм • *n* hippopotamus
гіпотенуза • *n* hypotenuse
гіпс • *n* cast
гíркий • *adj* bitter
гíрник • *n* miner
гірчúця • *n* mustard
гість • *n* guest
гітáра • *n* guitar
главá • *n* chapter
гладкúй • *adj* smooth
глек • *n* ewer
глечик • *n* ewer
глибинá • *n* depth
глибокий • *adj* deep
глóбус • *n* globe
глóтка • *n* larynx
глухар • *n* capercaillie
глухúй • *adj* deaf
глушнúк • *n* muffler, silencer
гнáти • *v* chase, drive
гнейс • *n* gneiss
гнида • *n* nit
гнів • *n* anger
гніздó • *n* nest
гній • *n* dung, manure, pus
гном • *n* dwarf
гнýти • *v* bend
гобой • *n* oboe
гóвір • *n* dialect, speech
говорити • *v* talk
говорúти • *v* say, speak

година • *adv* o'clock
годúна • *n* hour, time
годúнник • *n* clock, watch
годівниця • *n* manger
годувáти • *v* feed
гокей • *n* hockey
гол • *n* goal
голий • *adj* nude
гóлий • *adj* naked
голúти • *v* shave
голúтися • *v* shave
гóлка • *n* needle
гóлка-рúба • *n* needlefish
голкіпер • *n* goalkeeper
головá • *n* head
головоломка • *n* puzzle
гóлод • *n* famine, hunger
голóдний • *adj* hungry
голодомóр • *n* famine
голодувáти • *v* starve
гóлос • *n* voice, vote
голосний • *n* vowel
голóсний • *adj* loud
гóлосно • *adv* loudly
голосувáти • *v* vote
голуб • *n* dove
гóлуб • *n* pigeon
гóльмій • *n* holmium
гольф • *n* golf
гóмік • *n* fag
гомілка • *n* shin
гомосексуалíзм • *n* homosexuality
гомосексуалíст • *n* gay, homosexual
гомосексуáльний • *adj* homosexual
гомофóбія • *n* homophobia
гондола • *n* gondola
гонорéя • *n* gonorrhea
гончáр • *n* potter
горá • *n* mountain
гóрдий • *adj* proud
горе • *n* distress, misery
гóре • *n* disaster, sorrow, tragedy
горизóнт • *n* horizon
горила • *n* gorilla
горíлка • *n* vodka
горíти • *v* burn
горíх • *n* nut
горло • *n* throat
горностай • *n* ermine
горобина • *n* rowan
гóрод • *n* garden
горóх • *n* pea
горóшок • *n* pea
гортáнь • *n* larynx
госпіталізáція • *n* hospitalization
господáрство • *n* economy

господиня • *n* hostess
гостинність • *n* hospitality
гóстрий • *adj* sharp
готéль • *n* hotel, inn
готíвка • *n* cash
готóвий • *adj* ready
готувáти • *v* cook, prepare
гра • *n* game, play
грáблі • *n* rake
град • *n* hail
грáдус • *n* degree
грак • *n* rook
грам • *n* gram
грамáтика • *n* grammar
грамофóн • *n* gramophone
гранат • *n* pomegranate
гранáта • *n* grenade
гранатомéт • *n* launcher

границя • *n* border
грáппа • *n* grappa
грáти • *v* act
грáти • *v* play
грáфік • *n* schedule, timetable
грéбля • *n* barrage, dam
грéчка • *n* buckwheat
гриб • *n* fungus, mushroom
грибóк • *n* fungus
грива • *n* mane
гризти • *v* gnaw
грип • *n* flu, influenza
гриф • *n* griffin, vulture
грíзний • *adj* formidable, terrible
грім • *n* thunder
грíнго • *n* gringo

грíнго • *n* gringo

грíнка • *n* toast
гріх • *n* sin
грíшити • *v* sin
грíшник • *n* sinner
грíшниця • *n* sinner
гроб • *n* coffin
грозá • *n* thunderstorm
громадянин • *n* citizen
громадянка • *n* citizen
громадянство • *n* citizenship,
nationality
грош • *n* grosz
грóші • *n* cash, money
грýди • *n* breast, chest
грудь • *n* breast
грузило • *n* sinker
грузовик • *n* truck
ґрунт • *n* soil

ґрунт • *n* soil

грýпа • *n* group
грýша • *n* pear
грязь • *n* mud
гуáва • *n* guava
гуáш • *n* gouache

гуаява • *n* guava
губá • *n* lip
губити • *v* lose
гýбка • *n* sponge

ґу́дзик • *n* button

гуля́ти • *v* walk
гуля́ш • *n* goulash
ґу́ма • *n* rubber

гуманізм • *n* humanism
ґу́мка • *n* eraser

ґу́мка • *n* eraser

гурт • *n* herd
ґу́ртка • *n* mug
гусак • *n* gander
гуса́к • *n* goose
ґу́сениця • *n* caterpillar

ґу́ска • *n* goose
ґу́чний • *adj* loud
ґу́чно • *adv* loudly

дава́ти • *v* give
дайкон • *n* daikon
дактилі́чний • *adj* dactylic
далекий • *adj* extreme, remote
дале́кий • *adj* distant, far
далеко • *adv* widely
дале́ко • *adv* far
да́мба • *n* dam
да́ні • *n* data
данти́ст • *n* dentist
дар • *n* faculty, gift, talent
дарува́ти • *v* give
да́та • *n* date
да́ти • *v* give
дах • *n* roof
дача • *n* dacha, villa
двадця́тий • *adj* twentieth
двана́дцятий • *adj* twelfth
две́рі • *n* door
двигу́н • *n* crane, engine, motor
дві́йка • *n* two
двір • *n* court, yard
двічі • *adv* twice
двопала́тний • *adj* bicameral
дворик • *n* yard
дворя́нство • *n* nobility
де • *adv* where • *conj* where
дебе́лий • *adj* fat

девя́ностих • *adj* ninetieth
девя́тий • *adj* ninth
девя́тна́дцятий • *adj* nineteenth
дезертирство • *n* desertion
деїзм • *n* deism
декада́нс • *n* decadence
дельфі́н • *n* dolphin
демагог • *n* demagogue
демокра́тія • *n* democracy
демон • *n* demon
демонстра́нт • *n* demonstrator
демонстра́нтка • *n* demonstrator
денний • *adj* diurnal
день • *n* day
депорта́ція • *n* deportation
депресія • *n* depression
де́рвіш • *n* dervish
де́рево • *n* tree
дереворит • *n* woodcut
держа́ва • *n* country, nation, state
дерьмо́ • *n* shit
десерт • *n* dessert
десна́ • *n* gum
деспотизм • *n* despotism
десь • *adv* somewhere
деся́тий • *adj* tenth
десятилі́ття • *n* decade
десятирі́ччя • *n* decade

деталь • *n* detail
дефетизм • *n* defeatism
дефініція • *n* definition
дефіс • *n* hyphen
дехто • *pron* something
дещо • *pron* something
деякий • *pron* something
деякий • *pron* some
джаз • *n* jazz
джгут • *n* tourniquet
джгутик • *n* flagellum
джем • *n* jam, marmalade
джерело • *n* fountain
джерельце • *n* fontanelle
джин • *n* gin, jinn
джихад • *n* jihad
джміль • *n* bumblebee
джоуль • *n* joule
джунглі • *n* jungle
дзбан • *n* ewer
дзвін • *n* bell
дзвоник • *n* bell
дзвонити • *v* telephone
дзвонити • *v* call, phone, ring
дзеркало • *n* mirror
дзьоб • *n* beak, bill
дивак • *n* freak
диван • *n* carpet, sofa
дивина • *n* curiosity
дивитися • *v* watch
дивитися • *v* look
дивний • *adj* strange
диво • *n* wonder
диво • *n* miracle
дивуватися • *v* wonder
дизайнер • *n* designer
дикий • *adj* wild
дикобраз • *n* porcupine
диктатор • *n* dictator
диктатура • *n* dictatorship
дилема • *n* dilemma
дилетантизм • *n* dilettantism
дим • *n* smoke
димохід • *n* chimney
динаміт • *n* dynamite
динозавр • *n* dinosaur
диня • *n* melon
диплом • *n* diploma
директор • *n* director
дисидент • *n* dissident
дисидентка • *n* dissident
диск • *n* disk
дискримінація • *n* discrimination
дискусія • *n* discussion
дискутувати • *v* discuss
дислексія • *n* dyslexia

диспрозій • *n* dysprosium
дистанція • *n* distance
дисципліна • *n* science
дитина • *n* baby, child
дитинство • *n* childhood
дитя • *n* child
дихати • *v* breathe
диявол • *n* devil
диякон • *n* deacon
діабет • *n* diabetes
діагностичний • *adj* diagnostic
діалект • *n* dialect
діалог • *n* dialogue
діамант • *n* diamond
діаметрально • *adv* diametrically
діва • *n* maiden, virgin
дівер • *n* brother-in-law
дівчина • *n* maiden
дівчина • *n* girl, girlfriend
дід • *n* grandfather
дідусь • *n* grandfather
діетилетер • *n* ether
дієвість • *n* strength
дієйменник • *n* infinitive
дієслово • *n* verb
дієта • *n* diet
дієцезія • *n* diocese
дійти • *v* arrive, reach
ділити • *v* divide
діло • *n* company
дім • *n* building, home, house
діоцез • *n* diocese
дірка • *n* hole
діставати • *v* get
дістати • *v* get
дітище • *n* offspring
дітовбивство • *n* infanticide
дія • *n* act
діяти • *v* act
для • *prep* for
дно • *n* bottom
доба • *n* day
добовий • *adj* diurnal
добра • *n* dobra
добре • *adv* well
добриво • *n* fertilizer
добрий • *adj* good
добрий • *adj* good, kind
добро • *n* good
добровільно • *adv* voluntarily
доброволець • *n* volunteer
доброчесність • *n* virtue
довгий • *adj* long
довгий • *adj* long
довгоносик • *n* weevil
довгота • *n* longitude

довжина́ • *n* length
до́від • *n* proof
довідник • *n* handbook
довіряти • *v* trust
догматизм • *n* dogmatism
до́говір • *n* contract
догори • *adv* up
додава́ти • *v* add
дода́ти • *v* add
додатко́вий • *adj* additional
додекаедр • *n* dodecahedron
додому • *adv* homeward
додо́му • *adv* home
дож • *n* doge
доза • *n* dose
дозво́лити • *v* allow
дозволя́ти • *v* allow
дозрівати • *v* ripen
доїжджа́ти • *v* arrive, reach
доїхати • *v* arrive, reach
до́каз • *n* proof
докладний • *adj* accurate, exact, precise
доко́наний • *adj* perfective
до́ктор • *n* doctor
докуме́нт • *n* document, paper
документа́льний • *adj* documentary
документа́ція • *n* documentation
до́лар • *n* dollar
долина • *n* dale
доли́на • *n* valley
доло́нь • *n* palm
до́лото • *n* chisel
до́ля • *n* destiny, fate
домівка • *n* home
доміно • *n* dominoes
домкрат • *n* jack
домогоспода́рка • *n* housewife
дони́зу • *adv* down
допи́тливий • *adj* curious
допомага́ти • *v* assist, help
допомо́га • *n* assistance, help
допомогти́ • *v* assist, help
доро́га • *n* road
дороги́й • *adj* dear, expensive, precious
дорогоці́нний • *adj* precious
доро́слий • *n* adult • *adj* adult
до́свід • *n* experience
дослить • *pron* something
доста́ток • *n* plenty
досто́їнство • *n* dignity
досту́пний • *adj* available
досяга́ти • *v* achieve
досягти́ • *v* achieve
дот • *n* dot

до́тик • *n* touch
доторка́тися • *v* touch
доторкну́тися • *v* touch
дохо́дити • *v* arrive, reach
дочка́ • *n* daughter
до́шка • *n* blackboard
дошкуля́ти • *v* afflict
дощ • *n* rain
до́щик • *n* shower
дощовий • *adj* rainy, wet
дощови́к • *n* raincoat
дощовитий • *adj* wet
драби́на • *n* ladder
драко́н • *n* dragon
драхма • *n* drachma
дрі́жджі • *n* yeast
дрізд • *n* thrush
дріма́ти • *v* doze
дріт • *n* wire
дро́ва • *n* firewood
дромаде́р • *n* dromedary
друг • *n* boyfriend, friend
другий • *adj* second
дру́жба • *n* friendship
дружи́на • *n* wife
дружній • *adj* friendly
друшля́к • *n* colander
дуб • *n* oak
дуель • *n* duel
ду́же • *adv* very
ду́ма • *n* duma
думати • *v* think
думка • *n* thought
ду́мка • *n* idea
ду́па • *n* ass, butt
ду́рень • *n* fool
дури́світ • *n* charlatan
дуріан • *n* durian
дурний • *adj* stupid
дурни́й • *adj* foolish
ду́ти • *v* blow
духи́ • *n* perfume
духове́нство • *n* clergy
душ • *n* shower
душа́ • *n* soul
душогуб • *n* murderer
дьо́готь • *n* tar
дю́жина • *n* dozen
дюйм • *n* inch
дю́на • *n* dune
дя́дько • *n* uncle
дя́кувати • *v* thank
дякую • *interj* thanks
дя́тел • *n* woodpecker

еволю́ція • *n* evolution
евтаназія • *n* euthanasia
евфемі́зм • *n* euphemism
евфуї́зм • *n* euphuism
егоїзм • *n* egoism
ей • *interj* hey
ейнште́йній • *n* einsteinium
еква́тор • *n* equator
екза́мен • *n* examination
екзистенціалі́зм • *n* existentialism
екологія • *n* ecology
еконо́міка • *n* economics, economy
екосистема • *n* ecosystem
екра́н • *n* screen
ексгібіціоні́зм • *n* exhibitionism
екскава́тор • *n* excavator
екскреме́нти • *n* dung, excrement, feces
екскурсія • *n* excursion
екску́рсія • *n* hike
експресіоні́зм • *n* expressionism
екстрема́льний • *adj* extreme
екстремі́зм • *n* extremism
еласти́чний • *adj* elastic
еле́ктрика • *n* electricity
електрифіка́ція • *n* electrification
електромагнети́зм • *n* electromagnetism
електрон • *n* electron
електро́ніка • *n* electronics
елізія • *n* elision
еліпс • *n* ellipse
ель • *n* ale
ем • *n* em

емаль • *n* enamel
ембріо́н • *n* germ
емі́р • *n* emir
емо́ція • *n* emotion
емпіри́зм • *n* empiricism
ему • *n* emu
ендогамія • *n* endogamy
ене́ргія • *n* energy
ентерит • *n* enteritis
ентомологія • *n* entomology
ентропія • *n* entropy
ентузіазм • *n* enthusiasm
ентузіаст • *n* enthusiast
ентузіастка • *n* enthusiast
енциклопе́дія • *n* encyclopedia
епізо́д • *n* episode
епітелій • *n* epithelium
епопея • *n* epopee
епо́ха • *n* age
е́ра • *n* age
е́рбій • *n* erbium
ерекція • *n* erection
еротичний • *adj* erotic
еруди́ція • *n* erudition
ескала́тор • *n* escalator
ете́р • *n* ether
е́тика • *n* ethics
етимоло́гія • *n* etymology
е́тнос • *n* nationality
етноцентризм • *n* ethnocentrism
еякуля́т • *n* semen
еякуляція • *n* ejaculation

є • *v* is
єва́нгеліє • *n* gospel
євро́пій • *n* europium
єди́ний • *adj* only
єдиноріг • *n* unicorn
єнот • *n* raccoon

єпархія • *n* diocese
єпи́скоп • *n* bishop
єресь • *n* heresy
єрети́к • *n* heretic
єретичний • *adj* heretic, heretical

жа́ба • *n* frog, toad
жабри • *n* gill
жага • *n* thirst
жа́йворонок • *n* lark, skylark
жалити • *v* sting

жало • *n* stinger
жар • *n* fever
жа́рити • *v* fry
жарт • *n* joke
жартува́ти • *v* joke

жасми́н • *n* jasmine
жати • *v* reap, sickle
жах • *n* horror
жахливий • *adj* terrible
жахливість • *n* monstrosity
жда́ти • *v* await, wait
женитися • *v* marry
жени́х • *n* bridegroom
жеребе́ць • *n* foal, stallion
жертва • *n* sacrifice
же́ртва • *n* immolation, victim
жертвоприно́шення • *n* immolation
жертвувати • *v* sacrifice
живий • *adj* living
живи́й • *adj* alive
живити • *v* fertilize
живіт • *n* abdomen, stomach
живі́т • *n* belly
жи́ла • *n* vein
жиле́т • *n* vest, waistcoat
жир • *n* fat
жира́ф • *n* giraffe
жира́фа • *n* giraffe
жи́рний • *adj* fat
житель • *n* resident
жи́ти • *v* dwell, live, reside
житло • *n* dwelling
житло́ • *n* lodging
жито • *n* grain

жи́то • *n* rye
життя́ • *n* life
жі́нка • *n* female, wife, woman
жіно́чий • *adj* feminine
жме́ня • *n* handful
жо́вні́р • *n* soldier
жо́втий • *adj* yellow
жовтогарячий • *n* sunflower
жовток • *n* yolk
жовтяниця • *n* jaundice
жовч • *n* bile
жоден • *pron* neither
жолудь • *n* acorn
жона́ • *n* woman
жона́тий • *adj* married
жонглювання • *n* juggling
жо́па • *n* ass, butt
жорно • *n* millstone
жорстокий • *adj* cruel
жрець • *n* priest
жува́ти • *v* chew
жук • *n* beetle
жураве́ль • *n* crane
журавлина • *n* cranberry
журна́л • *n* magazine
журнали́стика • *n* journalism
журналі́ст • *n* journalist, reporter
журналі́стка • *n* journalist

з • *prep* from, since, with
зє́днання • *n* joint
зє́днувати • *v* connect
зя́ви́тися • *v* appear
зя́вля́тися • *v* appear
за • *prep* behind
заарешто́вувати • *v* arrest
заарештува́ти • *v* arrest
забава • *n* fun
забастовка • *n* strike
забезпека • *n* protection
забобо́н • *n* superstition
заборо́на • *n* prohibition
заборони́ти • *v* ban, forbid, prohibit
заборони́ти • *v* ban, forbid, prohibit
забра́ло • *n* visor
забува́ти • *v* forget
забу́ти • *v* forget
за́вя́зь • *n* germ
завбачливий • *adj* forethoughtful
завертка • *n* screwdriver
завжди • *adv* always

завзяття • *n* zest
завіса • *n* curtain
заво́д • *n* factory
за́втра • *n* tomorrow • *adv* tomorrow
завча́сний • *adj* early
завча́сно • *adv* early
за́вше • *adv* always
загадка • *n* puzzle
зага́дка • *n* mystery
загальмува́ти • *v* brake
загар • *n* tan
загарбник • *n* invader
загін • *n* detachment, force
загли́блювати • *v* duck
загроза • *n* distress
загро́за • *n* danger, threat
загуби́ти • *v* lose
зад • *n* butt
за́дниця • *n* ass
задній • *adj* hinder
задоволення • *n* pleasure
за́єць • *n* hare
заїкання • *n* stutter

займа́ти • *v* occupy
займе́нник • *n* pronoun
зайня́ти • *v* occupy
за́йнятий • *adj* busy
закаже́ння • *n* infection
закі́нчити • *v* end, finish
закі́нчувати • *v* end, finish
заклина́ння • *n* spell
закля́ття • *n* spell
закон • *n* legislation
зако́н • *n* law
законода́вець • *n* legislator
законода́виця • *n* legislator
законодавство • *n* legislation
законодавчий • *adj* legislative
закрива́ти • *v* close, shut
закри́ти • *v* close, shut
закри́тий • *adj* closed
зали́в • *n* bay, gulf
залишення • *n* abandonment, desertion
залі́зко • *n* iron
залі́зний • *adj* iron
залізни́ця • *n* railway
залі́зо • *n* iron
залоза • *n* gland
замирювач • *n* peacekeeper
замі́жня • *adj* married
за́мкнений • *adj* closed
замкну́тість • *n* aloofness
замо́к • *n* lock
за́мок • *n* castle
заморо́жений • *adj* frozen
заморо́жувати • *v* freeze
заморо́жуватися • *v* freeze
занаві́ска • *n* curtain
занедба́ність • *n* desertion, shabbiness
занепоко́єння • *n* anxiety
зану́рювати • *v* duck
зану́рюватися • *v* sink
запя́стя • *n* wrist
запада́ти • *v* sink
запал • *n* enthusiasm, zest
запали́ти • *v* light
запальни́чка • *n* lighter
запа́лювати • *v* light
запам'ятати • *v* memorize
запам'ятовувати • *v* memorize
за́пах • *n* scent, smell
запе́внити • *v* assure
запевня́ти • *v* assure
заперечення • *n* denial
заперечувати • *v* contradict
запита́ти • *v* ask
заплати́ти • *v* pay

заплі́днити • *v* fertilize
заплі́днювати • *v* fertilize
за́повідь • *n* commandment
запре́т • *n* veto
запроси́ти • *v* invite
запро́шення • *n* invitation
запро́шувати • *v* invite
запряга́ти • *v* harness
запу́щений • *adj* overgrown
зараже́ння • *n* infection
зараз • *adv* immediately
зараза • *n* infection
заріс • *adj* overgrown
заро́док • *n* germ
зарослий • *adj* overgrown
зарпла́та • *n* wage
зару́чник • *n* hostage
засі́дання • *n* meeting
засло́на • *n* protection
заспіва́ти • *v* sing
засра́нець • *n* asshole
засту́да • *n* cold
за́ступ • *n* spade
заступа • *n* protection
заступни́цтво • *n* protection
за́суха • *n* drought
затим • *adv* therefore
зато́ка • *n* gulf
затопи́ти • *v* sink
затоплення • *n* inundation
затримуватися • *v* stay
захворі́ти • *v* ache, hurt
захисни́к • *n* defender, guard
захисни́ця • *n* defender
захист • *n* protection
за́хист • *n* defense
захисти́ти • *v* defend, protect
захища́ти • *v* defend, protect
за́хід • *n* west
західний • *adj* western
за́хідний • *adj* west, westerly
заходи́ти • *v* sink
захо́плення • *n* admiration
захо́плювати • *v* fascinate
захо́плюватися • *v* admire
зачаро́ваний • *adj* spellbound
зачаровувати • *v* bewitch
зачаро́вувати • *v* enthrall, fascinate
зачарува́ти • *v* bewitch
зача́ття • *n* conception
зачи́нений • *adj* closed
зачини́ти • *v* close, shut
зачиня́ти • *v* close, shut
заши́йок • *n* nape
зая́ва • *n* advertisement
заяви́ти • *v* announce

заявля́ти • *v* announce
збайдужі́ння • *n* alienation
збайдужування • *n* alienation
збира́ти • *v* collect, gather
збира́тися • *v* intend
збі́жжя • *n* grain
збо́ри • *n* meeting
збро́я • *n* arm, weapon
збру́я • *n* harness
збудувати • *v* construct
збудува́ти • *v* build
зв'я́зка • *n* ligament
зв'я́зок • *n* nexus
зва́гом • *adv* deliberately
зва́жити • *v* weigh
зва́жувати • *v* weigh
зва́ти • *v* call
зви́вина • *n* gyrus
звинуватити • *v* accuse
звинувачувати • *v* accuse
звича́й • *n* custom
зви́чка • *n* habit
звідки́ • *adv* where • *conj* where
звізда́ • *n* star
звільнити • *v* liberate
звільня́ти • *v* liberate
звір • *n* animal, beast, mammal
зворушувати ся • *v* touch
звужений • *v* narrowed
звук • *n* sound
зга́рище • *n* conflagration
зґвалтува́ння • *n* rape
зґвалтува́ння • *n* rape
зґвалтува́ти • *v* rape
зґвалтува́ти • *v* rape
згина́ти • *v* bend
зго́джуватися • *v* agree
зго́дитися • *v* agree
згорі́ти • *v* burn
згоря́ти • *v* incinerate
зграя • *n* flock
згра́я • *n* school
здібність • *n* aptitude, faculty
здоро́в'я • *n* health
здоро́вий • *adj* healthy
зе́бра • *n* zebra
зеле́ний • *n* green • *adj* green
землерийка • *n* shrew
землероб • *n* farmer
землеро́бство • *n* agriculture
землетру́с • *n* earthquake
земля • *n* ground
земля́ • *n* country, earth, land, soil
земля́-пові́тря • *adj* surface-to-air
земново́дне • *n* amphibian
зерно • *n* grain

зефір • *n* marshmallow
зима́ • *n* winter
зимо́вий • *adj* wintry
зимородок • *n* kingfisher
зібра́ти • *v* collect, gather
зіва́ти • *v* yawn
зівну́ти • *v* yawn
зіни́ця • *n* pupil
зір • *n* eyesight, vision
зі́рка • *n* star
зі́рочка • *n* asterisk
зконструювати • *v* construct
зламати • *v* fracture
зламатися • *v* fracture
злива • *n* downpour
злий • *adj* angry, bad, evil
злі́ва • *adv* left
злість • *n* anger
зло • *n* evil
злові́щий • *adj* ominous
зло́дій • *n* thief
зло́дійка • *n* thief
злотий • *n* zloty
зло́чин • *n* crime
злочи́нець • *n* criminal
злочи́нниця • *n* criminal
зме́ншувати • *v* flag
зме́ншуватися • *v* flag
зміїха • *n* dragon
змій • *n* dragon, kite
змі́нений • *adj* modified
зміни́ти • *v* alter
зміни́тися • *v* change
змі́нювати • *v* alter
змі́нюватися • *v* change
змія́ • *n* adder, snake
змогти́ • *v* can
змокнути • *v* wet
зморшка • *n* wrinkle
змочувати • *v* wet
змусити • *v* force
знайо́мий • *adj* familiar
знайо́мити • *v* acquaint
знайти́ • *v* find
знак • *n* symbol
знаме́нник • *n* denominator
знамено • *n* banner, flag
знання́ • *n* knowledge, science
знань • *n* erudition
зна́рошне • *adv* deliberately
зна́рошна • *adv* deliberately
зна́ти • *v* know
знахідний • *n* accusative
знаходи́ти • *v* find
значення • *n* value
зна́чення • *n* meaning

значити • *v* mean
значний • *adj* important
зневажати • *v* despise
знижка • *n* discount
знижуватися • *v* sink
зникати • *v* disappear, vanish
знищити • *v* annihilate
знищувати • *v* annihilate
знімати • *v* photograph
знімок • *n* photo, photograph
знов • *adv* again
знову • *adv* again
зношеність • *n* shabbiness
зобовязання • *n* obligation
зобовязання • *n* debt
зозуля • *n* cuckoo
зола • *n* ash
золотий • *adj* golden
золото • *n* gold
зоологія • *n* zoology
зоопарк • *n* zoo
зоря • *n* dawn
зошит • *n* notebook
зправа • *adv* right
зрада • *n* treason
зраджувати • *v* betray
зрадити • *v* betray
зрадник • *n* traitor

зрадниця • *n* traitor
зречення • *n* abjuration
зрештою • *adv* finally
зрідка • *adv* seldom
зріти • *v* ripen
зробити • *v* do, make
зрозуміти • *interj* roger
зручний • *adj* convenient
зуб • *n* tooth
зубило • *n* chisel
зубожіти • *v* sink
зубочистка • *n* toothpick
зубр • *n* bison, wisent
зумисно • *adv* deliberately
зуміти • *v* can
зупинитися • *v* stop
зупинка • *n* stop
зупинятися • *v* stop
зустріти • *v* meet
зустріч • *n* encounter
зустріч • *n* meeting, summit
зустрічати • *v* meet
зцілити • *v* heal
зцілювати • *v* heal
зяблик • *n* finch
зябра • *n* gill
зять • *n* son-in-law

импресионист • *n* impressionist

і • *conj* and
іго • *n* yoke
ігра • *n* game
іграшка • *n* toy
ідеалізм • *n* idealism
ідея • *n* idea
ідіосинкразія • *n* idiosyncrasy
ієрей • *n* priest
ізоляціонізм • *n* isolationism
ізоляція • *n* isolation
ізоморфізм • *n* isomorphism
ізотоп • *n* isotope
ікати • *v* hiccup
ікра • *n* roe
іл • *n* slime
ільменіт • *n* ilmenite
імя • *n* name

імам • *n* imam
іменник • *n* noun
імла • *n* fog
імміґрант • *n* immigrant
імміґрантка • *n* immigrant
імміґрація • *n* immigration
імовірний • *adj* probable
імовірно • *adv* probably
імперія • *n* empire
імпічмент • *n* impeachment
імпортувати • *v* import
індекс • *n* index
індик • *n* turkey
індичка • *n* turkey
індій • *n* indium
індустріалізація • *n* industrialization
індустрія • *n* industry

інженéр • *n* engineer
інíй • *n* frost
інíнґ • *n* inning
іноді́ • *adv* sometimes
іноземéць • *n* foreigner
іноземка • *n* foreigner
іноземний • *adj* foreign
інститýт • *n* school
інструкція • *n* manual
інсулíн • *n* insulin
інтелігéнція • *n* intelligentsia
інтерв'ю́ • *n* interview
інтервéнція • *n* intervention
інтерéс • *n* interest
інтересувáти • *v* interest
інтернаціонáльний • *adj* international
інтонáція • *n* intonation
інфéкція • *n* infection
інфéкція • *n* contagion
інфінітíв • *n* infinitive
інфля́ція • *n* inflation

інформáція • *n* information
інцéст • *n* incest
íнший • *adj* different, other
іподром • *n* hippodrome
іпотéка • *n* mortgage
іредентизм • *n* irredentism
іржáти • *v* guffaw, neigh
ири́дій • *n* iridium
ири́с • *n* flag
íскра • *n* spark
існувáння • *n* being, existence
існувáти • *v* exist
íспит • *n* examination
істéблішмент • *n* establishment
істина • *n* truth
істóрія • *n* history
істóта • *n* being, creature
íти • *v* go
іти́ • *v* walk
іхтіологія • *n* ichthyology
ішáк • *n* donkey

їбáти • *v* fuck
їбáтися • *v* fuck
їдáльня • *n* cafeteria, canteen
їжа • *n* diet, food, meal
їжáк • *n* hedgehog
їздити • *v* go, travel

її • *pron* hers
íсти • *v* eat
їстівни́й • *adj* comestible, edible
їх • *pron* theirs
їхати • *v* go

й • *conj* and
ймовíрний • *adj* probable
ймовíрно • *adv* probably
йо-йо • *n* yo-yo
йóга • *n* yoga
його • *pron* him

йóгурт • *n* yogurt
йóгурт • *n* yogurt
йод • *n* iodine
йому • *pron* him
йти • *v* go

кабáк • *n* bar
кабáн • *n* boar
кабарé • *n* cabaret
кáбель • *n* cable
кабíнет • *n* cabinet
каблýк • *n* heel
кавя́р • *n* caviar
кáва • *n* coffee

кавýн • *n* watermelon
кáдмій • *n* cadmium
кажáн • *n* bat
казáрма • *n* barrack
казáти • *v* say
казинó • *n* casino
кáзка • *n* fable
какао • *n* cacao

кал • *n* dung, excrement, feces
каліфо́рній • *n* californium
каламáр • *n* inkwell
календáр • *n* calendar
календáрний • *adj* calendric
калина • *n* viburnum
кали́тка • *n* scrotum
кáлій • *n* potassium
калóша • *n* galosh
калькуля́тор • *n* calculator
кáльцій • *n* calcium
калю́жа • *n* pool, puddle
камбала • *n* flounder
кáмера • *n* camera, cell
камінець • *n* stone
кáмінь • *n* stone
кампáнія • *n* campaign
кáмпус • *n* campus
канава • *n* ditch
канáл • *n* canal, channel
кáнцлер • *n* chancellor
каньйóн • *n* canyon
канюк • *n* buzzard
капелю́х • *n* hat
капітáл • *n* capital
капіталíзм • *n* capitalism
каплиця • *n* chapel
кáптур • *n* hood
капуста • *n* cabbage
капюшóн • *n* hood
кáра • *n* punishment
каракáтиця • *n* cuttlefish
карáльний • *adj* punitive
карамель • *n* caramel
каратé • *n* karate
карáти • *v* punish
карбóванець • *n* ruble
карбюрáтор • *n* carburetor
кардамóн • *n* cardamom
кáрий • *adj* brown
карикатýра • *n* caricature
кáрлик • *n* dwarf
карнавáл • *n* carnival
кáрта • *n* card, map
картéч • *n* grapeshot
карти́на • *n* picture
кáртка • *n* card
картóн • *n* cardboard
картóпля • *n* potato
кáска • *n* helmet
касувати • *v* abolish, abrogate, annul, reverse
кат • *n* executioner
катаклíзм • *n* cataclysm
каталізáтор • *n* catalyst
катастрóфа • *n* accident, crash, disaster

катóд • *n* cathode
кáчка • *n* duck
качкодзьóб • *n* platypus
кáша • *n* kasha
кáша • *n* gruel, porridge
кáшель • *n* cough
кáшляти • *v* cough
каштáн • *n* chestnut
каштáновий • *adj* brown
квадрат • *n* square
квазар • *n* quasar
кварк • *n* quark
кварта • *n* quart
варти́ра • *n* apartment
кварц • *n* quartz
квас • *n* kvass, pickle
квáсити • *v* pickle
квасóля • *n* bean
квитóк • *n* ticket
квíтка • *n* flower
квíткарство • *n* floriculture
квітколóже • *n* receptacle
квітконíжка • *n* pedicel
квíтникарство • *n* floriculture
кволий • *adj* languid
кекс • *n* cake
кéльнер • *n* waiter
кельнерка • *n* waitress
кенгурý • *n* kangaroo
кентáвр • *n* centaur
кéпський • *adj* bad
керáміка • *n* ceramic
керувати • *v* manage
кефáль • *n* mullet
кидáти • *v* throw
кили́м • *n* carpet
кинджáл • *n* dagger
кисень • *n* oxygen
ки́слий • *adj* sour
кислотá • *n* acid
кислотнíсть • *n* acidity
кисляк • *n* clabber
кит • *n* whale
кишéня • *n* pocket
кишéчник • *n* intestine
киши́ти • *v* swarm
ки́шка • *n* intestine
кíборг • *n* cyborg
кíготь • *n* talon
кíготь • *n* claw
кіл • *n* stake
кілогрáм • *n* kilogram
кíлька • *pron* some
кíлькість • *n* quantity
кільцé • *n* ring
кімнáта • *n* room

кімоно́ • *n* kimono
кіне́ць • *n* end
кіно́ • *n* cinema, movie
кіноплі́вка • *n* film
кінотеа́тр • *n* cinema
кінофі́льм • *n* movie
кінча́ти • *v* end, finish
кінь • *n* horse, knight
кіоск • *n* kiosk
кір • *n* measles
кі́стка • *n* bone
кі́стка • *n* die
кі́сточка • *n* ankle
кіт • *n* cat, tom
кі́шка • *n* cat
клавесин • *n* harpsichord
клавесині́ст • *n* harpsichordist
клавесині́стка • *n* harpsichordist
клавіату́ра • *n* keyboard
кларне́т • *n* clarinet
клас • *n* class, classroom, year
класифіка́ція • *n* classification
кла́сти • *v* put
клей • *n* glue
клен • *n* maple
кле́цька • *n* dumpling
кли́кати • *v* call
клин • *n* wedge
кли́чка • *n* nickname
клі́мат • *n* climate
кліматоло́гія • *n* climatology
клі́ніка • *n* clinic
клітина • *n* cell
клі́тка • *n* cage
клі́тор • *n* clitoris
клі́торний • *adj* clitoral
кліф • *n* cliff
клішня́ • *n* claw
кліщ • *n* mite, tick
клоп • *n* bedbug, bug
кло́ун • *n* clown
клуа́тр • *n* cloister
клуб • *n* club
ключ • *n* key
кля́тва • *n* oath
кмин • *n* caraway
кна́йпа • *n* bar, pub
кни́га • *n* book
книга́рня • *n* bookshop
кни́жка • *n* book
кно́пка • *n* button
княгиня • *n* duchess
князівство • *n* duchy
князь • *n* duke, prince
ко́бальт • *n* cobalt
коби́ла • *n* mare

ко́бра • *n* cobra
кова́дло • *n* anvil
кова́ль • *n* blacksmith, smith
ковбаса́ • *n* sausage
ковбо́й • *n* cowboy
ко́вдра • *n* blanket
ковза́н • *n* skate
ковта́ти • *v* swallow
ковче́г • *n* ark
ко́гут • *n* rooster
код • *n* code
ко́жний • *pron* everybody, everyone
коза́ • *n* booger, goat
козачо́к • *n* boy
козе́л • *n* asshole, goat
козеня́ • *n* kid
козиро́к • *n* awning, visor
кокарда • *n* cockade
ко́кон • *n* cocoon
коко́с • *n* coconut
ко́ла • *n* cola
колаборціоні́ст • *n* collaborator
колаборціоні́стка • *n* collaborator
колго́сп • *n* kolkhoz
коле́га • *n* colleague
коле́дж • *n* school
колективіза́ція • *n* collectivization
колесо • *n* wheel
коли • *conj* as
коли́ • *conj* if, when • *adv* when
коли́-небудь • *adv* sometime
коли́ска • *n* cradle
колиско́ва • *n* lullaby
коли́сь • *adv* sometime
колі́но • *n* knee
ко́лір • *n* color
колія́ • *n* railway
коло • *n* round, wheel
ко́ло • *n* circle
коло́да • *n* log
колодязь • *n* well
колоніза́ція • *n* colonization
коло́нія • *n* colony
ко́лос • *n* ear
ко́ма • *n* coma, comma
кома́нда • *n* command
кома́р • *n* mosquito
кома́ха • *n* insect
кома́шка • *n* insect
коме́дія • *n* comedy
коме́рція • *n* commerce
коме́та • *n* comet
ко́мір • *n* collar
коміре́ць • *n* collar
коміте́т • *n* committee
комп'ю́тер • *n* computer
компа́нія • *n* company

ко́мпас • *n* compass
компліме́нт • *n* compliment
компози́тор • *n* composer
компоне́нт • *n* component
компроміс • *n* compromise
комуні́зм • *n* communism
конве́нція • *n* convention
конве́рт • *n* envelope
конво́й • *n* convoy
ко́ндор • *n* condor
ко́ник • *n* horsy
ко́ник • *n* grasshopper
ко́ні • *n* horse
коно́плі • *n* hemp
коно́пля́ • *n* cannabis
консервато́рія • *n* school
конструюва́ти • *v* construct
ко́нсульство • *n* consulate
конте́йнер • *n* container
контине́нт • *n* continent
конто́ра • *n* office
контра́кт • *n* contract
контррозві́дка • *n* counterespionage
конфедера́ція • *n* confederation
конфлі́кт • *n* conflict
конце́рт • *n* concert
конья́к • *n* brandy, cognac
конюши́на • *n* clover
копа́ти • *v* dig
копи́то • *n* hoof
копі́йка • *n* kopek
ко́пра • *n* copra
кора́ • *n* bark
кора́бел • *n* shipbuilder
корабе́ль • *n* ship
корве́т • *n* corvette
кордо́н • *n* boundary
кордо́н • *n* border
кореспонде́нт • *n* journalist, reporter
коридо́р • *n* corridor
кори́сний • *adj* beneficial, useful
користува́ч • *n* user
кори́стувач • *n* user
кори́сть • *n* advantage
кори́то • *n* trough
кори́чневий • *n* brown • *adj* brown
корі́ння • *n* root
ко́рінь • *n* root
корми́ти • *v* feed
корніше́н • *n* gherkin
коро́бка • *n* box
коро́ва • *n* cattle, cow
короле́ва • *n* queen
короле́вич • *n* prince
королі́вна • *n* princess
королі́вство • *n* kingdom

коро́ль • *n* king
коромисло • *n* yoke
коро́на • *n* crown
ко́роп • *n* carp
коро́ткий • *adj* short
корпора́ція • *n* corporation
кору́пція • *n* corruption
корчма́ • *n* inn, pub
коса́ • *n* plait, scythe
коса́ • *n* spit
коса́р • *n* spoonbill
коса́рик • *n* harvestman
коси́ти • *v* scythe
коси́ти • *v* mow
коси́ця • *n* flag
космі́чний • *adj* cosmic
космона́вт • *n* astronaut
ко́смос • *n* cosmos
котрий • *pron* which
кофеї́н • *n* caffeine
коха́на • *n* girlfriend
коха́нець • *n* lover
коха́ний • *n* boyfriend
коха́нка • *n* lover
коха́ння • *n* love
кочерга́ • *n* poker
кошеня́ • *n* kitten
ко́шик • *n* basket
кошикі́вка • *n* basketball
кошт • *n* price
кошто́вний • *adj* precious
ко́штувати • *v* cost
кошу́ля • *n* shirt
краб • *n* crab
крава́тка • *n* necktie
краді́ж • *n* theft
краді́жка • *n* theft
краєви́д • *n* scenery
краї́на • *n* country
край • *n* end
кра́йній • *adj* extreme
крамни́ця • *n* shop
кран • *n* crane
кра́пка • *n* dot
кра́пля • *n* drop
краса́ • *n* beauty
краси́вий • *adj* beautiful
красноті́рка • *n* rudd
кра́сти • *v* steal
красу́ня • *n* belle
красу́ня • *n* beauty
креве́тка • *n* prawn, shrimp
кре́йда • *n* chalk
крем • *n* cream
кремато́рій • *n* crematorium
кре́мній • *n* silicon

кремо́вий • *adj* cream
кре́чет • *n* gyrfalcon
кривавий • *adj* gory
кривити • *v* twist
криголам • *n* icebreaker
крижень • *n* mallard
крижина • *n* floe
кри́за • *n* crisis
крилатка • *n* samara
крило́ • *n* wing
криптон • *n* krypton
критика • *n* criticism, stab
крихітний • *adj* tiny
кри́хта • *n* crumb
кри́ця • *n* steel
крича́ти • *v* shout
кри́шка • *n* cover, lid
кріль • *n* rabbit
крім • *conj* but • *prep* except
кріп • *n* dill
крі́сло • *n* armchair, chair
крісло-каталка • *n* wheelchair
кріт • *n* mole
кров • *n* blood
кровожерливий • *adj* bloodthirsty
кровозмішення • *n* incest
кровопролиття • *n* bloodshed
крок • *n* pace, step
крокоди́л • *n* crocodile
кролик • *n* rabbit
кропива́ • *n* nettle
круг • *n* circle, round
круглий • *adj* round
крук • *n* raven
кря́чок • *n* tern
ксенон • *n* xenon
ксенофобія • *n* xenophobia
ксероко́пія • *n* photocopy
ксьондз • *n* priest
куб • *n* cube
кубізм • *n* cubism
куди • *adv* whither
куди́ • *adv* where • *conj* where

кудись • *adv* somewhere
кузе́н • *n* cousin
кузи́на • *n* cousin
кукуріку • *interj* cock-a-doodle-doo
кула́к • *n* fist
кулон • *n* pendant
кульба́ба • *n* dandelion
кульга́вий • *adj* lame
культ • *n* cult
культу́ра • *n* culture
ку́ля • *n* ball, bullet
куми́с • *n* koumiss
куни́ця • *n* marten
купа • *n* crowd
ку́па • *n* heap
купа́льня • *n* bath
купання • *n* bathe
купа́ння • *n* bath
купати • *v* bathe
ку́пиль • *n* bath
купи́ти • *v* buy
купува́ти • *v* buy
ку́рва • *n* prostitute, slut, whore
кури́ти • *v* smoke
курі́ння • *n* smoking
курка • *n* chicken
ку́рка • *n* hen
курс • *n* year
курти́на • *n* curtain
курча • *n* chicken
кусати • *v* sting
куса́ти • *v* bite
кут • *n* angle
куфер • *n* trunk
куха́р • *n* cook
куха́рка • *n* cook
кухарський • *adj* culinary
ку́хня • *n* kitchen
кухова́рити • *v* cook
куховарський • *adj* culinary
ку́холь • *n* mug
кущ • *n* bush
кюрій • *n* curium

лава • *n* lava
ла́вка • *n* bench
ла́вочка • *n* bench
ла́зер • *n* laser
ла́зити • *v* climb
лазни́чка • *n* bath
ла́зня • *n* bath, bathhouse
лайм • *n* lime

ла́ймовий • *adj* lime
лайно́ • *n* shit
лакросс • *n* lacrosse
ламати • *v* fracture
ламатися • *v* fracture
ла́мпа • *n* lamp
ла́мпочка • *n* lamp
ландша́фт • *n* scenery

ланка • *n* company
лантан • *n* lanthanum
ланцет • *n* lancet
ланцюг • *n* chain
ланцюжок • *n* chain
ланч • *n* lunch
лапа • *n* paw
ласка • *n* weasel
ластівка • *n* swallow
лат • *n* lat
лата • *n* patch
латка • *n* patch
латунь • *n* brass
лебідь • *n* swan
лев • *n* lev, lion
левиця • *n* lioness
легенда • *n* myth
легенда • *n* legend
легеня • *n* lung
легке • *n* lung
легкий • *adj* easy
легкий • *adj* light, simple
легко • *adv* easily
ледар • *n* lazybones
ледарство • *n* sloth
ледачий • *adj* lazy
ледве • *adv* hardly
лежати • *v* lie
лезо • *n* knife
лей • *n* leu
лексема • *n* lexeme
лелека • *n* stork
леопард • *n* leopard
лес • *n* loess
лесбійка • *n* homosexual, lesbian
лесбійський • *adj* lesbian
лесбіянка • *n* homosexual, lesbian
лещата • *n* vise
лижа • *n* ski
лижва • *n* skate
лико • *n* bast
лимон • *n* lemon
лин • *n* tench
лис • *n* fox
лисий • *adj* bald
лисиця • *n* vixen
лисиця • *n* fox
лисичка • *n* chanterelle
лист • *n* leaf, letter
листвениця • *n* larch
листівка • *n* flyer
листівка • *n* leaflet, postcard
листоноша • *n* mailman
лити • *v* pour
литовище • *n* airport
лихвар • *n* pawnbroker
лихо • *n* distress, evil

лихо • *n* disaster
лихоманка • *n* fever
лицар • *n* knight
лицарство • *n* chivalry
лице • *n* face
личинка • *n* larva
лишайник • *n* lichen
лише • *adv* merely, only
лівий • *adj* left
ліворуч • *adv* left
ліврея • *n* livery
ліга • *n* league
лід • *n* ice
ліжко • *n* bed
лізин • *n* lysine
лізти • *v* climb
лік • *n* medicine
лікар • *n* veterinarian
лікар • *n* doctor
лікарня • *n* hospital
лікарство • *n* medicine
лікер • *n* liqueur
ліки • *n* medicine
лікоть • *n* elbow
лікування • *n* medicine
лікувати • *v* heal
лілея • *n* lily
лімузин • *n* limousine
лінивець • *n* sloth
лінивий • *adj* lazy
лінощі • *n* sloth
лінь • *n* sloth
ліпше • *adj* better
ліс • *n* forest
лісок • *n* grove
літак • *n* aircraft, plane
літак • *n* airplane
літера • *n* letter
література • *n* literature
літературний • *adj* literary
літій • *n* lithium
літо • *n* summer
літургія • *n* liturgy
ліфт • *n* lift
ліфчик • *n* bra
ліхтар • *n* flashlight, lamppost, lantern
ліхтарик • *n* flashlight
ліцензія • *n* license
лічити • *v* count
лоб • *n* forehead
ловити • *v* catch
лодь • *n* boat
ложка • *n* spoon
локомотив • *n* locomotive
локшина • *n* noodle
ломбард • *n* pawnshop

лопа́та • *n* shovel, spade
лосо́сь • *n* salmon
лось • *n* moose
лотере́я • *n* lottery
лоуренсій • *n* lawrencium
ло́ша • *n* colt
лоша́ • *n* foal
лоша́к • *n* hinny
луб • *n* bast
луг • *n* meadow
лук • *n* bow, onion
лу́ковиця • *n* onion
луна́ • *n* echo
лунь • *n* harrier
лупа́ • *n* dandruff
лускунчик • *n* nutcracker
лу́чник • *n* archer
льодови́к • *n* glacier
льос • *n* destiny, fate
льо́тчик • *n* pilot
льо́тчиця • *n* pilot
льох • *n* cellar

льоха • *n* sow
любя́зний • *adj* kind
любя́зність • *n* compliment
люби́ти • *v* like
любо́в • *n* love
лю́бощі • *n* sex
люд • *n* nationality
лю́ди • *n* human, man, people
люди́на • *n* human, man, person
лю́дство • *n* mankind
люк • *n* manhole
лю́лька • *n* cradle
лю́ля • *n* cradle
люстра́ція • *n* lustration
лютеці́й • *n* lutetium
лю́тня • *n* lute
лягти́ • *v* lie
ляка́ти • *v* scare
ля́лька • *n* baby, doll
ля́рва • *n* whore

мю́зикл • *n* musical
мʼяз • *n* muscle
мʼяки́й • *adj* soft
мʼя́ко • *adv* softly
мʼя́со • *n* meat
мʼя́та • *n* mint
мʼяч • *n* ball
мʼя́ти • *v* crease
ма́буть • *adv* perhaps
ма́впа • *n* ape, monkey
ма́впувати • *v* ape
мавпува́ти • *v* parrot
маг • *n* magician, warlock
магази́н • *n* magazine, shop
магістра́ль • *n* highway
ма́гія • *n* magic
ма́гма • *n* magma
ма́гній • *n* magnesium
магні́т • *n* magnet
мази́ло • *n* grease
мазь • *n* cream, grease, salve
майбу́тнє • *n* future
майбу́тній • *adj* future
майда́н • *n* plaza, square
ма́йже • *adv* almost, approximately, nearly
ма́йка • *n* singlet
майно́ • *n* property
майоне́з • *n* mayonnaise
майсте́рня • *n* workshop

мак • *n* poppy
макаро́ни • *n* macaroni
маківка • *n* vertex
ма́ківка • *n* crown
мале́нький • *adj* little, small
мали́й • *adj* little, small
мали́на • *n* raspberry
малокрі́вʼя • *n* anemia
мальва • *n* mallow
малюва́ти • *v* draw
малю́нок • *n* drawing
маля́рія • *n* malaria
мама • *n* ma, mummy
ма́ма • *n* mother, mum
ма́монт • *n* mammoth
ма́мут • *n* mammoth
ма́мця • *n* mother
ма́нго • *n* mango
ма́нґо • *n* mango
мангу́ст • *n* mongoose
манда́ • *n* pussy
мандари́н • *n* tangerine
мандраго́ра • *n* mandrake
мандрува́ти • *v* travel
манже́та • *n* cuff
манікю́р • *n* manicure
маніфеста́нт • *n* demonstrator
маніфеста́нтка • *n* demonstrator
манул • *n* manul
ма́па • *n* map

мáра • *n* ghost
марганець • *n* manganese
маргарин • *n* margarine
мáрево • *n* ghost, mirage
марихуáна • *n* marijuana
маркíз • *n* marquess
марля • *n* gauze
мармелáд • *n* jam
мармеляда • *n* marmalade
мармур • *n* marble
мартин • *n* gull
марш • *n* march
маса • *n* mass
масáж • *n* massage
мáска • *n* mask
маслúна • *n* olive
масло • *n* grease
мáсло • *n* butter
маслянка • *n* buttermilk
мастило • *n* grease
мастúло • *n* cream
масть • *n* cream, suit
мат • *n* checkmate • *interj* checkmate
математика • *n* mathematics
материк • *n* continent, mainland
материнка • *n* oregano
матеріáл • *n* material
мати • *v* have
мáти • *n* mother • *v* own
мáтінка • *n* mum
мáтір • *n* mother
мáтка • *n* womb
матрáс • *n* mattress
матрáц • *n* mattress
матрос • *n* sailor
матуся • *n* mother
матýся • *n* mum
матч • *n* match
мáфін • *n* muffin
мафія • *n* mafia
мацá • *n* matzo
мачта • *n* mast
мачула • *n* bast
мáчуха • *n* stepmother
машúна • *n* automobile, car, machine
машиніст • *n* engineer
маяк • *n* lighthouse
мéблі • *n* furniture
мегаліт • *n* megalith
мегалітúчний • *adj* megalithic
мед • *n* honey
медаль • *n* medal
медицúна • *n* medicine
медсестрá • *n* nurse
медýза • *n* jellyfish
межа • *n* boundary
мелодрама • *n* melodrama

мем • *n* meme
мемуáри • *n* memoir
менделéвій • *n* mendelevium
мене • *pron* me
мені • *pron* me
менструáція • *n* menstruation
меню • *n* menu
мер • *n* mayor
мерéжа • *n* network
мертвéць • *n* corpse
мéртвий • *adj* dead
мести • *v* sweep
метáл • *n* metal
металевий • *adj* metallic
металічний • *adj* metallic
металобрýхт • *n* scrap
металург • *n* metallurgist
метéлик • *n* butterfly
метеор • *n* meteor
метеорúт • *n* meteorite
метіонін • *n* methionine
мéтод • *n* method
метро • *n* metro, subway
метрополія • *n* metropolis
механізм • *n* mechanism
меч • *n* sword
мечéть • *n* mosque
мешканець • *n* resident
мéшкання • *n* habitation
мéшкати • *v* dwell, live, reside
ми • *pron* we
мигдáлик • *n* tonsil
мúло • *n* soap
мúля • *n* mile
минýле • *n* past
минýлий • *adj* last
мир • *n* peace
миротвóрець • *n* peacemaker
мис • *n* cape
мúска • *n* bowl, dish, plate
мислúвець • *n* hunter
мислити • *v* think
мистéцтво • *n* art
мити • *v* wash
мúтися • *v* wash
мишяк • *n* arsenic
мúша • *n* mouse
мúшка • *n* mouse
мід • *n* honey
мідь • *n* copper
між • *prep* among, between
міжнарóдний • *adj* international
мій • *pron* mine
мікрóб • *n* germ, microbe
мікрометр • *n* micrometer
мікроскоп • *n* microscope
мікрофóн • *n* microphone

мікрохви́ля • *n* microwave
мілина • *n* shallow
мілина́ • *n* beach
мілісекунда • *n* millisecond
міліціоне́р • *n* militiaman, policeman
міліція • *n* militia
міліція • *n* police
міліція́нт • *n* militiaman
мілкий • *adj* shallow
міль • *n* moth
мільйоне́р • *n* millionaire
мільйоне́рка • *n* millionaire
мі́на • *n* mine
мінаре́т • *n* minaret
міндобриво • *n* fertilizer
мінерало́гія • *n* mineralogy
мінет • *n* fellatio
міністерство • *n* ministry
міністр • *n* minister
міра́ж • *n* mirage
місіоне́р • *n* missionary
місіоне́рка • *n* missionary
місія • *n* mission
міст • *n* bridge
місткий • *adj* capacious
мі́сто • *n* city, town
мі́сце • *n* place
місцеполо́ження • *n* location, situation
мі́сяць • *n* month, moon
мітинг • *n* rally
мітла́ • *n* broom
мітоз • *n* mitosis
мітохондрія • *n* mitochondrion
міф • *n* myth
міфологія • *n* mythology
міхур • *n* bladder
міху́р • *n* bubble
мі́цний • *adj* powerful, strong
міць • *n* force, strength
мішень • *n* target
мішо́к • *n* bag, sack
млин • *n* mill
млине́ць • *n* pancake
млинці • *n* blini
множення • *n* multiplication
множина́ • *n* plural
мобіліза́ція • *n* mobilization
мобі́льний • *adj* movable
мова • *n* language
мо́ва • *n* language, speech
мовозна́вство • *n* linguistics
мовча́ння • *n* silence
моги́ла • *n* grave
могти́ • *v* can
могу́тній • *adj* powerful

мо́да • *n* fashion
моде́м • *n* modem
модри́на • *n* larch
моє • *pron* mine
мо́же • *adv* perhaps
можли́вість • *n* chance, opportunity, possibility
можли́во • *adv* perhaps
моза́їка • *n* mosaic
мозковий • *adj* cerebral
мо́зок • *n* brain
мокнути • *v* wet
мо́крий • *adj* wet
мокри́ця • *n* woodlouse
молібде́н • *n* molybdenum
моле́кула • *n* molecule
моли́тва • *n* prayer
моли́тися • *v* pray
молода́ • *n* bride
молоди́й • *adj* small, young
мо́лодіж • *n* youth
мо́лодість • *n* youth
молодший • *adj* junior, younger
мо́лодь • *n* youth
моло́зиво • *n* colostrum
мо́лот • *n* hammer
молоти • *v* grind
молото́к • *n* hammer
мона́рхія • *n* monarchy
мона́х • *n* monk
моне́та • *n* coin
мони́сто • *n* necklace
монотеї́зм • *n* monotheism
монуме́нт • *n* monument
мопед • *n* moped
морг • *n* morgue
мо́ре • *n* sea
морж • *n* walrus
мо́рква • *n* carrot
мороження • *adj* frozen
мороз • *n* frost
морок • *n* darkness
морфема • *n* morpheme
мости́ти • *v* flag
моте́ль • *n* motel
мотика • *n* hoe
мото́р • *n* engine, motor
мотоци́кл • *n* motorcycle
мох • *n* moss
мочити • *v* wet
мошо́нка • *n* scrotum
моя • *pron* mine
мрець • *n* corpse
мрі́я • *n* dream
муда́к • *n* asshole
мудрець • *n* sage
му́дрий • *adj* sage, wise

мудрість • *n* wisdom
муедзин • *n* muezzin
муж • *n* husband, man
мужність • *n* courage
музей • *n* museum
музика • *n* music
музикант • *n* musician
музичний • *adj* musical
мука • *n* flour
мука • *n* suffering
мулла • *n* mullah
мумія • *n* mummy
мур • *n* wall
мураха • *n* ant
мурахоїд • *n* anteater
мурашка • *n* ant

мурашник • *n* anthill
мурин • *n* black
муринка • *n* negress
муринка • *n* black
мусити • *v* force
мусити • *v* must
мускул • *n* muscle
мусон • *n* monsoon
муфлон • *n* mouflon
муфтій • *n* mufti
муха • *n* fly
муха • *n* fly
мухомор • *n* amanita
мушкетон • *n* blunderbuss
мушля • *n* seashell
муштарда • *n* mustard

нікель • *n* nickel
ніобій • *n* niobium
на • *prep* on
набережна • *n* quay
навік • *adv* forever
навіс • *n* awning
навмисний • *adj* deliberate, intentional
навмисно • *adv* deliberately
наводити • *v* adduce
навчати • *v* school
навчатися • *v* study
нагий • *adj* naked
наглий • *adj* sudden
наголос • *n* accent
нагота • *n* nudity
над • *prep* above
надійність • *n* quality, reliability
надіти • *v* wear
надія • *n* hope
надіятися • *v* hope
надмірний • *adj* extreme
надмор'я • *n* beach
наднова • *n* supernova
надягати • *v* wear
наживо • *adv* live
назавжди • *adv* forever
назад • *adv* back
назалізація • *n* nasalization
назва • *n* name
називатися • *v* hight
назнарошки • *adv* deliberately
назнарошне • *adv* deliberately
наїзник • *n* invader
найвищий • *adj* supreme

найманець • *n* mercenary
найманка • *n* mercenary
наймит • *n* mercenary
наймитка • *n* mercenary
найпростіш • *n* protist
наказ • *n* command
наказати • *v* bid
наказувати • *v* bid, punish
наклеп • *n* calumny
наклепницький • *adj* defamatory
нактоуз • *n* binnacle
наливати • *v* pour
налити • *v* pour
наліво • *adv* left
наложниця • *n* concubine
намагатися • *v* attempt, try
намалювати • *v* draw
намет • *n* tent
намисто • *n* necklace
наміритись • *v* intend
намотувати • *n* spool
напад • *n* attack
нападати • *v* attack
напалм • *n* napalm
напасти • *v* attack
напилок • *n* file
написати • *v* write
напиток • *n* beverage
напій • *n* beverage
наплювати • *v* spit
направо • *adv* right
напрям • *n* direction
напрямок • *n* direction
нарвал • *n* narwhal
нарди • *n* backgammon

наре́чена • n bride
нарисува́ти • v draw
нарі́ччя • n dialect
нарколепсія • n narcolepsy
наро́д • n nation, nationality, people
народження • n birth
наро́дність • n nationality
нароком • adv deliberately
наро́чито • adv deliberately
наро́шне • adv deliberately
нару́чники • n handcuffs
наряд • n detail
нас • pron us
насе́лення • n population
насіни́на • n seed
насі́ння • n seed, semen
насл́дник • n heir
насл́дниця • n heir
наслідування • n inheritance
насл́дувати • v parrot
насо́с • n pump
насті́льки • adv as
насторо́женість • n watchfulness
на́ступ • n offensive
натовп • n crowd, throng
на́товп • n swarm
на́трій • n sodium
нау́ка • n science
науко́вий • adj scientific
на́фта • n oil
нацизм • n fascism
націоналі́зм • n nationalism
націона́льність • n nationality
на́ція • n nation, nationality, people
наш • pron ours
наши́йник • n necklace
наща́дки • n offspring
наща́док • n descendant, offspring
наща́док • n scion
не • n no • adv not
небезпека • n distress
небезпе́ка • n danger, threat
небезпечний • adj harmful, injurious
небезпе́чний • adj dangerous
небеса́ • n heavens, paradise, sky
не́бо • n ether, palate, sky
невдаха • n loser
невимо́вний • adj ineffable
неви́нність • n chastity
невіѓластво • n ignorance
невіруючий • adj unbelieving
неві́стка • n daughter-in-law
невралгі́чний • adj neuralgic
невро́з • n neurosis
неврологічний • adj neurological
невто́мний • adj indefatigable

негайно • adv immediately
негі́дник • n worm
неглибокий • adj shallow
негр • n black
негритянка • n negress
негритя́нка • n black
не́ділка • n atom
недоко́наний • adj imperfective
недокрів́я • n anemia
недоста́тньо • adv insufficiently
недоста́ча • n lack
недосту́пний • adj unavailable
не́друг • n enemy
нежона́тий • adj unmarried
незаба́ром • adv soon
незабу́дка • n forget-me-not
неза́ймана • n maiden, virgin
неза́йманець • n virgin
неза́йманість • n virginity
незале́жність • n independence, nationality
незамі́жня • adj unmarried
неземний • adj unearthly
незнання́ • n ignorance
незру́чний • adj inconvenient, uncomfortable
нейлон • n nylon
неймові́рний • adj incredible
нейробіоло́гія • n neuroscience
нейтрон • n neutron
неквапливо • adv deliberately
некрома́нтія • n necromancy
нема́тода • n nematode
немовля́ • n baby
ненави́діти • v hate
нена́висть • n hatred
не́нька • n mum
неня • n mother
не́ня • n mum
необме́жений • adj absolute
необхі́дність • n need
неоди́м • n neodymium
нео́н • n neon
неосла́бний • adj indefatigable
непере́хідний • adj intransitive
непокі́рний • adj disobedient
непоко́ра • n rebellion
непоро́чність • n chastity
непра́вда • n lie
непра́вильний • adj wrong
неприє́днаний • adj nonaligned
непрони́кний • adj impenetrable
непту́ній • n neptunium
нерв • n nerve
несква́пно • adv deliberately
неслухня́ний • adj disobedient

несподіваний • *adj* sudden
несподівано • *adv* suddenly
неспокій • *n* anxiety
нести • *v* bear, carry
нетерпляче • *adv* impatiently
нетовариськість • *n* aloofness
неуцтво • *n* ignorance
нешкідливий • *adj* innocuous
нещастя • *n* misery
нещастя • *n* disaster, tragedy
неясний • *adj* unclear
нижче • *prep* below
низький • *adj* humble
низький • *adj* low, short
нині • *adv* nowadays
нині • *adv* now
нирка • *n* kidney
ниряти • *v* dive
нитка • *n* thread
нігілізм • *n* nihilism
ніготь • *n* fingernail, nail
ніде • *adv* nowhere
ніж • *n* knife • *prep* than
ніздря • *n* nostril
ніколи • *adv* never
нікуди • *adv* nowhere
нікчемність • *n* shabbiness
німий • *n* mute • *adj* mute
німота • *n* muteness
нірвана • *n* nirvana

ніс • *n* nose
ніч • *n* night
нічний • *adj* nocturnal
нічого • *pron* nothing
ніщо • *pron* nothing
ніщо • *pron* anything
нобелій • *n* nobelium
новела • *n* novel
новий • *adj* new
новини • *n* news
новосілля • *n* housewarming
нога • *n* foot, leg
ножиці • *n* scissors
ножівка • *n* handsaw
нокаут • *n* knockout
номенклатура • *n* nomenclature
номер • *n* number
нора • *n* burrow
норма • *n* norm
носити • *v* bear, carry, wear
носій • *n* carrier
носок • *n* sock
носоріг • *n* rhinoceros
нотаріус • *n* notary
ну • *interj* well
нудний • *adj* slow
нужда • *n* need
нянька • *n* nanny
няня • *n* nanny
няня • *n* nurse

о • *interj* o
об'єкт • *n* object
об'яття • *n* hug
обговорити • *v* discuss
обговорювати • *v* discuss
обдуманість • *n* forethought
оберега • *n* protection
обережно • *adv* carefully
оберемок • *n* armful
обичай • *n* custom
обід • *n* lunch
обід • *n* dinner
обіймання • *n* hug
обіймати • *v* hug
обійми • *n* hug
обійняти • *v* hug
область • *n* province
облачний • *adj* cloudy
обличчя • *n* face
обман • *n* deception
обманути • *v* deceive

обманювати • *v* deceive
обмежувальний • *adj* restrictive
обмілина • *n* beach
обнімати • *v* hug
обняти • *v* hug
обов'язковий • *adj* compulsory
обов'язок • *n* duty
оболонь • *n* sapwood
оборона • *n* protection
оборона • *n* defense
оборонити • *v* defend
обороняти • *v* defend
ображати • *v* insult
образ • *n* image
образ • *n* image
образа • *n* contumely, insult
образити • *v* insult
образливий • *adj* offensive
образний • *adj* transitive
обрізання • *n* circumcision
обруч • *n* hoop

обряд • *n* rite, ritual
обсерваторія • *n* observatory
обстановка • *n* situation
обшлаг • *n* cuff
овід • *n* botfly
овес • *n* oat
овоч • *n* vegetable
огірок • *n* cucumber
оголосити • *v* announce
оголошення • *n* advertisement
оголошувати • *v* announce
огорожа • *n* fence
одежа • *n* clothes, clothing, dress
одеколон • *n* cologne
одержувати • *v* get
один • *adv* alone
одинадцятий • *adj* eleventh
одиниця • *n* unit
однак • *adv* however • *conj* only
однина • *n* singular
одноманітний • *adj* same
однопалатний • *adj* unicameral
одружений • *adj* married
одруження • *n* marriage
одуд • *n* hoopoe
одяг • *n* clothes, clothing, dress
одягати • *v* dress
одягатися • *v* dress
ожина • *n* blackberry
ожиріння • *n* obesity
озеро • *n* lake
означати • *v* mean
означення • *n* definition
озон • *n* ozone
океан • *n* ocean
око • *n* eye
околиці • *n* neighborhood
окорок • *n* ham
окріп • *n* dill
округа • *n* neighborhood
окружність • *n* circle
окуляри • *n* spectacles
окунь • *n* bass, perch
окупант • *n* occupant, occupier
окупантка • *n* occupant, occupier
окупація • *n* occupation
окупувати • *v* occupy
олень • *n* deer
оленятко • *n* fawn
оливка • *n* olive
олівець • *n* pencil
олія • *n* oil
олово • *n* tin
омар • *n* lobster
омела • *n* mistletoe
ондатра • *n* muskrat

онкологія • *n* oncology
ономастика • *n* onomastics
онук • *n* grandson
онучка • *n* granddaughter
опалення • *n* heating
опера • *n* opera
оперета • *n* operetta
опис • *n* description
описати • *v* describe
описувати • *v* describe
опір • *n* resistance
оплакувати • *v* mourn
оповідь • *n* story
ополченець • *n* militiaman
опускатися • *v* sink
орангутан • *n* orangutan
оранжевий • *n* orange
оранжевий • *adj* orange
оранжерея • *n* greenhouse
орати • *v* plough
ораторія • *n* oratorio
оргазм • *n* orgasm
органела • *n* organelle
організація • *n* organization
організм • *n* organism
органічний • *adj* organic
органоїд • *n* organelle
орден • *n* order
орел • *n* eagle
оркестр • *n* orchestra
орфографія • *n* orthography
оса • *n* wasp
освіта • *n* education
осел • *n* donkey
оселедець • *n* herring
оселедець • *n* topknot
осетер • *n* sturgeon
осідати • *v* sink
осінній • *adj* autumn
осінь • *n* autumn
оскільки • *conj* as
оскільки • *conj* because
осмій • *n* osmium
особа • *n* person
особливо • *adv* chiefly
осот • *n* thistle
останній • *adj* last, recent
острів • *n* island
острог • *n* prison
осцилювати • *v* oscillate
отець • *n* father, priest
отримати • *v* receive
отримувати • *v* get, receive
отруєння • *n* poisoning
отруїти • *v* poison
отруйний • *adj* poisonous

отру́та • *n* poison
отру́ювати • *v* poison
о́фіс • *n* office
офіце́р • *n* bishop, officer
офіціа́нт • *n* waiter
офіціа́нтка • *n* waitress
офіціа́нтка • *n* waiter
охолодження • *n* cooling
охорона • *n* protection

охоро́на • *n* guard
охоро́нець • *n* guard, guardian
оцві́тина • *n* perianth
оцет • *n* vinegar
оцифро́вування • *n* digitization
очеви́дець • *n* eyewitness
очеви́дний • *adj* apparent, obvious
очі́кувати • *v* await

пія́вка • *n* leech
пія́ний • *adj* drunk
пія́ниця • *n* drinker
пія́та́ • *n* heel
пія́тидеся́тий • *adj* fiftieth
пія́тий • *adj* fifth
пія́тка • *n* heel
пія́тна́дцятий • *adj* fifteenth
пістри́й • *adj* variegated
паб • *n* pub
пави́ч • *n* peacock
паву́к • *n* spider
пагода • *n* pagoda
па́горб • *n* hill
паго́рок • *n* hill
падальник • *n* vulture
па́дати • *v* fall, sink
па́дуб • *n* holly
падчерка • *n* stepdaughter
пазл • *n* puzzle
паке́т • *n* packet
пакунок • *n* package
палади́й • *n* palladium
пала́тка • *n* tent
пала́ц • *n* palace
па́лець • *n* finger, toe
паливо • *n* fuel
пали́ти • *v* burn, smoke
палиця • *n* stick
палі́ння • *n* smoking
пало́мник • *n* pilgrim
палтус • *n* halibut
пальто́ • *n* coat
пам'я́та́ти • *v* remember
па́м'ятник • *n* monument
па́м'ять • *n* memory
пампу́шка • *n* doughnut
пан • *n* gentleman, mister, sir
панегірик • *n* eulogy
па́ні • *n* madam
панікувати • *v* panic
па́нна • *n* maiden, miss

пантофля • *n* slipper
панчо́ха • *n* stocking
папа • *n* pope
па́па • *n* dad
папа́йя • *n* papaya
паперо́вий • *adj* paper
папі́р • *n* paper
папіро́с • *n* cigarette
папіро́са • *n* cigarette
папороть • *n* fern
папу́га • *n* parrot
пар • *n* steam, vapor
пара • *n* pair
па́ра • *n* steam, vapor
пара́д • *n* parade
парадокс • *n* paradox
паралізувати • *v* paralyze
парасо́лька • *n* umbrella
парашу́т • *n* parachute
парк • *n* park
паркан • *n* fence
парла́мент • *n* parliament
паро́ль • *n* password
паропла́в • *n* steamboat, steamer, steamship
партиза́н • *n* guerrilla
партиза́нка • *n* guerrilla
партиза́нський • *adj* partisan
па́ртія • *n* party
паруб́о́к • *n* bachelor
па́рубок • *n* boyfriend, youth
па́рус • *n* sail
паруси́на • *n* duck
парфу́м • *n* perfume
пасажи́р • *n* passenger
пасажи́рка • *n* passenger
пасерб • *n* stepson
пасербиця • *n* stepdaughter
пасинок • *n* stepson
пасі́ка • *n* apiary
па́сквіль • *n* lampoon
па́спорт • *n* passport

пасти • *v* graze
пастир • *n* shepherd
пастух • *n* shepherd
патефон • *n* gramophone
патріот • *n* patriot
патріотка • *n* patriot
патронім • *n* patronymic
паха • *n* armpit
пахва • *n* armpit
пахлава • *n* baklava
пацифізм • *n* pacifism
паша • *n* pasha
певний • *pron* something
певно • *adv* probably
педаль • *n* pedal
педераст • *n* pederast
педик • *n* fag
педік • *n* fag
пейзаж • *n* scenery
пекар • *n* baker
пекарка • *n* baker
пекарня • *n* bakery
пекти • *v* bake
пелікан • *n* pelican
пельмень • *n* dumpling
пемза • *n* pumice
пеніс • *n* penis
пеніцилін • *n* penicillin
пень • *n* stump
пеня • *n* fine
пердіти • *v* fart
перевага • *n* advantage
перевести • *v* translate
переводити • *v* translate
передача • *n* program
передбачення • *n* forecast, foresight
передбачливий • *adj* forethoughtful
передбачливість • *n* forethought
передмістя • *n* suburb
передмова • *n* preface
передпередостанній • *adj* antepenultimate
переживати • *v* survive
пережити • *v* survive
переїзд • *n* crossing
переклад • *n* translation, version
перекладати • *v* translate
перекладач • *n* translator
перекладач • *n* interpreter
перекладачка • *n* interpreter
перекласти • *v* translate
перелюбство • *n* adultery
перемагати • *v* conquer
перемир'я • *n* armistice, truce
перемога • *n* victory
переможець • *n* winner

перенісся • *n* bridge
переодягатися • *v* change
переодягнутися • *v* change
переозброєння • *n* rearmament
перепел • *n* quail
переправа • *n* crossing
перепросити • *v* apologize
перепрошувати • *v* apologize
перепрошую • *interj* sorry
перерісший • *adj* overgrown
перерослий • *adj* overgrown
переселенець • *n* immigrant
переселенка • *n* immigrant
пересідати • *v* change
пересісти • *v* change
переслідувати • *v* persecute
перетин • *n* crossing
перетинка • *n* comma
перетравлювати • *v* digest
перехід • *n* crossing
перехідний • *adj* movable, transitive
перехресток • *n* crossroads, intersection
перехрестя • *n* crossing
перехрестя • *n* crossroads, intersection
перехрещення • *n* crossing
перехрещування • *n* crossing
перець • *n* pepper
перешийок • *n* isthmus
перешкоджати • *v* inhibit
перистальтика • *n* peristalsis
перла • *n* pearl
перламутр • *n* mother-of-pearl
перлина • *n* pearl
перо • *n* feather, pen, quill
перон • *n* platform
персик • *n* peach
персона • *n* person
перстень • *n* ring
перука • *n* wig
перукар • *n* hairdresser
перукарка • *n* hairdresser
перукарня • *n* barbershop
перун • *n* lightning
перчатка • *n* glove
перша • *adv* o'clock
перший • *n* first • *adj* first
пес • *n* dog
петля • *n* loop, noose
петрушка • *n* parsley
печаль • *n* sadness, sorrow
печать • *n* seal
печера • *n* cave
печінка • *n* liver

пивна́ • *n* bar, pub
пивни́ця • *n* bar, pub
пи́во • *n* beer
пивова́р • *n* brewer
пивова́рка • *n* brewer
пизда́ • *n* cunt, pussy
пил • *n* dust
пила́ • *n* saw
пилка • *n* file
пильність • *n* vigilance
пиляк • *n* anther
пир • *n* banquet
пиріг • *n* pie
пиро́жне • *n* cake
писа́ти • *v* write
писемність • *n* writing
письме́нник • *n* writer
письмо • *n* writing
пита́ння • *n* question
пита́ти • *v* ask
пи́ти • *v* drink
питни́й • *adj* drinkable, potable
південні́ше • *prep* below
пі́вдень • *n* south
пі́вдень • *n* noon
пі́вень • *n* rooster
пі́вники • *n* flag
пі́вніч • *n* north
пі́вніч • *n* midnight
пі́вні́чний • *adj* north, northerly, northern
піво́нія • *n* peony
піво́стрів • *n* peninsula
піґу́лка • *n* pill
під • *prep* below, beneath, under
піде́днувати • *v* connect
підборі́ддя • *n* chin
підва́л • *n* cellar
підвіко́ння • *n* windowsill
підготува́ти • *v* prepare
піджа́к • *n* coat
підземний • *adj* subterranean
підкова • *n* horseshoe
підко́рювати • *v* conquer, enthrall
підкорятися • *v* obey
пі́дкуп • *n* bribe
підли́ва • *n* sauce

підли́вка • *n* gravy
підлі́ток • *n* adolescent
підло́га • *n* floor
підмести • *v* sweep
пі́дмет • *n* subject
підме́тка • *n* sole
підмі́тати • *v* sweep
підмножина • *n* subset
піднебі́ння • *n* palate
піднос • *n* tray
пі́дор • *n* fag
підора́с • *n* asshole, fag
підо́шва • *n* sole
пі́дпис • *n* signature
підписа́ти • *v* sign
підписа́тися • *v* sign
підпи́сувати • *v* sign
підпи́суватися • *v* sign
підприє́мець • *n* businessman, entrepreneur
підприє́мниця • *n* entrepreneur
підприє́мство • *n* business, company, enterprise
підру́чник • *n* textbook
підсумок • *n* summary
підши́пник • *n* bearing
піжа́ма • *n* pajamas
пі́зній • *adj* late
пі́зно • *adv* late
пійма́ти • *v* catch
пік • *n* summit
пікні́к • *n* picnic
пі́ксель • *n* pixel
піло́т • *n* pilot
пі́на • *n* foam, salve
пінгві́н • *n* penguin
піоне́р • *n* pioneer
піоне́рка • *n* pioneer
піп • *n* priest
піра́нья • *n* piranha
піра́т • *n* pirate
піратство • *n* piracy
пірникоза • *n* grebe
піроте́хніка • *n* pyrotechnics
пірс • *n* pier
пі́руза • *n* turquoise
пірузовий • *n* turquoise

пісня • *n* song
пісок • *n* sand
пістолет • *n* pistol
пістолет • *n* gun
піська • *n* cunt, pussy
пісюн • *n* prick
пісюн • *n* dick
піт • *n* sweat
піти • *v* go
пітон • *n* python
піхва • *n* vagina
піхта • *n* fir
піца • *n* pizza
піч • *n* fire, oven, stove
пічка • *n* oven, stove
піщаний • *adj* sandy
плавання • *n* swimming
плавати • *v* swim
плазма • *n* plasma
плазун • *n* reptile
плакати • *v* weep
плакати • *v* cry
планета • *n* planet
планета • *n* planet
планувати • *v* intend
пласт • *n* reconnoiter, scouting
пластинка • *n* disk
пластування • *n* reconnoiter, scouting
пластувати • *v* reconnoiter
платина • *n* platinum
платити • *v* pay
плаття • *n* dress
платформа • *n* platform
плащ • *n* raincoat
плем'я • *n* nationality, tribe
племінник • *n* nephew
племінниця • *n* niece
пленарний • *adj* plenary
плести • *v* weave
плече • *n* shoulder
пліска • *n* wagtail
плисти • *v* swim
плита • *n* flag, stove
плитка • *n* stove
плитняк • *n* flag
плівка • *n* film
плід • *n* fruit, offspring
пліснь • *n* mildew, mold
пліснява • *n* mildew, mold
пліт • *n* raft, wattle
плоский • *adj* flat
площа • *n* plaza, square
плуг • *n* plough
плутоній • *n* plutonium
плювати • *v* spit
плювок • *n* spit

плюндрувати • *v* plunder
плюнути • *v* spit
плюш • *n* plush
пляж • *n* beach
пляжа • *n* beach
пляшка • *n* bottle
пневмонія • *n* pneumonia
побажати • *v* wish
побережжя • *n* coast
побити • *v* beat
повезти • *v* carry
поверхневий • *adj* shallow
поверхня • *n* surface
повести • *v* lead
повечеряти • *v* dine
повзати • *v* crawl
повзик • *n* nuthatch
повзти • *v* crawl
повидло • *n* marmalade
повинен • *v* have
повиний • *v* must
повиснути • *v* flag
повід • *n* rein
повідомити • *v* announce
повідомити • *v* inform
повідомлення • *n* message
повідомляти • *v* announce, inform
повідь • *n* inundation
повіка • *n* eyelid
повільний • *adj* slow
повільно • *adv* deliberately, slowly
повінь • *n* flood, inundation
повір'я • *n* myth
повісити • *v* hang
повість • *n* novel
повітря • *n* air
повітря-земля • *adj* air-to-surface
повітря-повітря • *adj* air-to-air
повія • *n* prostitute, whore
повний • *adj* whole
повний • *adj* complete, entire, full, utter
поводити • *v* lead
поводитись • *v* act
поводитися • *v* behave
повозити • *v* carry
поволі • *adv* deliberately
повстанець • *n* rebel
повстанець • *n* insurgent
повстання • *n* rebellion
повстання • *n* insurrection, uprising
повсюди • *adv* everywhere
повторювати • *v* repeat, revise
поганий • *adj* bad
поганяти • *v* chase
поглинати • *v* absorb

поглинути • *v* absorb
погнати • *v* chase
погода • *n* weather
погоджуватися • *v* agree
погодитися • *v* agree
погреб • *n* funeral
погріб • *n* cellar
погроза • *n* threat
погром • *n* pogrom
подарувати • *v* give
подарунок • *n* gift
податок • *n* tax
подзвонити • *v* telephone
подзвонити • *v* call, phone, ring
подивитися • *v* look
подібний • *adj* akin
подібність • *n* similarity
подія • *n* event
подобатися • *v* like
подорож • *n* journey, travel
подорожувати • *v* journey, travel
подруга • *n* friend, girlfriend
подушка • *n* cushion
подушка • *n* pillow
подякувати • *v* thank
поезія • *n* poetry
поема • *n* poem
поет • *n* poet
поетеса • *n* poetess
поєдинок • *n* duel
пожежа • *n* conflagration, fire
пожинати • *v* reap
поза • *prep* behind
позаблоковий • *adj* nonaligned
позвати • *v* call
поздоровити • *v* congratulate
поздоровляти • *v* congratulate
позитрон • *n* positron
позичати • *v* borrow, lend

позичити • *v* borrow, lend
позіхати • *v* yawn
позіхнути • *v* yawn
познайомити • *v* acquaint
поїзд • *n* train
поїздка • *n* travel
показати • *v* point, show
показувати • *v* display, point, show
покарання • *n* punishment
покарати • *v* punish
поки • *conj* as
покидати • *v* abandon
покинути • *v* abandon
покинутий • *adj* abandoned
покій • *n* room
покірний • *adj* submissive
покірний • *adj* obedient
покірність • *n* obedience
покликати • *v* call
покоління • *n* generation
покора • *n* obedience
покража • *n* theft
покривало • *n* blanket
покривати • *v* cover
покрити • *v* cover
полазити • *v* climb
поле • *n* field
полегшувати • *v* soothe
полекс • *n* thumb
полеміка • *n* polemic
полин • *n* mugwort
полин • *n* wormwood
полиця • *n* shelf
поліглот • *n* polyglot
поліетилен • *n* polyethylene
полізти • *v* climb
політ • *n* flight
політбюро • *n* politburo

Політбюро • *n* politburo

політеїзм • *n* polytheism
політик • *n* politician
політика • *n* politics
поліц14 • *n* police
поліцейський • *n* policeman
поліціянт • *n* policeman

полова • *n* chaff
половина • *n* half
пологи • *n* birth
пологий • *adj* flat
положення • *n* location, situation
полоній • *n* polonium
полонений • *n* captive

полтергейст • *n* poltergeist
по́лудень • *n* noon
по́лумя́ • *n* flame
полуни́ця • *n* strawberry
полуни́чний • *adj* strawberry
полюва́ння • *n* hunt
полюва́ти • *v* hunt
поляна • *n* glade
поля́на • *n* meadow
помага́ти • *v* help
пома́да • *n* cream
помара́нчевий • *adj* orange
помело • *n* pomelo
поме́рти • *v* die
помешкання • *n* dwelling
поме́шкання • *n* habitation
помили́тися • *v* err
поми́лка • *n* mistake
помиля́тися • *v* err
помідо́р • *n* tomato
помогти́ • *v* help
помоли́тися • *v* pray
по́мпа • *n* pump
по́мста • *n* revenge
понево́лювати • *v* enslave, enthrall
понести́ • *v* carry
пони́кнути • *v* flag
по́ні • *n* pony
поноси́ти • *v* carry
по́нчик • *n* doughnut
поняття • *n* notion
поп • *n* pope
по́па • *n* butt
попелиця • *n* aphid
попере́дження • *n* warning
попередити • *v* warn
по́піл • *n* ash
попільни́чка • *n* ashtray
попко́рн • *n* popcorn
попла́вати • *v* swim
поплисти́ • *v* swim
попроси́ти • *v* ask
пора́да • *n* advice
пора́дити • *v* advise
пора́зка • *n* defeat
порина́ти • *v* duck
порі́внювати • *v* compare
порі́вняння • *n* comparison
порівня́ти • *v* compare
поріг • *n* threshold
порнографі́чний • *adj* pornographic
порнографі́я • *n* pornography
порожні́й • *adj* empty
поро́м • *n* ferry
порослий • *adj* overgrown
порося́ • *n* piglet

порося́тко • *n* piglet
по́рох • *n* gunpowder
порошо́к • *n* powder
порт • *n* port
портре́т • *n* portrait
портфе́ль • *n* briefcase
портьє́ра • *n* curtain
порцеля́на • *n* porcelain
поря́док • *n* order
порятунок • *n* rescue
поряту́нок • *n* salvation
поса́да • *n* situation
поса́дка • *n* landing
посила́ти • *v* send
посла́ння • *n* message
посла́ти • *v* send
послу́хати • *v* listen
послу́шність • *n* obedience
посміха́тися • *v* smile
посміхну́тися • *v* smile
посмі́шка • *n* smile
посо́л • *n* ambassador
посо́льство • *n* embassy
посприя́ти • *v* assist
пості́льга • *n* kestrel
по́стіль • *n* bed
постмодернізм • *n* postmodernism
по́стріл • *n* shot
постскриптум • *n* postscript
потво́рний • *adj* ugly
потерпі́лий • *n* victim
поти́лиця • *n* nape
потік • *n* stream
потім • *adv* then
поті́ти • *v* sweat
потіха • *n* fun
потомство • *n* offspring
потоп • *n* inundation
пото́п • *n* flood
потре́ба • *n* need
потупа́ти • *v* sink
потяг • *n* zest
по́тяг • *n* attraction
потяга́ти • *v* pull
потягну́ти • *v* pull
потягти́ • *v* pull
похвала́ • *n* compliment
похід • *n* hike
похітливий • *adj* salacious
похіть • *n* lust
похмі́лля • *n* hangover
похмурий • *adj* gloomy
по́хорони • *n* funeral
поцілува́ти • *v* kiss
поцілу́нок • *n* kiss
почати • *v* start

почати • *v* begin, commence
початися • *v* start
початися • *v* begin, commence
початок • *n* start
початок • *n* beginning
почерк • *n* writing
починати • *v* start
починати • *v* begin, commence
починатися • *v* start
починатися • *v* begin, commence
почистити • *v* clean
почувати • *v* feel
почути • *v* feel
почуття • *n* emotion, feeling
пошкодження • *n* injury
поштар • *n* mailman
пошук • *n* search
пояс • *n* belt
пояснити • *v* explain
пріч • *adv* away
правда • *n* truth
правдоподібний • *adj* probable
правий • *adj* right
правило • *n* rule
правильний • *adj* correct, right
правитель • *n* ruler
правителька • *n* ruler
правопис • *n* orthography, spelling
празеодим • *n* praseodymium
пральня • *n* laundry
праля • *n* washer
прання • *n* laundry
прапор • *n* banner, flag
праска • *n* iron
прасувати • *v* iron
прати • *v* wash
працівник • *n* worker
працівниця • *n* worker
працювати • *v* work
праця • *n* job, work
предикат • *n* predicate
предмет • *n* object
предок • *n* ancestor
представляти • *v* adduce
презерватив • *n* condom
президент • *n* president
прекрасний • *adj* great
прелат • *n* prelate
препуцій • *n* prepuce
префікс • *n* prefix
при • *prep* at
приблизно • *adv* approximately
приборкувати • *v* harness
прибуття • *n* arrival
привабливість • *n* allure
привезти • *v* bring
привести • *v* bring

привид • *n* ghost
привіт • *interj* hello, hi
приводити • *v* bring
привозити • *v* bring
приголосна • *n* consonant
приголосний • *n* consonant
пригород • *n* suburb
приготувати • *v* prepare
придатність • *n* fitness
приєднання • *n* accession, annexation
приєднати • *v* annex
приєднувати • *v* annex
приземлення • *n* landing, touchdown
приземлитися • *v* land
приземлятися • *v* land
приїжджати • *v* arrive, come
приїзд • *n* arrival
приїздити • *v* arrive
приїхати • *v* arrive, come
приймати • *v* accept
прийменник • *n* preposition
прийняти • *v* accept
прийом • *n* method
прийти • *v* arrive, come
приклад • *n* example
прикметник • *adj* adjectival • *n* adjective
прикривати • *v* cover
прикрити • *v* cover
прикриття • *n* protection
прилив • *n* tide
приліт • *n* arrival
примара • *n* ghost
примус • *n* coercion
принести • *v* bring
принижувати • *v* humiliate
принизити • *v* humiliate
приносити • *v* bring
принтер • *n* printer
принц • *n* prince
принцеса • *n* princess
приправа • *n* seasoning
приправа • *n* condiment
природа • *n* nature
присідання • *n* squat
прискорення • *n* acceleration
прискорення • *n* acceleration
прискорити • *v* accelerate
прискорювати • *v* accelerate
прискорюватися • *v* accelerate
прислівник • *n* adverb
присмерк • *n* twilight
пристань • *n* pier, wharf
пристрій • *n* device
присудок • *n* predicate
присяга • *n* oath

притулок • *n* refuge
притýлок • *n* asylum
прихíд • *n* arrival
прихóдити • *v* arrive, come
причиняти • *v* afflict
прищ • *n* pimple
приятель • *n* boyfriend
приятель • *n* friend
приятелька • *n* friend, girlfriend
прíзвисько • *n* nickname
прíзвище • *n* surname
пробáч • *interj* sorry
пробачáти • *v* forgive
пробáчити • *v* forgive
пробáчте • *interj* sorry
прóбувати • *v* attempt, try
провестí • *v* lead
прóвід • *n* wire
провíнція • *n* country, province
провісницький • *adj* ominous
проводúти • *v* guide
провóдити • *v* lead
провокатор • *n* provocateur
провýлок • *n* alley, lane
прогнóз • *n* forecast
проголосувáти • *v* vote
програвáти • *v* lose
програвáч • *n* gramophone
програма • *n* syllabus
прогрáма • *n* program
прогрáти • *v* lose
прогрес • *n* progress
прогулянка • *n* walk
продавáти • *v* sell
продавець • *n* salesperson
продáти • *v* sell
продовжити • *v* continue
продовжувати • *v* continue
продуманість • *n* forethought
проект • *n* project
проживáння • *n* habitation
проживáти • *v* dwell, live, reside
прозвáти • *v* nickname
прозивáти • *v* nickname
пройдúсвіт • *n* charlatan
проквóлисто • *adv* deliberately
прокладáти • *v* flag
проклятий • *pron* something
пролúв • *n* channel, strait
промежина • *n* perineum
прометій • *n* promethium
промислóвість • *n* industry
промінь • *n* beam, ray
промóва • *n* speech
промóвець • *n* orator
проникливість • *n* perspicacity

пропагáнда • *n* propaganda
пропáн • *n* propane
пропозиція • *n* suggestion
пророк • *n* prophet
пророчий • *adj* ominous
пророчиця • *n* prophet, prophetess
просипáтися • *v* awake
просúти • *v* ask
прóсо • *n* millet
прóстий • *adj* simple
простúти • *v* forgive
проститýтка • *n* prostitute
проституція • *n* prostitution
прóсто • *adv* merely
просторий • *adj* capacious, roomy
простýда • *n* cold
протактúній • *n* protactinium
протé • *adv* however • *conj* only
протекціонізм • *n* protection
протест • *n* protest
прóти • *prep* against
протúвник • *n* enemy
протилéжний • *adj* opposite
протитáнковий • *adj* antitank
протóка • *n* channel, strait
прóтягом • *prep* during
профéсія • *n* profession
профéсор • *n* professor
професура • *n* faculty
прохолóдний • *adj* chilly, cool
процéнт • *n* interest
процéсор • *n* processor
прочáнин • *n* pilgrim
прочитáти • *v* read
прощáти • *v* forgive
прутень • *n* prick
пряжа • *n* yarn
пряжа • *n* wool
прямúй • *adj* right
прямокутник • *n* rectangle
прясти • *v* spin
психоз • *n* alienation
психолóгія • *n* psychology
псувати • *v* spoil
птах • *n* bird
пташеня • *n* nestling
пташка • *n* birdie
птúця • *n* bird
публікувáти • *v* publish
пýтоловок • *n* tadpole
пудель • *n* poodle
пузúр • *n* bubble
пулóвер • *n* sweater
пульсáр • *n* pulsar
пунктуáція • *n* punctuation
пуп • *n* navel
пупóк • *n* navel

пу́рпурний • *adj* magenta
пусте́ля • *n* desert
пусти́й • *adj* empty
пусти́ня • *n* desert

пшени́ця • *n* wheat
пшоно́ • *n* millet

раб • *n* slave
раби́н • *n* rabbi
раби́ня • *n* slave
ра́бі • *n* rabbi
рави́н • *n* rabbi
ра́влик • *n* snail
ра́да • *n* advice, soviet
раджа • *n* rajah
ра́дити • *v* advise
радіа́тор • *n* radiator
ра́діо • *n* radio
радіоакти́вний • *adj* radioactive
ра́дість • *n* joy
радо́н • *n* radon
раз • *adv* once • *n* time
ра́зом • *adv* together
рай • *n* paradise
ра́йдуга • *n* rainbow
рак • *n* cancer, crayfish
ра́ка • *n* shrine
раке́та • *n* missile
ра́ковина • *n* seashell
ракоподі́бні • *n* crustacean
ра́на • *n* injury, wound
ра́нець • *n* backpack
раніше • *adv* already
ра́нній • *adj* early
ра́но • *adv* early
ра́нок • *n* morning
рантье́ • *n* rentier
рапто́вий • *adj* abrupt, sudden
раптово • *adv* suddenly
раси́зм • *n* racism
рахівни́к • *n* accountant
рахівниця • *n* abacus
рахівни́ця • *n* accountant
рахува́ти • *v* count
раху́нок • *n* account, bill, check
рва́ти • *v* vomit
реакція • *n* reaction
ре́бе • *n* rabbi
ребро́ • *n* rib
ребус • *n* rebus
реві́нь • *n* rhubarb
ревнивий • *adj* jealous
револю́ція • *n* revolution
регіт • *n* guffaw
ре́ґіт • *n* laughter

реготати • *v* guffaw
редис • *n* radish
редиска • *n* radish
режисер • *n* director
резерфо́рдій • *n* rutherfordium
результа́т • *n* result
рейс • *n* flight
реквізит • *n* property
рекла́ма • *n* advertisement
рекогнозцировка • *n* reconnoiter
рекогносцировка • *n* scouting
рекогносцирувати • *v* reconnoiter
релі́гія • *n* religion
ремесло́ • *n* handicraft
ремі́нь • *n* belt
ре́ній • *n* rhenium
репертуа́р • *n* repertoire
репортер • *n* journalist, reporter
репти́лія • *n* reptile
репута́ція • *n* name
респу́бліка • *n* republic
ресторан • *n* restaurant
рети́на • *n* retina
рето́рика • *n* rhetoric
реторта • *n* retort
референдум • *n* referendum
рефері • *n* referee
рефері́ • *n* judge
реце́пт • *n* recipe
реце́пт • *n* prescription
ре́чення • *n* sentence
решето • *n* sieve
ре́шта • *n* rest
ри́ба • *n* fish
риба-мі́сяць • *n* sunfish
риба́к • *n* fisherman
риба́лка • *n* fisherman, fishing
рибка • *n* fishy
рига́ти • *v* belch, burp, vomit
риж • *n* rice
ри́кша • *n* rickshaw
ри́нок • *n* bazaar, market
рис • *n* rice
рисува́ти • *v* draw
рисунок • *n* drawing
рись • *n* lynx
ри́ти • *v* dig
ритм • *n* rhythm

ритуал • *n* rite, ritual
риф • *n* reef
ри́цар • *n* knight
риштування • *n* scaffold
рів • *n* ditch
рі́вний • *adj* flat
рівнина • *n* plain
рівновага • *n* equilibrium
рівнова́га • *n* balance
рівня́ння • *n* equation
ріг • *n* antler, horn
рід • *n* gender, tribe, type
рі́дкий • *adj* rare
рі́дкість • *n* curiosity
рі́дко • *adv* seldom
рі́жок • *n* shoehorn
рі́зати • *v* cut
рі́зний • *adj* different
рі́зниця • *n* difference
різнорі́дність • *n* heterogeneity
рій • *n* swarm
рік • *n* year
ріка́ • *n* river
рі́па • *n* turnip
рі́пка • *n* turnip
річ • *n* file, thing
рі́чка • *n* stream
рі́чка • *n* river
річни́ця • *n* anniversary
роби́ти • *v* work
роби́ти • *v* do, make
робі́тник • *n* worker
робі́тниця • *n* worker
робо́та • *n* job, work
рога́тий • *adj* horned
ро́дій • *n* rhodium
роджє́нство • *n* sibling
роди • *n* delivery, parturition
ро́ди • *n* childbirth
роди́мка • *n* birthmark, mole
роди́на • *n* family
роди́нний • *adj* familial
роди́тель • *n* parent
родови́й • *n* genitive
родовід • *n* pedigree
роже́вий • *n* pink
роже́вий • *adj* pink, rose
роже́н • *n* skewer, spit
розє́днання • *n* detachment
ро́за • *n* rose
розарій • *n* rosary
розбі́йник • *n* bandit
розбі́рливий • *adj* legible
розвага • *n* fun
розвива́тися • *v* develop
розви́нутися • *v* develop
розві́дка • *n* reconnoiter, scouting
розві́дка • *n* intelligence
розві́дувати • *v* reconnoiter
розвіювати • *v* dispel
ро́зділ • *n* chapter
роздорі́жжя • *n* crossing
розкла́д • *n* timetable
ро́зклад • *n* schedule, timetable
розлу́чення • *n* estrangement
розлютовувати • *v* enrage
ро́змір • *n* size
розмова • *n* discussion
розмо́ва • *n* chat, conversation, dialogue
розмо́вити • *v* converse
розмовляти • *v* talk
розмовля́ти • *v* converse, speak
розп'я́ття • *n* cross
розповіда́ти • *v* reply
розпові́сти • *v* reply
розрив • *n* estrangement
розсіювати • *v* dispel
розташува́ння • *n* location, situation
ро́зум • *n* mind
розумі́ти • *v* understand
розу́мний • *adj* clever, smart
розумовий • *n* erudition
роль • *n* role
ром • *n* rum
рома́н • *n* novel
ромб • *n* rhombus
ропу́ха • *n* toad
роса́ • *n* dew
росли́на • *n* plant
росома́ха • *n* wolverine
рости́ • *v* grow
рот • *n* mouth
ротор • *n* rotor
ртуть • *n* mercury
руба́ти • *v* cut
рубє́ць • *n* scar, tripe
рубі́дій • *n* rubidium
рубі́н • *n* ruby
рубль • *n* ruble
руда • *n* ore
рудни́к • *n* mine
руйнівний • *adj* consumptive
рука • *n* hand
рука́ • *n* arm
рука́в • *n* sleeve
рукави́ця • *n* glove
руно́ • *n* fleece
рупа́ • *n* pickle
руте́ній • *n* ruthenium
рух • *n* traffic

рухли́вий • *adj* movable
рухо́мий • *adj* movable
ру́чка • *n* pen
рушни́к • *n* towel
рушни́ця • *n* shotgun
рушни́ця • *n* rifle

рюкза́к • *n* backpack
ря́са • *n* cassock, habit
рятува́ти • *v* rescue
рятува́ти • *v* save
рятуйте • *interj* help

сагайда́к • *n* quiver
сад • *n* garden, orchard
сайга́к • *n* saiga
саке́ • *n* sake
салама́ндра • *n* salamander
сала́т • *n* lettuce, salad
сала́т-лату́к • *n* lettuce
сале́ра • *n* celery
сало • *n* grease, lard, tallow
салямі • *n* salami
сам • *adv* alone
сама́рій • *n* samarium
сами́ця • *n* female
са́міт • *n* summit
са́мка • *n* female
самова́р • *n* samovar
самого́н • *n* moonshine
самогу́бство • *n* suicide
самообслу́га • *n* self-service
самообслуго́вування • *n* self-service
самості́йність • *n* nationality
самоцві́т • *n* gem
саму́м • *n* simoom
самура́й • *n* samurai
санато́рій • *n* sanatorium
са́ни • *n* sledge
са́нки • *n* sledge
са́нкція • *n* sanction
сап • *n* glanders
сапса́н • *n* kestrel
сарана́ • *n* locust
сарга́н • *n* needlefish
сарди́нка • *n* sardine
сарка́зм • *n* sarcasm
саркофа́г • *n* sarcophagus
са́рна • *n* chamois
сати́ра • *n* satire
са́уна • *n* sauna
саші́мі • *n* sashimi
сва́ритися • *v* quarrel
сва́рка • *n* quarrel
сва́стика • *n* swastika
све́кор • *n* father-in-law
свекру́ха • *n* mother-in-law
светр • *n* sweater
свине́ць • *n* lead

свини́на • *n* pork
свиня́ • *n* hog, sow
свиня́ • *n* pig
свист • *n* whistle
свисті́ти • *v* whistle
свисто́ • *n* whistle
свисто́к • *n* whistle
сві́домо • *adv* deliberately
сві́жий • *adj* fresh
свій • *adj* own
світ • *n* kingdom, world
світа́нок • *n* dawn
світи́ти • *v* shine
сві́тлий • *adj* bright, light
світло́ • *n* light
світля́к • *n* firefly
світови́й • *adj* worldwide
сві́чка • *n* candle
свобо́да • *n* freedom
сволота́ • *n* asshole
свята • *n* saint
святи́й • *adj* sacred • *n* saint
святи́й • *adj* holy
святи́ня • *n* shrine
свя́то • *n* holiday
свяще́ник • *n* priest
свяще́нний • *adj* sacred
свяще́нний • *adj* holy
свяще́нник • *n* priest
себе́ • *pron* myself
сейсмоло́гія • *n* seismology
сейф • *n* safe
секре́т • *n* secret
секс • *n* sex
сексизм • *n* sexism
се́кта • *n* sect
се́кта • *n* cult
секу́нда • *n* second
селезі́нка • *n* spleen
селе́н • *n* selenium
селе́ра • *n* celeriac, celery
село • *n* village
село́ • *n* country
селяни́н • *n* farmer
селя́нин • *n* peasant
селя́нка • *n* peasant

селянство • *n* peasantry
сенат • *n* senate
сепаратист • *n* separatist
сепаратистка • *n* separatist
сепаратистський • *adj* separatist
сервант • *n* cupboard
серветка • *n* napkin, tissue
сервітут • *n* easement
серга • *n* earring
сердечний • *adj* kind
сердитий • *adj* angry
серед • *prep* among
середина • *n* center
середній • *adj* neuter
серёжка • *n* earring
серйозний • *adj* serious
серйозно • *adv* seriously
серна • *n* chamois
серп • *n* sickle
серпанок • *n* mist
серце • *n* heart
серцевидка • *n* cockle
сестра • *n* nurse, sister
сецесія • *n* secession
сеча • *n* urine
сечовід • *n* ureter
сибірка • *n* anthrax
сигарета • *n* cigarette
сидіти • *v* sit
сидня • *n* buttock
сила • *n* strength
сильний • *adj* strong
символ • *n* symbol
симетрія • *n* symmetry
симонія • *n* simony
симфонія • *n* symphony
син • *n* son

синагога • *n* synagogue
синиця • *n* chickadee
синій • *n* blue • *adj* blue
синонім • *n* synonym
синяк • *n* bruise
сир • *n* cheese, quark
сирена • *n* horn
сироватка • *n* whey
сироп • *n* cordial, syrup
сирота • *n* orphan
система • *n* system
ситий • *adj* full
сито • *n* sieve
ситуація • *n* situation
сич • *n* owl
сідло • *n* saddle
сідниця • *n* butt, buttock
сік • *n* juice, sap
сікти • *v* mow
сіль • *n* salt
сім'я • *n* family
сім'я • *n* seed, semen
сім'я • *n* seed
сім'явиверження • *n* ejaculation
сімейний • *adj* familial
сінник • *n* hayloft
сіно • *n* hay
сіновал • *n* hayloft
сірий • *adj* gray
сірка • *n* sulfur
сірник • *n* match, matchstick
сісти • *v* sit
сітківка • *n* retina
сіть • *n* network

Січ • *n* sich

січка • *n* chaff
сіяти • *v* sow
скаженіти • *v* enrage
сказати • *v* say, speak
скакати • *v* jump
скандій • *n* scandium
сканер • *n* scanner
скасувати • *v* abolish, abrogate, annul,
rescind, reverse

скат • *n* ray
скатерка • *n* tablecloth
скатерть • *n* tablecloth
скаутінг • *n* scouting
скейтборд • *n* skateboard
скелет • *n* skeleton
скеля • *n* cliff, crag
скептицизм • *n* skepticism
скін • *n* skinhead

скінхе́д • *n* skinhead
скі́нчити • *v* end, finish
скло • *n* glass
скля́нка • *n* glass
скорбо́ти • *v* mourn
скорий • *adj* quick
ско́ро • *adv* soon
скороти́ти • *v* abbreviate, abridge, shorten
скоро́чувати • *v* abbreviate, abridge, shorten
скорпіон • *n* scorpion
скотина • *n* livestock
скоти́на • *n* cattle
скребти • *v* scrape
скриня • *n* case, trunk
скри́ня • *n* box
скрипка • *n* violin
скро́мний • *adj* humble
скроня • *n* temple
ску́мбрія • *n* mackerel
сла́бий • *adj* weak
слабки́й • *adj* weak
слабша́ти • *v* sink
сла́бшати • *v* flag
слава • *n* fame, glory • *interj* hurrah
сла́ти • *v* send
слива • *n* plum
сливе́ • *adv* almost, nearly
сливовиця • *n* slivovitz
слиз • *n* mucus, slime
слизень • *n* slug
слизняк • *n* slug
слимак • *n* slug
сли́на • *n* saliva, spit
сліпи́й • *adj* blind
сло́вник • *n* dictionary
сло́во • *n* word
словосполучення • *n* collocation
слон • *n* bishop, elephant
слоник • *n* weevil
слони́ха • *n* elephant
слуга́ • *n* servant
служба • *n* service
службо́вець • *n* official
службо́вка • *n* official
служни́ця • *n* servant
слух • *n* hearing
слухати • *interj* hello
слу́хати • *v* listen
слу́хатися • *v* listen
слуха́ч • *n* listener
слуха́чка • *n* listener
слухня́ний • *adj* obedient
сльоза́ • *n* tear
смага • *n* tan, thirst
сма́жити • *v* fry

смак • *n* taste
смалець • *n* lard
смара́гд • *n* emerald
смара́гдовий • *n* emerald • *adj* emerald
смарка́ль • *n* snot
сма́чний • *adj* delicious
смерді́ти • *v* stink
смере́ка • *n* spruce
сме́ртний • *adj* mortal
смерть • *n* death, departure
смета́на • *n* cream
сметанко́вий • *adj* cream
смичо́к • *n* bow
сміл́ивість • *n* bravery, courage
сміття́ • *n* garbage
сміх • *n* laughter
смішни́й • *adj* comical
смія́тися • *v* laugh
смокінг • *n* tuxedo
смоктати • *v* suck
смола́ • *n* tar
смолоскип • *n* torch
сморід • *n* reek, stench
смородина • *n* currant
сму́тний • *adj* sad
сму́ток • *n* sadness, sorrow
сна́йпер • *n* sniper
сніг • *n* snow
сніговик • *n* snowman
сніда́нок • *n* breakfast
сніжи́нка • *n* snowflake
сніжок • *n* snowball
сніп • *n* sheaf
сновиді́ння • *n* dream
сну́кер • *n* snooker
собака • *n* dog
соба́ка • *n* dog
собі́ • *pron* myself
собо́р • *n* cathedral
собо́ю • *pron* myself
сова • *n* owl
сове́т • *n* soviet
совість • *n* conscience
сово́к • *n* dustpan
сойка • *n* jay
со́кер • *n* football
сокіл • *n* kestrel
со́кіл • *n* falcon
солда́т • *n* soldier
солове́й • *n* nightingale
солове́йко • *n* nightingale
соло́дкий • *adj* sweet
соло́ма • *n* straw
солоний • *adj* salty
сом • *n* catfish

сон • *n* dream, sleep
сонет • *n* sonnet
сонце • *n* sun
соня • *n* dormouse
соняx • *n* sunflower
сонячний • *adj* sunny
соняшник • *n* sunflower
соплі • *n* snot
сорока • *n* magpie
сороковий • *adj* fortieth
сорочка • *n* shirt
сосиска • *n* sausage
сосна • *n* pine
сосок • *n* nipple
сотня • *n* company
соус • *n* gravy, sauce
софа • *n* sofa
соціалізм • *n* socialism
соціаліст • *n* socialist
соціалістка • *n* socialist
союз • *n* alliance, union
спадок • *n* inheritance
спалити • *v* burn
спальня • *n* bedroom
спаржа • *n* asparagus
спасибі • *interj* thanks
спасіння • *n* salvation
спати • *v* sleep
спекотний • *adj* hot
сперма • *n* sperm
сперма • *n* semen
спина • *n* back
спирт • *n* alcohol
спис • *n* spear
список • *n* list
співак • *n* singer
співати • *v* sing
співачка • *n* singer
співбесіда • *n* interview
співвітчизник • *n* compatriot
співвітчизниця • *n* compatriot
співробітник • *n* colleague
співробітниця • *n* colleague
спідниця • *n* skirt
спільний • *adj* joint
спільно • *adv* together
спірний • *adj* moot
спірний • *adj* controversial
сповідальня • *n* confessional
сповіщення • *n* notification
сподіватися • *v* hope
споживач • *n* consumer
спойлер • *n* spoiler
спокій • *n* calmness
спокій • *n* peace
сполучник • *n* conjunction

спора • *n* spore
споріднений • *adj* akin
спорт • *n* sport
споруда • *n* building
спосіб • *n* method
справжнє • *n* present
спрага • *n* thirst
спраглий • *adj* thirsty
сприяти • *v* assist
сприятливий • *adj* advantageous
спроба • *n* stab
спроба • *n* attempt
спускати • *v* drain
спускатися • *v* descend
спустити • *v* drain
спуститися • *v* descend
супутнік • *n* sputnik
срака • *n* ass
срати • *v* shit
срібло • *n* argent
срібло • *n* silver
сріблястий • *n* silver
срібний • *adj* silver
ссавець • *n* mammal
ссати • *v* suck
став • *n* pond
ставати • *v* become
ставлення • *n* attitude
стадіон • *n* stadium
стадо • *n* herd
сталь • *n* steel
стамеска • *n* chisel
стан • *n* condition, situation, state
становище • *n* state
станція • *n* station
старатися • *v* try
старий • *adj* old
стародавній • *adj* ancient
старший • *adj* elder
стати • *v* become
статися • *v* happen
стаття • *n* article
статуя • *n* statue
стать • *n* gender, sex
стая • *n* flock
створіння • *n* being, creature
стегно • *n* hip, thigh
стеля • *n* ceiling
степ • *n* steppe
стерва • *n* bitch
стерти • *v* erase
стетоскоп • *n* stethoscope
стирати • *v* erase
стіг • *n* haystack
стіл • *n* table
стілець • *n* chair

стíльник • *n* honeycomb
стінá • *n* wall
стовп • *n* post
столáр • *n* carpenter
столíтній • *adj* centenary
столíття • *n* century
сторíнка • *n* page
стоя́ти • *v* stand
стрáва • *n* meal
страждáння • *n* distress, suffering
страждáючий • *adj* suffering
страйк • *n* strike
страсть • *n* passion
стрáус • *n* ostrich
страх • *n* fear, horror
страшний • *adj* terrible
стрекозá • *n* dragonfly
стрéмено • *n* stirrup
стрептокок • *n* streptococcus
стрибáти • *v* jump
стрілá • *n* arrow
стрíлка • *n* hand
стрíлка • *n* arrow, needle
стрільбá • *n* shooting
стріляни́на • *n* shooting
стріля́ти • *v* shoot
стрíчка • *n* tape
стрíчка • *n* ribbon
строк • *n* time
строкáтий • *adj* variegated
стрóнцій • *n* strontium
структура • *n* structure
струмок • *n* stream
стручок • *n* silique
студент • *n* student
студентка • *n* student
стýкати • *v* knock
стýкнути • *v* knock
ступня́ • *n* foot
ступор • *n* stupor
стяг • *n* banner, flag
субстрат • *n* substrate
субстрáт • *n* substratum
сувій • *n* scroll
суглоб • *n* joint
суд • *n* court, tribunal
суддя • *n* referee
суддя́ • *n* judge
суднó • *n* ship
суднобудівник • *n* shipbuilder
сузíря́ • *n* constellation
суї́ци́д • *n* suicide
сук • *n* bough
сýка • *n* bitch
сýкня • *n* dress
султáн • *n* sultan
сум • *n* spleen

сýма • *n* sum
сумíсний • *adj* joint
сýмка • *n* bag
сумлíння • *n* conscience
сумний • *adj* gloomy
сýмнів • *n* doubt
сумнівáтися • *v* doubt
суни́ця • *n* strawberry
суничний • *adj* strawberry
суперечити • *v* contradict
суперечли́вий • *adj* contradictory
супермаркет • *n* supermarket
супроти́вник • *n* enemy
супýтник • *n* satellite, sputnik
сурмá • *n* antimony
сурóдженець • *n* sibling
сусíдство • *n* neighborhood
суспíльство • *n* society
сутенер • *n* pimp
сути́чка • *n* fight
сутíнки • *n* twilight
сýтність • *n* essence
суть • *n* essence
суфíкс • *n* suffix
сухий • *adj* dry
сухожи́лля • *n* tendon
сухотний • *adj* consumptive
суцвíття • *n* inflorescence
сучасний • *adj* modern
сучасник • *n* contemporary
сучасниця • *n* contemporary
сушáрка • *n* dryer
сýші • *n* sushi
сфера • *n* sphere
сфínктер • *n* sphincter
сфотографувáти • *v* photograph
схи́льність • *n* aptitude
схід • *n* east
схíдний • *adj* eastern
схíдний • *adj* easterly
схóди • *n* staircase, stairs
сходинка • *n* step
схожість • *n* similarity
схрещення • *n* crossing
сьогодні • *n* today
сьогóдні • *adv* today
сьóгун • *n* shogun
сьóмий • *adj* seventh
сюди́ • *adv* here, hither
сюї́та • *n* suite
сюрчáти • *v* whistle
сюрчóк • *n* whistle
ся́йво • *n* glitter
сякий-такий • *pron* something
ся́яти • *v* glitter
ся́ти • *v* shine

та • *conj* and
табака • *n* pussy
та́бір • *n* camp
табли́ця • *n* table
табли́чний • *adj* tabular
табу́н • *n* herd
таврува́ти • *v* stigmatize
таємни́ця • *n* mystery, secret
таємни́чий • *adj* mysterious
таємно • *adv* secretly
таз • *n* basin, pelvis
тайга́ • *n* taiga
тайфу́н • *n* typhoon
так • *adv* as, sic, so
також • *adv* too
тако́ж • *adv* also
такса • *n* dachshund
таксі • *n* taxi
таксі́вка • *n* taxi
талі́й • *n* thallium
тала́нт • *n* gift, talent
там • *adv* there
тампо́н • *n* tampon
та́нець • *n* dance
танк • *n* tank
та́нкер • *n* tanker
танкі́ст • *n* tanker
танкі́стка • *n* tanker
та́нок • *n* dance
танта́л • *n* tantalum
танцюва́ти • *v* dance
танцюри́ст • *n* dancer
танцюри́стка • *n* dancer
тапіо́ка • *n* tapioca
тарга́н • *n* cockroach
тарі́лка • *n* dish, plate
та́то • *n* dad, daddy, father
та́тусь • *n* dad, daddy
та́чка • *n* wheelbarrow
твари́на • *n* animal
твари́на • *n* being, creature
тварь • *n* being, creature
тве́рдий • *adj* hard
твій • *pron* thine, yours
твір • *n* writing
творо́г • *n* quark
тво́рчий • *adj* creative
теа́тр • *n* theater
теж • *adv* also, too
текст • *n* text
текти́ • *v* flow
телеба́чення • *n* television
телеві́зор • *n* television

телегра́ма • *n* telegram
телегра́ф • *n* telegraph
телепа́тія • *n* telepathy
телеско́п • *n* telescope
телефо́н • *n* phone, telephone
телефонува́ти • *v* telephone
телу́р • *n* tellurium
те́льбух • *n* tripe
теля́ • *n* calf
те́мний • *adj* dark
темни́ця • *n* prison
темно-си́ній • *adj* navy
темнота • *n* darkness
температу́ра • *n* temperature
температу́ра • *n* fever
те́мпура • *n* tempura
темрява • *n* darkness
те́ніс • *n* tennis
теорбо • *n* theorbo
теоре́ма • *n* theorem
теорети́чний • *adj* theoretical
теософія • *n* theosophy
тепер • *adv* nowadays
тепе́р • *adv* now
те́плий • *adj* warm
тепли́ця • *n* greenhouse
тербі́й • *n* terbium
терито́рія • *n* territory
те́рка • *n* grater
термі́н • *n* time
термі́т • *n* termite
те́рмос • *n* thermos
терори́зм • *n* terrorism
терори́ст • *n* terrorist
терористи́чний • *adj* terrorist
терпели́вий • *adj* patient
терпля́чий • *adj* patient
те́рція • *n* third
те́сля • *n* carpenter
тесть • *n* father-in-law
тета • *n* theta
тетерев'я́тник • *n* goshawk
технеці́й • *n* technetium
те́хніка • *n* technology
те́хнікум • *n* school
техноло́гія • *n* technology
те́ща • *n* mother-in-law
ти • *pron* thou, you
тигр • *n* tiger
тигри́ця • *n* tigress
ти́ждень • *n* week
тик • *n* teak
тин • *n* fence

тип • *n* phylum, type
тиранити • *v* tyrannize
тис • *n* yew
тисячеліття • *n* millennium
титан • *n* titanium
тихий • *adj* quiet
тихо • *adv* quietly, softly
тичинка • *n* stamen
тиша • *n* silence
тіло • *n* body
тілоохоронець • *n* bodyguard
тільки • *adv* merely, only
тімя́ • *n* vertex
тімя́ • *n* crown
тімячко • *n* fontanelle
тінь • *n* shadow
тісно • *adv* closely
тістечко • *n* cake
тісто • *n* dough
тітка • *n* aunt
ткати • *v* weave
тліти • *v* smolder
тля • *n* aphid
товариство • *n* company
товариш • *n* comrade
товкти • *v* grind
товстий • *adj* thick
товстий • *adj* fat
тоді • *adv* then
томагавк • *n* tomahawk
томат • *n* tomato
тому • *adv* therefore
тому́ • *conj* because
тонкий • *adj* thin
тонна • *n* ton
тонути • *v* sink
топити • *v* sink
тополя • *n* poplar
торій • *n* thorium
торба • *n* bag
торгівля • *n* commerce, trade
торт • *n* cake
тортура • *n* torture
торф • *n* peat
тост • *n* toast
точка • *n* dot
точний • *adj* accurate, exact, precise
точність • *n* reliability
точно • *adv* exactly
трава́ • *n* grass
травити • *v* digest
травлення • *n* digestion
травма • *n* trauma
травма • *n* injury
трагедія • *n* tragedy
традиційний • *adj* traditional
традиція • *n* tradition
трактир • *n* inn, pub
трактор • *n* tractor
трамвай • *n* tram
транслітерація • *n* transliteration
трахея • *n* windpipe
требник • *n* breviary
требух • *n* tripe
тренер • *n* trainer
третій • *adj* third
трибунал • *n* tribunal
тривога • *n* alarm
тривога • *n* anxiety
тридцятий • *adj* thirtieth
тризубець • *n* trident
трилисник • *n* trefoil
тримати • *v* hold
триместр • *n* trimester
тринадцятий • *adj* thirteenth
трирічний • *adj* triennial
триріччя • *n* triennium
тритон • *n* newt
тричі • *adv* thrice
трійка • *n* three, troika
тріска́ • *n* cod
троль • *n* troll
тромбон • *n* trombone
трон • *n* throne
тронка • *n* cowbell
тротуар • *n* pavement, sidewalk
тротуар • *n* flag
трофей • *n* trophy
трохи • *pron* some
троянда • *n* rose
труба • *n* trumpet
трудитися • *v* work
трудний • *adj* difficult
трудящий • *n* worker
труїти • *v* poison
труна • *n* coffin
труп • *n* corpse
труси • *n* underpants
труси́ • *n* pants
трутень • *n* drone
трущоба • *n* slum
трюм • *n* hold
трясовина • *n* quagmire
тсуга • *n* hemlock
туалет • *n* toilet
тубільний • *adj* aboriginal
туди • *adv* thither
туди́ • *adv* there
туземський • *adj* aboriginal
тулій • *n* thulium
туман • *n* mist
туман • *n* fog
туманність • *n* nebula

тýндра • *n* tundra
тунель • *n* tunnel
тупий • *adj* blunt, stupid
тупúй • *adj* dull
тура • *n* rook
туризм • *n* tourism
туркус • *n* turquoise
туркусова • *n* turquoise
туркусовий • *n* turquoise
тут • *adv* here
туш • *n* mascara
тхір • *n* ferret
тьма • *n* darkness
тьóтя • *n* aunt

тюк • *n* bale
тюлень • *n* seal
тюль • *n* tulle
тюльпан • *n* tulip
тюрбáн • *n* turban
тюрмá • *n* prison
тютюн • *n* tobacco
тягáр • *n* burden
тягáти • *v* pull
тягнýти • *v* pull
тягтú • *v* pull
тятивá • *n* bowstring

у • *prep* at, in • *v* have
убивця • *n* murderer
убúвця • *n* killer
убогість • *n* shabbiness
увя́знення • *n* imprisonment
увáга • *n* attention
увезти • *v* import
увійтú • *v* enter
увозити • *v* import
угноювати • *v* manure
удáв • *n* boa
удавати • *v* pretend
удар • *n* punch
удáрити • *v* beat
ударя́ти • *v* beat
удобрювати • *v* fertilize
ужалити • *v* sting
ужé • *adv* already
уживáти • *v* use
ужúти • *v* use
узмóря́ • *n* beach
узя́ти • *v* take
уїк-éнд • *n* weekend
указáти • *v* point
укáзувати • *v* point
украсти • *v* steal
укривáти • *v* cover
укрúти • *v* cover
укусити • *v* sting
укусúти • *v* bite
умéрти • *v* die
умирáти • *v* die
умисний • *adj* deliberate, intentional
умисно • *adv* deliberately
умíти • *v* can
умлáут • *n* umlaut
умóва • *n* condition
унаслíдок • *conj* because

уникáти • *v* avoid
унúкнути • *v* avoid
університéт • *n* school, university
унітáз • *n* toilet
упáсти • *v* fall
упúр • *n* vampire
уплúв • *n* influence
уповати • *v* hope
упокíй • *n* departure
упокóєння • *n* departure
управляти • *v* manage
ýпряж • *n* harness
ура • *interj* hurrah
ураган • *n* hurricane
урагáн • *n* hurricane
уран • *n* uranium
урóк • *n* lesson
ýряд • *n* government
урядовий • *adj* governmental
усе • *pron* everything
усí • *pron* everybody, everyone
успíх • *n* success
успíшний • *adj* successful
усюди • *adv* everywhere
утрóба • *n* womb
ухилúтися • *v* avoid
ухиля́ти • *v* duck
ухиля́тися • *v* avoid
уходúти • *v* enter
участь • *n* participation
учéний • *n* scientist
учениця • *n* pupil
учень • *n* pupil
учúлище • *n* school
учитель • *n* teacher
учителька • *n* teacher
учити • *v* study
учитися • *v* study

учи́тися • *v* learn
учо́ра • *n* yesterday • *adv* yesterday
ущелина • *n* ravine

уявити • *v* fancy
уявляти • *v* fancy

фа́брика • *n* factory
фавори́т • *n* minion
фаго́т • *n* bassoon
фа́за • *n* phase
фазан • *n* pheasant
факс • *n* fax
факт • *n* fact
факульте́т • *n* faculty
факульте́т • *n* school
фаланга • *n* phalanx
фалоімітатор • *n* dildo
фанто́м • *n* ghost
фа́ра • *n* headlight
фара́д • *n* farad
фарао́н • *n* pharaoh
фа́рба • *n* color
фармацевти́чний • *adj* pharmaceutical
фа́ртух • *n* apron
фарфо́р • *n* porcelain
фарш • *n* mince
фасо́ля • *n* bean
фах • *n* profession
фашизм • *n* fascism
фаши́ст • *n* fascist
фаши́стка • *n* fascist
фаши́стський • *adj* fascist
фаянс • *n* faience
федера́ція • *n* federation
фека́лії • *n* excrement, feces
фелляція • *n* fellatio
фемінізм • *n* feminism
фе́рмій • *n* fermium
фе́рма • *n* farm
фермер • *n* farmer
фиаско • *n* fiasco
фі́зик • *n* physicist
філателі́я • *n* philately
фі́лія • *n* branch
філоло́гія • *n* philology
філо́соф • *n* philosopher
філосо́фія • *n* philosophy
фільм • *n* movie

фі́нік • *n* date
фіоле́товий • *adj* purple
фі́рма • *n* company
фіруза • *n* turquoise
флаг • *n* banner, flag
фламі́нго • *n* flamingo
фле́йта • *n* flute
флогістон • *n* phlogiston
флот • *n* navy
флотський • *adj* navy
фля́га • *n* flag
фля́га • *n* flag
фо́бія • *n* phobia
фо́кус • *n* magic
фольклор • *n* folklore
фондю • *n* fondue
фонта́н • *n* fountain
форель • *n* trout
форма • *n* uniform
форт • *n* fort
фортепіа́но • *n* piano
форте́ця • *n* fortress
фосфат • *n* phosphate
фо́сфор • *n* phosphorus
фоте́ль • *n* armchair
фо́тка • *n* photo
фо́то • *n* photo, photograph
фотоапара́т • *n* camera
фото́граф • *n* photographer
фотогра́фія • *n* photo, photograph, photography
фотографува́ти • *v* photograph
фотозні́мок • *n* photo, photograph
фото́н • *n* photon
фра́за • *n* sentence
фра́нцій • *n* francium
фрукт • *n* fruit
фтор • *n* fluorine
функція • *n* function
фурго́н • *n* van
фут • *n* foot
футбо́л • *n* football, soccer

хабáр • *n* bribe
хадж • *n* hajj
хазя́їн • *n* owner
хакер • *n* hacker
халепа • *n* trouble
халíф • *n* caliph
халіфáт • *n* caliphate
халупа • *n* shack
халцедон • *n* chalcedony
хамелеóн • *n* chameleon
хан • *n* khan
хаóс • *n* chaos
харчування • *n* nutrition
харчувáння • *n* food
харчувáти • *v* feed
хáта • *n* house, room
хатинка • *n* shack
хаща • *n* thicket
хвилерíз • *n* breakwater
хвилерíз • *n* bulwark
хвилина • *n* minute
хвіст • *n* tail
хвóрий • *adj* ill
хворíти • *v* ache, hurt
хвороба • *n* illness
хворóба • *n* disease
хибно • *adv* awry
хíмія • *n* chemistry
хірург • *n* surgeon
хлíб • *n* bread
хлопець • *n* lad
хлóпець • *n* boy, boyfriend, youth
хлóпчик • *n* boy
хлор • *n* chlorine
хлороформ • *n* chloroform
хмара • *n* cloud
хмáрний • *adj* cloudy
хмарочос • *n* skyscraper
хобі • *n* hobby
хобот • *n* trunk
ховáти • *v* hide
ховрáх • *n* gopher, suslik
ховрашóк • *n* gopher, suslik
хода • *n* step
ходити • *v* go
ходи́ти • *v* walk
хокей • *n* hockey

холодець • *n* aspic
холоди́льник • *n* refrigerator
холóдний • *adj* cold
холостя́к • *n* bachelor
хомя́к • *n* hamster
хомýт • *n* yoke
хор • *n* choir
хорóбрий • *adj* brave
хорóбрість • *n* bravery, courage
хоругвá • *n* flag
хороший • *adj* good
хорóший • *adj* good
хоругвá • *n* flag
хотíти • *v* fancy
хотíти • *v* want
храм • *n* shrine, temple
храп • *n* snore
хрест • *n* cross, crossing
хрещéння • *n* baptism
хризантема • *n* chrysanthemum
хрін • *n* horseradish
хробак • *n* worm
хробáк • *n* insect
хром • *n* chromium
хропíти • *v* snore
хрущ • *n* cockchafer
хрящ • *n* cartilage
хтивий • *adj* lascivious, prurient, salacious
хти́вий • *adj* lewd
хто • *pron* who
хтось • *pron* somebody
худи́й • *adj* skinny
худоба • *n* cattle, livestock
худóжник • *n* artist, painter
хуй • *n* dick, penis, prick
хуйлó • *n* asshole
хуліган • *n* hooligan
хуліганка • *n* hooligan
хунта • *n* junta
хурмá • *n* persimmon
хустка • *n* headscarf
хýстка • *n* handkerchief, kerchief
хýсточка • *n* handkerchief
хутрó • *n* fur
хýтро • *n* fur

цаль • *n* inch
цап • *n* goat
цапеня́ • *n* kid
цар • *n* king, tsar
царéвич • *n* prince

цари́ця • *n* queen
царíвна • *n* princess
цáрство • *n* kingdom
цвіль • *n* mildew, mold

цвіркун • *n* cricket
цвісти • *v* bloom
цвіт • *n* flower
цвях • *n* nail
це • *pron* this
цегла • *n* brick
цедра • *n* zest
цей • *pron* this
цензурувати • *v* censor
цент • *n* cent
центр • *n* center
центрифуга • *n* centrifuge
церій • *n* cerium
церемонія • *n* ceremony
церква • *n* church
цибулина • *n* bulb, onion
цибуля • *n* onion
цивілізація • *n* civilization
циган • *n* gypsy
циганка • *n* gypsy
цигарка • *n* cigarette
цимбали • *n* dulcimer
цинізм • *n* cynicism
цинк • *n* zinc
цирк • *n* circus, cirque
цирконій • *n* zirconium

цифра • *n* number
цицька • *n* boob, tit
цікавий • *adj* curious, interesting
цікавити • *v* interest
цікавитися • *v* wonder
цікавість • *n* curiosity
цікавість • *n* interest
цілий • *adj* whole
цілий • *adj* entire
цілковитий • *adj* absolute
цілковитий • *adj* utter
цілковито • *adv* perfectly
цілком • *adv* perfectly
цілувати • *v* kiss
цілуватися • *v* kiss
ціна • *n* value
ціна • *n* price
цінність • *n* value
ціп • *n* flail
цнота • *n* virginity
цнотливість • *n* virtue
цнотливість • *n* chastity, virginity
цукерка • *n* candy
цукор • *n* sugar
цуценя • *n* puppy

чай • *n* tea
чайка • *n* gull, lapwing
чайник • *n* teakettle, teapot
чаклун • *n* warlock
чаклунство • *n* magic
чалма • *n* turban
чао • *interj* ciao
чапля • *n* heron
чари • *n* spell
чарівник • *n* wizard
чарівник • *n* magician, warlock
чарівництво • *n* magic
чарівниця • *n* sorceress
чарнакніжнік • *n* warlock
чарувати • *v* fascinate
час • *n* age, time
часник • *n* garlic
часом • *adv* sometimes
часопис • *n* magazine
частий • *adj* frequent
частина • *n* part
частинка • *n* particle
частиця • *n* particle
частка • *n* particle
часто • *adv* often
чат • *n* chat

чаша • *n* bowl
чашечка • *n* calyx
чашка • *n* cup
чашолисток • *n* sepal
чверть • *n* quarter
чек • *n* cheque
чекати • *v* await, wait
чемний • *adj* polite
чемодан • *n* valise
черв • *n* worm
червяк • *n* worm
червоний • *adj* red
червонопірка • *n* rudd
черга • *n* line
черга • *n* queue
черевик • *n* boot, shoe
черево • *n* stomach
черево • *n* intestine
череда • *n* herd
череп • *n* skull
черепаха • *n* tortoise, turtle
черепашка • *n* seashell
черешня • *n* cherry
черешок • *n* petiole
честь • *n* glory, honor
четвертий • *adj* fourth

чи • *conj* or, whether
чибис • *n* lapwing
чиж • *n* siskin
чий • *pron* whose
чинити • *v* act
чино́вник • *n* official
чисе́льний • *adj* plural
чисе́льник • *n* numerator
числі́вник • *n* number
число • *n* number
число́ • *n* number
чи́стий • *adj* clean
чистилище • *n* purgatory
чи́стити • *v* clean
чи́стість • *n* cleanliness
чистка • *n* purge
чистота́ • *n* cleanliness
чита́ти • *v* read
чита́ч • *n* reader
чиха́ти • *v* sneeze
чихну́ти • *v* sneeze
членистоно́ге • *n* arthropod
членство • *n* membership
чо́біт • *n* boot
чо́вен • *n* boat
чого-небудь • *pron* something

чоло́ • *n* forehead
чолові́к • *n* husband, man, person
чолові́чий • *adj* masculine
чому́ • *adv* why
чо́рний • *n* black • *adj* black
чорнило • *n* ink
чорни́льниця • *n* inkwell
чорниця • *n* bilberry
чорнобиль • *n* mugwort
чорногуз • *n* stork
чорнокни́жник • *n* warlock
чорт • *n* demon, devil
чортополох • *n* thistle
чотирна́дцятий • *adj* fourteenth
чотки • *n* rosary
чре́во • *n* womb
чуб • *n* topknot
чуде́сний • *adj* great
чудо • *n* wonder
чу́до • *n* miracle
чудовий • *adj* excellent
чудо́вий • *adj* great
чу́ти • *v* feel, hear, listen
чха́ти • *v* sneeze
чхну́ти • *v* sneeze

шаблон • *n* template
шавлія • *n* sage
шаг • *n* shah
шайта́н • *n* shaitan
шакал • *n* jackal
шамані́зм • *n* shamanism
шампа́нське • *n* champagne
шампу́нь • *n* shampoo
шампу́р • *n* skewer, spit
шанс • *n* chance, opportunity
шанта́ж • *n* blackmail
ша́пка • *n* hat
шарж • *n* caricature
шарм • *n* allure
шарф • *n* scarf
шасі́ • *n* chassis
шатро́ • *n* tent
шафа • *n* cupboard
ша́фа • *n* closet, wardrobe
шах • *n* shah
ша́хи • *n* chess
шахта • *n* shaft
ша́хта • *n* mine
шахтар • *n* miner
ша́шки • *n* draughts
швабра • *n* mop

швидкий • *adj* quick
швидки́й • *adj* fast
швидкість • *n* velocity
шви́дко • *adv* quickly
шви́дко • *adv* fast
швидкоплинний • *adj* fleeting
шеде́вр • *n* masterpiece
шейх • *n* sheik
шелесті́вка • *n* consonant
ше́піт • *n* whisper
шепну́ти • *v* whisper
шепта́ти • *v* whisper
шериф • *n* sheriff
шерсть • *n* fleece, wool
шерстяний • *adj* woolen
ше́ршень • *n* hornet
шестидеся́тих • *adj* sixtieth
ши́бениця • *n* gallows
шизофренія • *n* schizophrenia
ши́ло • *n* awl
шимпанзе́ • *n* chimpanzee
ши́на • *n* tyre
ши́нка • *n* ham
ши́нок • *n* pub
шипі́ння • *n* hiss
шипі́ти • *v* hiss

шипши́на • *n* rose
ширина • *n* width
широкий • *adj* wide
широко • *adv* widely
широта́ • *n* latitude
ши́ти • *v* sew
ши́шка • *n* cone
ши́я • *n* neck
шкі́ра • *n* skin
шкарпе́тка • *n* sock
шкідливий • *adj* harmful, injurious
шкі́ра • *n* leather
шкло • *n* glass
шкода • *n* harm
шко́ла • *n* school
шкрябати • *v* scratch, squiggle
шку́ра • *n* skin
шлам • *n* slime
шланг • *n* hose
шліфувати • *v* grind
шлу́нок • *n* stomach
шльо́ндра • *n* slut, whore
шлюб • *n* marriage
шлюз • *n* sluice
шлюп • *n* sloop
шлю́ха • *n* prostitute, slut
шлях • *n* road
шма́рклі • *n* snot
шнапс • *n* schnapps
шні́цель • *n* schnitzel

шнуро́к • *n* lace, shoelace
шовк • *n* silk
шовковиця • *n* mulberry
шокола́д • *n* chocolate
шоло́м • *n* helmet
шо́рти • *n* shorts
шосе́ • *n* highway
шостий • *n* sixth
шо́стий • *adj* sixth
шофе́р • *n* chauffeur, driver
шпіта́ль • *n* hospital
шпак • *n* starling
шпалери • *n* wallpaper
шпигун • *n* spy
шпинат • *n* spinach
шпіхлір • *n* granary
шприц • *n* syringe
шрам • *n* scar
шрифт • *n* font
штанга • *n* barbell
штани́ • *n* pants
штовхати • *v* push
штопор • *n* corkscrew
штраф • *n* fine
шука́ти • *v* search, seek
шулі́ка • *n* kite
шум • *n* noise
шу́рин • *n* brother-in-law
шуру́п • *n* screw

щабель • *n* step
ща́вель • *n* sorrel
щасли́вий • *adj* happy
ща́стя • *n* happiness
щедрість • *n* generosity, largess
щелепа • *n* jaw
щеня • *n* puppy
щенячий • *adj* puppyish
щиглик • *n* goldfinch
щиго́ль • *n* goldfinch
щи́колотка • *n* ankle
щит • *n* shield
щі́тка • *n* brush

що • *conj* that • *pron* what
що-небудь • *pron* something
що-не́будь • *pron* anything
щогла • *n* mast
щоденний • *adj* diurnal
щоде́нник • *n* diary
щока́ • *n* cheek
щорічний • *adj* yearly
щорі́чно • *adv* yearly
щось • *pron* something
щука • *n* pike
щупальце • *n* tentacle

юа́нь • *n* yuan
ювіле́й • *n* anniversary
югу́рт • *n* yogurt
юна́к • *n* youth

юна́цтво • *n* youth
ю́ний • *adj* young
ю́ність • *n* youth
юрба́ • *n* swarm

юри́ст • *n* lawyer
юри́стка • *n* lawyer

ю́рта • *n* yurt

я́блуко • *n* apple
я́вний • *adj* apparent, obvious
ягня́ • *n* lamb
я́года • *n* berry
яд • *n* poison
я́дерний • *adj* nuclear
я́дерце • *n* nucleolus
ядро́ • *n* ball
я́єчко • *n* ball
я́єчник • *n* ovary
язи́к • *n* tongue
язичо́к • *n* uvula
яйце́ • *n* ball, egg
яйцеклі́тина • *n* egg
як • *adv* as, how, like • *conj* as • *prep* as, like
яки́й • *pron* which
яки́й • *pron* what
я́кір • *n* anchor
які́сний • *adj* quality
я́кість • *n* quality
я́кість • *n* property
якщо́ • *conj* if
яли́на • *n* fir, spruce
яли́ця • *n* fir, spruce

яліве́ць • *n* juniper
ялове́ць • *n* juniper
я́ловичина • *n* beef
я́ма • *n* pit
я́нгол • *n* angel
яничар • *n* janissary
янта́р • *n* amber
яр • *n* ravine
ярд • *n* yard
ярмо́ • *n* yoke
ярму́лка • *n* yarmulke
яскра́вий • *adj* bright
ясла • *n* manger
ясна́ • *n* gum
ясні́сть • *n* clarity
ясновиді́ння • *n* clairvoyance
я́спис • *n* jasper
я́струб • *n* hawk
ятаган • *n* yataghan
ячмі́нь • *n* barley
я́шма • *n* jasper
я́щик • *n* box
я́щірка • *n* lizard

Made in the USA
Monee, IL
21 September 2022

14424746R00066